From Mom, With Love

◆

REAL HOME COOKING

KAY SPICER

DOUBLEDAY CANADA LIMITED, TORONTO

Canadian Cataloguing in Publication Data

Spicer, Kay
    From mom, with love: real home cooking

ISBN 0-385-25261-7

1. Cookery.   I. Title.   II. Title: From mom, with love.

TX714.S75 1990   641.5   C90-093663-0

Editor: Laurie Coulter
Design: Tania Craan
Photography: Curtis Lantinga
Styling: Jennifer McLagan, Kay Spicer
Props: Friday Myers
Manager, editorial, production
    and design: Maggie Reeves

Printed on acid free paper. ∞
Printed and bound in the USA

Photo credits: Antique furniture supplied by Inquisitive; milkpaint
cupboard supplied by Nitty Gritty Reproductions; wrought iron table
supplied by Hearth House; various dishware pieces supplied by En
Provence; other kitchen props supplied by Sinful Pleasures.

Published in Canada by
    Doubleday Canada Limited
    105 Bond Street
    Toronto, Ontario
    M5B 1Y3

CONTENTS

◆

INTRODUCTION

I was prompted to write this cookbook by a phone call I received years ago. It was a Sunday night and my 24-year-old son, Bob, was calling from Calgary.

His first words were, "Mom, how do you cook a duck?" I asked how much it weighed. There was a pause; then, "It cost $9.50."

That didn't help. While I tried to imagine the size of a $9.50 duck, I asked a few more questions. It turned out that the duck, stuffed with an apple concoction, was already roasting in his oven. He was preparing it as a special treat for his girlfriend, Judith. It was quite a major cooking adventure for him, and the anxiety of waiting had got to him. It was obvious that he needed a little reassurance from Mom.

Most Moms my age receive similar calls about cooking. When we least expect it, we're asked to quote recipes verbatim for family favorites. I think our kids see us as an ongoing reference file with all the formulas for preparing and serving food.

So this collection of recipes is for Bob and my daughters, Patti and Susan. It's also for all their Spicer cousins, and my Mighton step-children, Cathy, Laura and Steve. And, for my grandchildren, especially dear Morgan, my first granddaughter.

It's actually for all kids — past, present and future generations of them — who are building their own and creating good food in their kitchens.

I love closing my eyes and thinking about the things Mom, Belle Bergman, cooked for my Dad, my sister, Mary Ellen, and me. Often the food was not fancy; yet, it was special, because Mom prepared all meals in a special way, with love and care. What she did with ordinary ingredients amazed me. I have memories of the best of *real home cooking* — baked macaroni and cheese, rich with chunks of Cheddar; the world's best stew, full of stewing beef; roast chicken jacketed in crisp skin; syrupy butter tarts oozing with sweetness; creamy rice pudding dotted with plump raisins; and flapper pie, elegant with curly meringue.

The recipes Mom used were tucked in a big kitchen drawer. Some were clipped from magazines and newspapers, but most of them were scribbled in her pretty handwriting on backs of envelopes, three-holed lined paper, writing paper and even on paper napkins. Others were written in the unfamiliar handwriting of friends. Recipes were traded at church suppers, bridge parties, picnics, and wherever family and friends gathered to share and enjoy good company and good food.

Mom was born to cook. She seemed to know exactly what to do by feel and touch even when the recipes called for butter the size of a walnut or an egg, and enough flour to make a stiff dough. To her, one cup meant a teacupful. She didn't own proper measuring cups until I bought them for her, after they were introduced to me in my first home economics cooking classes. The assortment of mixing bowls, baking pans and utensils which she used were limited compared to what I have in my kitchen today.

Oven temperatures were simple – low, moderate and hot. Even after she started using her first General Electric range, she'd hold her hand in the oven to feel the temperature. When she pulled her hand away, she knew how hot it was. When she needed a cake tester, she simply pulled a straw out of the broom. (No wonder our brooms were thin when they were replaced!)

These were just some of the tricks taught to my mother by her mother and older sisters. It was at their apron strings that Mom learned to cook.

For me, learning to cook was also part of growing up. It was sharing time with Mom, communicating with her over ingredients, food and warmth. Besides, the joy of food and the joy of cooking came naturally. There was no television to distract me. Cooking was fun, especially the sampling sessions around Mom's pristine, white kitchen table.

Thinking about these times, I remember our first kitchen. It was in a small cottage in Radisson, Saskatchewan, where I first lived.

There were four wooden chairs around the table, which sat in front of a window. Across from it there was a Hossier cupboard, which held all of Mom's cooking and baking supplies, and a tall, built-in cupboard, where the firewood and broom were kept. A pail of fresh water with its dipper sat on top of that cupboard. (Our well was outside near the back door.) A free-standing painted cupboard full of pots and pans stood against the wall opposite the black wood-burning stove. And that was it. Quite a contrast to the kitchens I've cooked in for my family.

I'll always remember the good food we enjoyed at Mom's table. And, she always managed to keep us well-nourished, even during those lean years following the depression. For me, I guess that's one of the reasons there's a feeling of security and great comfort in eating "Mom" foods. The examples you'll find in this book are that kind of food — soul-satisfying and full of love.

These recipes are adaptations from my huge collection of cookbooks and food magazines, and the best of the recipes I've developed while on assignment over the years for food companies, commodity associations, television presentations, and magazine and newspaper features. I'm happy to share them with you. They're worth cherishing along with the other eating traditions of the past. Prepare them with, and for, your family and friends. And pass them on to the next generation — full of warmth, comfort and memories.

For all of you and especially Susan, Patti and Bob, these recipes are here for you to enjoy.

From Mom, with love.

APPETIZERS & SNACKS

◆

My Mom's repertoire of snacks was limited. Stuffed celery, pigs-in-blankets, small sandwiches and her own toasted tidbits are ones I remember.

My parents didn't have cocktail parties. Tea parties, yes, but not parties with alcoholic drinks. The only spirits I ever remember seeing were sherry and wine around Christmas, and now and then some brandy for medicinal purposes.

Cocktail parties became the big social thing for me in the '50s, after I was married. That's when I became aware of the wonderful little hot and cold morsels called canapes and hors d'oeuvres.

Over the years, I've served a great assortment of cocktail party and pre-dinner finger foods. The following are a few of my favorites. As well, some of the recipes are for starters I like to serve on little plates at sit-down dinners.

SESAME CHEESE LOG

Even though cheese balls became very fashionable in the '70s, I always preferred forming flavored cheese mixtures into logs. A little slice of a log is so easy to transfer to a cracker or even eat by hand. However, any of these mixtures can be formed into a large ball or into tiny ones that I call nuggets.

♦

2 cups	shredded Cheddar, Gouda, Edam or Havarti cheese ($^1/_2$ lb/250 g)	500 mL
$^1/_2$ cup	butter or cream cheese	125 mL
1 tsp	Dijon-style mustard	5 mL
1 tbsp	white wine, brandy or gin	15 mL
1 cup	sesame seeds, toasted	250 mL

- In food processor or by hand, combine cheese, butter, mustard and wine. Process or cream until smooth.
- Shape firmly into a log, about $1^1/_2$ inches (4 cm) in diameter.
- Roll in sesame seeds, pressing seeds into log. Wrap well and chill.
- Remove 20 minutes before serving.
- Serve at room temperature.
- To store: Wrap in plastic wrap; refrigerate for up to 2 weeks.

Makes 18 servings.

♦

HELPFUL HINT

To toast sesame seeds, coconut or nuts
Place in a shallow baking pan or dish. Bake, stirring once or twice, in 350 F (180 C) oven for about 10 minutes or until golden brown. Or stir in a nonstick skillet over medium heat for about 5 minutes or until golden brown.

CHEESE AND CHUTNEY SPREAD OR DIP

The cheese I like best for this and the following spreads is a red-coated ball of imported Holland Edam. Once a small slice is taken off the top and the cheese is scooped out, the remaining shell (about $^1/_2$ inch/ 1 cm) thick makes a perfect container, which looks grand surrounded with crisp veggies or crackers.

◆

2 cups	shredded Edam, Cheddar, Gouda or Havarti cheese ($^1/_2$ lb/250 g)	500 mL
$^1/_3$ cup	chutney	75 mL
$^1/_4$ cup	milk or mayonnaise	50 mL
$^1/_2$ tsp	curry powder	2 mL

• In food processor or blender, combine cheese, chutney, milk and curry powder. Process, scraping down bowl occasionally, for about 2 minutes or until smooth. (If using a blender, this works best if the chutney and milk are put into the container before the cheese.)
• Spoon into serving container.
• Best served at room temperature as a spread on crisp crackers or toast wedges or as a thick dip for raw vegetables — celery, carrot and turnip sticks, broccoli and cauliflower florets, green and red sweet pepper chunks, zucchini slices, radishes, mushrooms and green onions.
• For a thinner dip, blend in more milk, 1 tsp (5 mL) at a time, until mixture is the desired consistency.
• To store: Place in covered container. Refrigerate for up to 1 week.

Makes 2 cups (500 mL).

Variations

CHEESE AND BEER SPREAD OR DIP

- In place of chutney, milk and curry, with the cheese use:

$^{1}/_{3}$ cup	beer	75 mL
$^{1}/_{4}$ cup	mayonnaise	50 mL
$^{1}/_{2}$ tsp	Dijon-style mustard	2 mL
$^{1}/_{2}$ tsp	caraway seeds (optional)	2 mL

POTTED CHEESE SPREAD OR DIP

- In place of chutney, milk and curry, with the cheese use:

$^{1}/_{3}$ cup	port, sherry, brandy or rum	75 mL
$^{1}/_{4}$ cup	mayonnaise	50 mL
$^{1}/_{4}$ cup	chopped pecans or walnuts	50 mL
Pinch	nutmeg	Pinch

CHEESE AND FRUIT SPREAD

- In place of chutney, milk and curry, with the cheese use:

$^{1}/_{2}$ cup	chopped dried apricots or raisins	125 mL
$^{1}/_{2}$ cup	mayonnaise	125 mL

HELPFUL HINT

To crack peppercorns
Place peppercorns in a small plastic bag. On a hard surface, with a mallet or bottom of a small heavy saucepan, bang them until each one is cracked into 3 or 4 pieces.

BOURSIN BALL

The flavor of this homemade Boursin is close to the creamy one that my food-loving pals, Mary and Mona, and I savored during the week we spent drifting along the Canal du Midi on a barge. Whenever I taste it, memories of other glorious French specialties run through my head.

◆

1 cup	cream cheese ($^1\!/_2$ lb/250 g)	250 mL
1	clove garlic, minced	1
2 tsp	chopped fresh parsley	10 mL
2 tsp	chopped fresh dill or	10 mL
	$^1\!/_2$ tsp (2 mL) dried dillweed	
$^1\!/_4$ tsp	ground cumin	1 mL
$^1\!/_4$ tsp	crumbled dried thyme	1 mL
1 to 2 tsp	whole black peppercorns, cracked	5 to 10 mL
$^1\!/_2$ tsp	salt	2 mL

• In food processor or by hand, combine cream cheese, garlic, parsley, dill, cumin and thyme; process for 1 to 2 minutes or cream until well mixed and smooth.

• Form into a large ball. (Or mixture can be shaped into a log or 16 small balls.) Sprinkle all over with pepper and salt. Press into cheese. Wrap and chill.

• Remove about 20 minutes before serving and serve at room temperature.

• To store: Wrap in plastic wrap; refrigerate for up to 2 weeks.

Makes 16 servings.

DEVILED EGGS

Stuffed eggs turn into deviled ones as soon as mustard is added to the mashed yolk mixture.

◆

8	hard-cooked eggs	8
1/4 cup	mayonnaise	50 mL
1 tsp	Dijon-style mustard	5 mL
1/2 tsp	Worcestershire sauce	2 mL
1/4 tsp	salt	1 mL
Pinch	white pepper	Pinch
	Red lumpfish caviar or	
	paprika or chopped parsley	

• Cut eggs crosswise or lengthwise in half; remove yolks to small bowl. Reserve whites.
• Mash yolks and stir in mayonnaise, mustard, Worcestershire sauce, salt and pepper; mix well.
• Spoon and mound mixture in egg white halves. (If halves do not want to sit straight, cut a wee slice from the bottom.)
• Cover and refrigerate until serving time.
• Garnish with caviar, paprika or chopped parsley.
• To store: Deviled eggs can be made ahead and stored for up to 2 days as long as they are covered and refrigerated.

Makes 16 deviled eggs.

Variations

ANCHOVY DEVILED EGGS

• Add 2 finely chopped anchovy fillets to the mashed egg yolk mixture. Garnish with chopped fresh dill or parsley.

DILLY DEVILED EGGS

• Add 2 tbsp (25 mL) chopped fresh dill to the egg yolk mixture.

SPINACH AND BACON STUFFED EGGS

• Cook 2 strips side bacon until crisp. Drain on paper towels and crumble. Add to egg yolk mixture with $^1/_4$ cup (50 mL) finely chopped fresh spinach and 2 tsp (10 mL) minced green onions.

HELPFUL HINTS

To Hard-Cook Eggs
In saucepan, place eggs. Add cold or room temperature water until it is 1 inch (2.5 cm) above eggs. Bring to a boil rapidly over medium-high heat. As soon as water boils, remove saucepan from heat. Cover and let eggs stand for 12 minutes. Drain and cool quickly under cold running water. This rapid chilling prevents a dark ring from forming around the egg yolk.

To Soft-Cook Eggs
Follow the instructions for hard-cooked eggs. Let eggs stand 3 to 5 minutes, depending on how soft you like your eggs. Immediately cool in cold water for a few seconds to stop cooking and make handling easier.

PÂTÉ TRUFFLES

This recipe idea came to me when I was working on a *Canadian Living* food feature. Turns out, it's one of the easiest ways to serve pâté.

———————————————— ◆ ————————————————

¼ cup	butter	50 mL
2	onions, finely chopped	2
2	cloves garlic, minced	2
1 lb	chicken livers, trimmed and patted dry	500 g
1 tsp	salt	5 mL
1 tsp	dried thyme	5 mL
2 tbsp	brandy	25 mL
½ lb	cream cheese	250 g
	Freshly ground black pepper	
1 cup	whole wheat bread crumbs	250 mL
¼ cup	chopped walnuts or pistachios, toasted	50 mL
2 cups	shredded lettuce or other greens	

• In heavy skillet, melt butter. Add onions and garlic; sauté for about 5 minutes or until tender and golden.
• Add chicken livers; cook, stirring occasionally, for 4 minutes. Add salt, thyme and brandy; cook for about 5 minutes longer or just until livers are no longer pink. Let cool slightly.
• In food processor, purée liver mixture or press mixture through sieve using wooden spoon. Cut cream cheese into pieces; add to liver purée. Process until smooth. Season with pepper to taste.
• Turn into bowl, cover and refrigerate for 4 hours or until firm.
• In shallow pan, combine bread crumbs and walnuts. Form spoonfuls of pâté into ³/₄-inch (2 cm) balls; roll in crumb-nut mixture.
• To store: Place in covered container, in layers separated with waxed paper, and refrigerate for up to 3 days.
• Place on serving plate lined with greens.

Makes 48 pâté truffles.

LIGHT PÂTÉ

Pâté is usually full of lots of butter or cream cheese. Not this one. The only fat comes from the eggs and chicken livers.

◆

¹/₂ lb	chicken livers	250 g
¹/₂ tsp	salt	2 mL
1	onion, chopped	1
1	clove garlic, minced (optional)	1
¹/₂ cup	tomato sauce	125 mL
4	medium mushrooms, chopped	4
2	hard-cooked eggs, chopped	2
2 tbsp	chopped fresh parsley	25 mL
1 tsp	Worcestershire sauce	5 mL
¹/₈ tsp	nutmeg	0.5 mL
	Freshly ground black pepper	

• Rinse chicken livers and remove any visible fat; place in small saucepan. Cover with cold water and add salt. Bring to a boil, reduce heat and simmer for 5 minutes. Drain and chop.
• Meanwhile, in another saucepan, simmer onion and garlic, if using, in tomato sauce for about 7 minutes or until tender.
• In container of blender or food processor, combine liver, onion mixture, mushrooms, hard-cooked eggs, parsley, Worcestershire sauce and nutmeg. Process for about 2 minutes or until smooth. Blend in pepper to taste. (If you do not have a blender or food processor, press the hot chopped liver through a coarse sieve using a wooden spoon. You'll find the liver is soft and easy to work with when it has just been freshly simmered and is still hot. Blend in remaining ingredients.)
• Pack into small bowl or crockery pot. Cover and chill.
• To store: Keep, covered, in refrigerator for up to 3 days.

Makes 1¹/₂ cups (375 mL).

JELLIED PÂTÉ

This quick-to-fix trick with deli pâté made its rounds at cottage "happy hours" in the late '60s.

————————————— ◆ —————————————

1	envelope unflavored gelatin	1
¼ cup	water	50 mL
1	can (10 oz/284 mL) consommé	1
1 tbsp	dry white or red wine	15 mL
¼ tsp	Worcestershire sauce	1 mL
	Salt and pepper	
½ lb	fine liver sausage	250 g
	Crackers or lightly buttered French bread	

- Sprinkle gelatin over water; set aside for 5 minutes to soften.
- In saucepan, heat consommé, wine and Worcestershire sauce. Stir in softened gelatin until it dissolves. Season with salt and pepper, to taste. Pour a small amount into small (3 cup/750 mL) mold to thickly coat bottom. Refrigerate for about 15 minutes or until just set.
- Mash pâté and combine with remaining consommé mixture. Pour over set gelatin in mold. Cover and refrigerate for at least 4 hours or until firmly set.
- Unmold on serving tray or board. Surround with assorted crackers and/or small pieces of lightly buttered, thinly sliced French bread.
- To store: Cover with plastic wrap; refrigerate for up to 4 days.

Makes 12 to 16 appetizer servings.

Variation
—————————

FLOATING PÂTÉ

- Coat bottom of mold as above then allow remaining consommé mixture to chill for about 30 minutes or until partially set (mounds slightly on a spoon.)

- Cut chilled pâté or liverwurst into bite-size pieces. Gently fold into partially set gelatin. Pour into mold.
- Chill for at least 4 hours or until firmly set before serving.

SMOKED SALMON
PÂTÉ

For quick canapés, spread this pâté on melba toast or place in English cucumber or zucchini cups. Make the latter by scooping out a little of the seed section of a $^1/_2$-inch (1 cm) slice. A small wedge of a cherry tomato makes a great garnish.

♦

$^1/_4$ lb	smoked salmon	125 g
1 cup	cream cheese ($^1/_2$ lb/250 g)	250 mL
2 tsp	lemon juice	10 mL
2 tsp	minced onion	10 mL
1 tsp	chopped fresh dill	5 mL
	or $^1/_2$ tsp (2 mL) dried dillweed	
2	drops hot pepper sauce	2

- In container of food processor, combine smoked salmon, cream cheese, lemon juice, onion, dill and hot pepper sauce. Process for about 2 minutes, scraping down bowl frequently, until puréed and smooth. Spoon into serving crock or dish.
- Cover and refrigerate overnight for flavors to blend.
- To store: Place in covered container and refrigerate for up to 4 days.

Makes 1$^1/_4$ cups (300 mL).

Variations

SMOKED TROUT PÂTÉ

• In place of salmon, use smoked trout; in place of dill and hot pepper sauce, use $^1/_2$ tsp (2 mL) Dijon-style mustard.

SMOKED OYSTER PÂTÉ

• In place of salmon, use 1 can ($3^1/_2$ oz/ 92 g) smoked oysters, well drained; in place of dill, use chopped fresh parsley.

SMOKED SALMON, TROUT OR OYSTER DIP

• To the Smoked Salmon, Trout or Oyster Pâté , blend in $^1/_4$ cup (50 mL) light or regular mayonnaise and $^1/_4$ cup (50 mL) light or regular sour cream.

HELPFUL HINT

Lighter Pâtés
For lighter pâtés with fewer calories per serving, in place of cream cheese, use $^1/_2$ cup (125 mL/125 g) light cream cheese and $^1/_2$ cup (125 mL) 1% cottage cheese.

CAVIAR AND EGG MOUSSE

If you have a yen for caviar but feel it's too extravagant, this creation is for you. A little bit goes a long way.

◆

¹/₄ cup	dry sherry	50 mL
2 tbsp	lemon juice	25 mL
1	envelope unflavored gelatin	1
1 cup	mayonnaise	250 mL
2	rinsed anchovy fillets, minced	2
1 tsp	Worcestershire sauce	5 mL
6	hard-cooked eggs	6
1	green onion, minced	1
2	jars (1³/₄ oz/50 g) lumpfish caviar	2
1	jar (1³/₄ oz/50 g) small black caviar	1
	Fresh dill or parsley sprigs	

• In small saucepan, combine sherry and lemon juice. Sprinkle gelatin over top; let stand for 5 minutes to soften.

• In bowl, beat mayonnaise, sour cream, anchovy and Worcestershire sauce.

• Place gelatin mixture over low heat, stirring until dissolved. Stir ¹/₂ cup (125 mL) mayonnaise mixture into gelatin. Stir this into remaining mayonnaise mixture until well blended.

• In food processor or with knife, finely chop eggs. Fold eggs and green onion into mayonnaise mixture until well blended. Gently fold in half of the lumpfish caviar.

• Spoon into a rinsed 8-inch (20 cm) round flat-bottomed baking dish or flan pan.

• Refrigerate, covered, for at least 4 hours or until firm.

• Unmold on round platter or serving dish.

• Arrange black caviar in circle in center of mold; place remaining lumpfish caviar around edge of black caviar. Garnish with dill.

• Surround with French and rye bread.

Makes 12 to 16 servings.

CHEESE AND HAM PINWHEELS

For a savory biscuit to serve with a smooth vegetable soup, cut the pinwheel dough into 1 inch (2.5 cm) slices and bake.

———————————————— ◆ ————————————————

1	batch Baking Powder or Whole Wheat Baking Powder Biscuit dough (see pages 190-91)	1

Filling:

2 cups	shredded Cheddar, Edam, Gouda or Swiss cheese ($^1/_2$ lb/250 g)	500 mL
1 cup	finely chopped cooked ham	250 mL
$^1/_4$ cup	minced celery	50 mL
$^1/_4$ cup	mayonnaise or low-fat yogurt	50 mL

• On lightly floured surface, roll biscuit dough into an oblong about 12 x 18 inches (30 x 45 cm).
• *Filling:* In bowl, combine cheese, ham, celery and mayonnaise; mix well. Spread evenly over dough.
• Starting at one long side, roll up dough jelly-roll fashion into a long cylinder. Cut into $^1/_2$-inch (1 cm) slices. Place on nonstick or lightly buttered baking sheets.
• Bake in 375 F (190 C) oven for 15 minutes or until golden brown.

Variations

CHEESE AND SEAFOOD PINWHEELS

• In place of ham, use 1 cup (250 mL) finely chopped cooked shrimp, crab or scallops.

CHEESE SHORTBREAD

These crunchy cheese cookies store well in an airtight container for 2 to 3 weeks. For variety turn them into little sandwiches, using one of the Cheese Spreads (see page 3).

---

1 1/2 cups	shredded Cheddar, Edam, Gouda or Swiss cheese (1/3 lb/175 g)	375 mL
1 cup	butter	250 mL
2 cups	all-purpose flour	500 mL
1/4 tsp	salt	1 mL
1 tbsp	milk	15 mL
3	drops hot pepper sauce	3

• In mixing bowl or food processor, cream together cheese and butter. Work in flour, salt, milk and hot sauce. Form into a ball.
• On lightly floured surface, roll out to 1/8 inch (3 mm) thickness. With cookie cutter, cut into 1 1/2 inch (4 cm) rounds.
• Place on unbuttered baking sheet. With fork, prick each one.
• Bake in 350 F (180 C) oven for 10 minutes or until golden.
• Remove from baking sheets to wire racks to cool.

Makes 5 dozen.

Variations

CHEESE WHOLE WHEAT SHORTBREAD

• In place of 1 cup (250 mL) of the all-purpose flour, use 1 cup (250 mL) whole wheat or graham flour.

SEED OR NUT CHEESE SHORTBREAD

• Before baking, press a few caraway, fennel, sunflower, sesame or poppy seeds, pinenuts or chopped nuts (walnuts, pecans, hazelnuts) in center of each cookie.

TINY CHEESE PUFFS

French cooks would call these *petit gougères*. Serve the puffs warm or at room temperature. Or split them and use halves as tiny carriers for fillings such as egg, chicken or salmon salad.

◆

1 cup	water	250 mL
1/3 cup	butter	75 mL
1/2 tsp	salt	2 mL
1 cup	all-purpose flour	250 mL
4	eggs	4
1 cup	shredded Swiss, Gouda, Edam or Cheddar cheese (1/4 lb/125 g)	250 mL

Topping:

1	egg	1
1 tsp	water	5 mL
1/2 cup	sesame seeds	125 mL

• In 6-cup (1.5 L) saucepan, heat water, butter and salt to boiling. Add flour all at once. With wooden spoon, stir vigorously until mixture no longer sticks to the side of the pan and forms a ball. Remove from heat and allow to cool for about 5 minutes.

• Add eggs, one at a time, beating thoroughly after each addition until egg is completely blended into the cooked dough. Stir in shredded cheese. (Or the cooked dough can be transferred to the food processor. Add the eggs, processing until smooth. Add cheese, process for a few seconds.)

• Take up teaspoonfuls (5 mL) of the dough and with another spoon push them onto nonstick or lightly buttered baking sheets 2 inches (5 cm) apart.

• *Topping:* Beat egg with water and lightly brush on tops of dollops of dough. Sprinkle with sesame seeds.

- Bake in 400 F (200 C) oven for 10 minutes. Reduce heat to 350 F (180 C) and bake for about 25 minutes longer or until puffs have lightly browned and are firm to touch.
- With small, sharp knife, cut a slash on one side of each puff as soon as they come out of the oven to allow steam to escape. Cool away from drafts.
- Serve hot or at room temperature.
- To store: Pack in airtight plastic bags; store in freezer for up to 2 months.
- To reheat: Place on baking sheet and warm in 350 F (180 C) oven for about 10 minutes or until outside is firm to touch.

Makes 4 to 5 dozen 2-inch (5 cm) puffs.

Variations

HAM AND CHEESE PUFFS

- Add $^3/_4$ cup (175 mL) finely chopped ham and 1 tbsp (15 mL) minced onion to cooked dough after eggs are beaten into it. Omit topping.

SEAFOOD AND CHEESE PUFFS

- Add $^3/_4$ cup (175 mL) finely chopped crab meat, shrimp or scallops and 1 tbsp (15 mL) minced celery to cooked dough after eggs are beaten into it. Omit topping.

PETITES CROUSTADES

These are little toast cups for tantalizing hot or cold mixtures that can whet the appetite or even satisfy it as a small meal.

$\blacklozenge$

8	slices thinly sliced white or whole wheat bread	8
2 tbsp	melted butter	25 mL

- Remove crusts from bread. With rolling pin, flatten each slice. With cookie cutter, cut into 2-inch (5 cm) diameter circles.
- Press into buttered $1^1/_4$ to $1^1/_2$ inch (3 to 4 cm) muffin cups.
- Brush lightly with melted butter.
- Bake in 375 F (190 C) oven for 10 minutes or until crisp.
- To store: Layer in container with tight-fitting lid. Label and store in refrigerator for up to 4 weeks, in freezer for up to 3 months.

Makes 16.

MUSHROOM OYSTER CROUSTADES

$\blacklozenge$

16	Petites Croustades (see above)	16
2 tbsp	butter	25 mL
2 tbsp	minced onion	25 mL
$1/_4$ tsp	minced garlic	1 mL
12	button mushrooms, quartered	12
2 tbsp	all-purpose flour	25 mL
1	can (5 oz/142 g) oysters	1
$1/_2$ cup	whipping cream	125 mL
	Salt and freshly ground black pepper	

- Prepare and bake Petites Croustades.
- In small saucepan, heat butter. Add onion and garlic; sauté for 2 to 3 minutes until tender.
- Add mushrooms. Cook, stirring, for 5 minutes or until moisture evaporates.
- Add flour, stirring until all lumps disappear.
- Pour in oyster liquid; reserve oysters. Add cream. Cook, stirring, for about 2 minutes until sauce thickens. Add oysters; stir and cook until heated through. Season with salt and pepper, to taste.
- Divide evenly among croustades. Serve immediately while still hot or keep warm for 5 to 10 minutes in 300 F (150 C) oven.

Makes 16.

CHEESY CRAB OR SHRIMP CROUSTADES

◆

16	Petites Croustades (see page 18)	16
1	can (5 oz/ 142 g) crab or baby shrimp or 1 cup (250 mL) cooked	1
1 cup	shredded Cheddar, Edam, Gouda or Havarti cheese ($^1/_4$ lb/125 g)	250 mL
$^1/_4$ cup	shredded carrot	50 mL
$^1/_4$ cup	mayonnaise	50 mL
2 tsp	lemon juice	10 mL
Pinch	granulated sugar	Pinch
Pinch	curry powder	Pinch

- Prepare and bake Petites Croustades.
- Drain crab thoroughly. In small bowl, combine crab, cheese, carrot, mayonnaise, lemon juice, sugar and curry powder; mix well.
- Spoon evenly into croustades.
- Serve cold or bake in 375 F (190 C) oven for 10 minutes or until cheese melts and mixture is heated through.

Makes 16.

SEAFOOD AND CHEESE HOT SALAD

Yes, this unique salad is wonderful served hot as an appetizer.

◆

2 cups	coarsely shredded Gouda, Edam or Cheddar cheese (¹/₂ lb/250 g)	500 mL
2 cups	coarsely chopped cooked crabmeat and shrimp (1 lb/500 g shrimp and ¹/₂ lb/250 g crabmeat)	500 mL
1	onion, finely chopped	1
1 cup	finely chopped celery	250 mL
¹/₄ cup	finely chopped sweet green pepper	50 mL
¹/₄ cup	slivered almonds, toasted	50 mL
1 cup	mayonnaise	250 mL
¹/₄ cup	lemon juice	50 mL
1 tbsp	grated lemon rind	15 mL
¹/₂ tsp	salt	2 mL
¹/₄ tsp	dry mustard	1 mL
¹/₂ cup	dry bread crumbs	125 mL
2 tbsp	butter, melted	25 mL

• In bowl, combine cheese, seafood, onion, celery, green pepper and almonds. Set aside.
• In another bowl, mix together mayonnaise, lemon juice and rind, salt and mustard. Stir into seafood mixture. Spoon about 1 cup (250 mL) into each of 6 individual serving shells or ramekins.
• Combine crumbs and butter for topping and sprinkle over mixture in each shell.
• Bake in 300 F (150 C) oven for 10 to 12 minutes or until just heated through. (Or mixture may be heated in 6-cup (1.5 L) casserole for 20 to 25 minutes.)

Makes 6 servings.

GINGER SHRIMP AND BABY CORN

The shrimp, corn and celery look best arranged — or composed as they say in nouvelle cuisine circles — on the lettuce leaves.

◆

2 tbsp	olive oil or butter	25 mL
1	clove garlic, minced	1
1½ lb	medium raw shrimp, shelled and deveined (thaw if frozen)	750 g
2	stalks celery, thinly and diagonally sliced	2
1	can (14 oz/398 mL) sweet baby corn cobs	1
	Juice of ½ lime or lemon	
2 tbsp	grated fresh ginger root or 1 tsp (5 mL) ground ginger	25 mL
2 tbsp	soy sauce	25 mL
½ tsp	granulated sugar	2 mL
6	small lettuce leaves	6
	Slivers of sweet red pepper	

- In heavy skillet or wok, heat oil. Add garlic, shrimp, celery and corncobs. Stir-fry for about 10 minutes or just until shrimps turn pink and curl and celery is tender-crisp. Add lime juice.
- Stir in ginger root, soy sauce and sugar. Cook for 2 minutes longer.
- Serve immediately on lettuce leaves in scallop shells or on small plates. Garnish with slivers of red pepper.

Makes 4 servings.

Variation

MANDARIN ORANGE SCALLOPS

- In place of shrimp and sweet baby corn, use scallops (sea or larger ones, quartered) and 1 can (10 oz/284 mL) drained mandarin oranges.

Pigs in Blankets

In the '40s, as soon as the snow was crunchy, I remember both Mom and Aunt Mary baking these little sausage rolls, piling them into jam pails and putting them out in the back porch. It became their instant freezer. All winter long they kept edibles — pies, cookies, tarts, even roasting chickens — out there.

◆

8	breakfast sausages	8
1	batch Flaky Pastry (see page 271)	1
	Dijon-style mustard	

• Place sausages on rack in shallow roasting pan. Bake in 350 F (180 C) oven for 15 minutes or until no longer pink. Cool.
• Prepare Flaky Pastry. Wrap and freeze half for later use.
• On lightly floured surface, roll out remaining pastry to about $^1/_8$ inch (3 mm). Cut into 2 x 3-inch (5 x 8 cm) rectangles. Spread small amount of mustard down middle parallel to short side.
• Cut each sausage into 3 pieces about 2 inches (5 cm) long.
• Place piece of sausage on pastry rectangle and wrap pastry around sausage. Place seam side down on nonstick baking sheet. With fork, prick each roll several times. (Or cut pastry into $2^1/_2$-inch (6.5 cm) squares, spread with mustard, place sausage diagonally across square, roll up, wet overlapping edge and seal.
• Bake in 375 F (190 C) oven for 12 to 15 minutes or until golden.
• Serve warm or at room temperature.
• To store: Cool; pack in airtight container or plastic wrap. Refrigerate for up to 5 days; freeze for up to 6 weeks.
• To reheat: Defrost; bake in 375 F (190 C) oven for 7 minutes.

Makes 24.

MEATBALLS IN PIQUANT SAUCE

Over the years meatballs have been a consistently popular item at cocktail parties. It's the men who seem to love them.

◆

1	can (14 oz/398 mL) tomato sauce	1
½ cup	fruit jelly (apple, raspberry or currant)	125 mL
1 tbsp	Worcestershire sauce	15 mL
1	clove garlic, minced	1
1 tbsp	cornstarch	15 mL
1 tsp	curry powder	5 mL
1	batch cooked Zesty Meatballs (see page 94)	1

• In small saucepan, combine tomato sauce, jelly, Worcestershire sauce and garlic.
• In small bowl, combine cornstarch and curry powder. Mix in ½ cup (125 mL) tomato mixture until well blended with no lumps. Stir into mixture in saucepan until well blended.
• Bring to a boil. Cook, stirring constantly, for about 3 minutes or until thickened. Add meatballs. Warm until heated through.
• Spoon into serving or chafing dish.
• Have wooden picks handy for spearing meatballs.

Makes 16 servings.

Variation

SAUSAGES OR WEINERS IN PIQUANT SAUCE

• In place of meatballs, heat 1 lb (500 g) cooked cocktail sausages, or bite-size pieces of weiners or cooked sausages, in Piquant Sauce.

STICKY SESAME RIBS

There's only one problem with these: everyone tends to eat too many.

◆

3 lb	pork back ribs	1.5 kg
8 cups	water	2 L
8	whole black, peppercorns	8
3	cloves garlic, cut in half	3
1	onion stuck with 4 whole cloves	1
1	bay leaf	1
Marinade:		
1	can (10 oz/284 mL) consommé	1
$^1/_2$ cup	corn syrup	125 mL
2 tbsp	brown sugar	25 mL
2 tbsp	sesame oil	25 mL
2	cloves garlic, minced	2
1 tbsp	soy sauce	15 mL
1 tsp	salt	5 mL
2 tbsp	sesame seeds, toasted	25 mL

• Ask butcher to cut strips of ribs crosswise in half, then cut strips into single rib portions.

• In medium saucepan, combine ribs, water, peppercorns, halved garlic cloves, onion studded with cloves and bay leaf.

• Bring to a boil; reduce heat and simmer for 30 minutes or until nearly tender. Drain well, rinse under running water and pat dry. (Pre-cooked ribs can be wrapped and stored in refrigerator for up to 3 days or in freezer for up to 3 months.)

• Place pre-cooked ribs in large shallow baking dish or roasting pan in as close to a single layer as possible.

• *Marinade:* In bowl, mix together consommé, corn syrup, brown sugar, sesame oil, minced garlic, soy sauce and salt. Pour over ribs; cover and allow to marinate in refrigerator for 4 to 6 hours or overnight. Turn several times to coat meat completely with marinade.

- Drain marinade into saucepan. Bring to a boil and cook for 3 minutes or until slightly reduced. Pour back over ribs.
- Bake in 350 F (180 C) oven, turning occasionally, for 45 minutes or until ribs are browned and well coated with sticky sauce.
- Place on serving platter and sprinkle with sesame seeds.

Makes 30 servings.

Variations

Honey Garlic Ribs

- In place of corn syrup, use liquid honey; add 2 more minced garlic cloves.

Sticky Sesame Chicken Wings

- In place of pork ribs, use chicken wings. With sharp knife or poultry shears, separate each wing at its joints into 3 pieces. Add all pieces to pot for simmering. Drain off and reserve simmering broth for another use. (It is great chicken broth.) Keep pre-cooked wings in covered container in refrigerator for 3 days, in freezer for 3 months. Discard wing tips before marinating the other wing pieces.

Honey Garlic Chicken Wings

- In place of corn syrup, use liquid honey; add 2 more minced garlic cloves. Follow above directions.

MOM'S TIDBITS

These toasted tidbits go down by the handfuls. It was a great snack when the kids were teenagers and had gangs of their friends at the cottage or house. Mom had bowls of it around in the '50s when she and Dad had friends in to play canasta. This is her recipe, probably a variation of one taken from a package.

◆

2 cups	Shreddies cereal	500 mL
2 cups	Cheerios cereal	500 mL
2 cups	thin stick pretzels	500 mL
2 cups	salted peanuts or almonds	500 mL
$^1/_3$ cup	vegetable oil	75 mL
2 tsp	Worcestershire sauce	10 mL
1 tsp	celery salt	5 mL
$^1/_2$ tsp	garlic salt	2 mL

• In roasting pan, combine cereals, pretzels and peanuts.
• In cup measure, mix together oil, Worcestershire sauce, celery and garlic salt. Gradually pour over and toss lightly into cereal mixture.
• Bake in 250 F (120 C) oven, stirring every 20 minutes, for about 1 hour or until toasted. Spread on brown paper or paper towels to cool.
• To store: Pack into airtight container or plastic bags. Keeps in dry place for up to 6 weeks.

Makes 8 cups (2 L).

SOUPS

◆

If there is one food category that epitomizes comfort, it's soothing soup — hot or cold, chunky or smooth.

With that in mind, there was no question about which soup would lead this parade of recipes. It had to be Chicken Rice Soup that I make with tomatoes — our family's pacifier over the years. It was the first recipe each one of my children asked for when they headed out on their own. The original one came from my Mom and called for egg noodles and no tomatoes. But now we all prefer my version.

All of these soups are easy to make. Once you've mastered them I hope you'll add your own touch and create new variations of this comfort food.

MOM'S CHICKEN RICE SOUP

Nine times out of ten the broth from simmering two chickens becomes the base for my family's favorite, comfy chicken soup. Leftovers store well and the potion tastes even better the second time around.

◆

8 cups	strong chicken broth	2 L
2	stalks celery, diced	2
1	onion, finely chopped	1
1	carrot, diced	1
1	can (19 oz/540 mL) tomatoes, undrained	1
1/2 cup	long-grain rice	125 mL
1 cup	diced cooked chicken	250 mL
	Salt and pepper	

• In large saucepan, combine chicken broth, celery, onion, carrot, tomatoes and long-grain rice. (If tomatoes are whole, break up with a fork.)
• Bring to a boil, reduce heat and simmer for 20 to 25 minutes or until rice is tender.
• Add chicken bits. Simmer until heated through. Season with salt and pepper, to taste.
• To store: Refrigerate in covered containers for up to 4 days; freeze for up to 2 months.

Makes 6 to 8 servings.

Variation

CHICKEN NOODLE SOUP

• In place of long-grain rice, use 3/4 cup (175 mL) fine egg noodles.

MOM'S CORN CHOWDER

This supper soup was an old standby for Mom. It uses leftover boiled potatoes. (I'm sure she planned the leftovers — it's what I'd do — and she always had several cans of creamed corn standing by in her pantry along with canned salmon for the variation I really like.) It's perfect with Grilled Cheese Sandwiches (page 104).

♦

4	slices side bacon	4
1	onion, finely chopped	1
1	stalk celery, thinly sliced	1
1	can (19 oz/540 mL) cream-style corn	1
1 cup	fresh frozen or canned kernel corn	250 mL
1 cup	diced cooked potatoes	250 mL
2 cups	milk	500 mL
$^1/_2$ tsp	salt	2 mL
$^1/_8$ tsp	white pepper	0.5 mL

• In medium saucepan, cook bacon until crisp. Remove from pan, drain on paper towels, crumble and set aside.

• Add onion and celery to pan drippings; sauté for about 5 minutes or until tender.

• Stir in cream-style and kernel corn, potatoes, milk, salt and pepper. Bring to a boil, reduce heat and simmer for 3 minutes until thoroughly heated.

• Ladle into soup bowls. Garnish with crumbled bacon.

Makes 4 to 6 servings.

Variations

CORN AND SALMON CHOWDER

• Add 1 can (7$\frac{1}{2}$ oz/213 g) canned salmon or tuna packed in water to corn mixture and simmer for 3 minutes.

CORN AND CLAM CHOWDER

• Add 1 can (5 oz/142 g) clams to corn mixture and simmer for 3 minutes.

MELBA TOAST

◆

• Toast whole wheat or white bread. Remove crusts and reserve for bread crumbs. With serrated knife, cut toast slices crosswise in half. (Split pieces of toast can be buttered before drying in the oven. They'll be tastier, but the addition of butter adds calories.)
• Place on baking sheet or directly on oven rack. Bake in 350 F (180 C) oven for about 15 minutes or until dry and golden. (Bake crusts as well to crush for dry bread crumbs.)
• Serve with appetizer spreads, salads or soup.
• Store any extra toast in airtight containers or sealed plastic bags.

◆

HELPFUL HINT

To Store Cooked Soups and Chowders
Ladle into containers with lids. Refrigerate for up to 4 days; freeze for up to 4 months.

ATLANTIC CHOWDER

My friend Shirley Moase in Charlottetown makes wonderful fish chowder. The tip she shared with me is that she adds a smidgen of sugar to hers.

◆

¹/₄ lb	salt pork, slab bacon or ham	125 g
1 cup	chopped onions	250 mL
¹/₂ cup	chopped celery	125 mL
6	small potatoes, peeled and diced	6
1 tsp	salt	5 mL
¹/₄ tsp	white pepper	1 mL
1 cup	chicken or fish broth	250 mL
1¹/₂ lb	cod or haddock fillets, fresh or frozen (thawed)	750 g
1	can (5 oz/142 g) baby clams, undrained	1
3 cups	milk	750 mL
¹/₂ tsp	granulated sugar	2 mL
2 tbsp	chopped fresh parsley	25 mL

- Dice salt pork.
- In large heavy saucepan or soup kettle, fry it over medium heat until golden; remove bits of pork and set them aside.
- Add onions, and celery to pan and sauté for 5 minutes or until tender. Add potatoes, salt, pepper and broth; bring to a boil.
- Cut fish into bite-size squares. Add to broth, cover and simmer for about 20 minutes or until potatoes are tender.
- Add clams, their juice and milk. Heat to simmering. Stir in sugar. Taste and season with more salt and pepper, if desired.
- Ladle into warm bowls. Garnish with fried pork and parsley.

Makes 8 servings.

SPLIT PEA SOUP

Hearty soups like this one make substantial one-pot meals, especially when there are more than snippets clinging to the ham bone.

◆

1 lb	dry split peas	500 g
	Water	
1	leftover ham bone with meat	1
3	onions, chopped	3
3	carrots, chopped	3
2	stalks celery, chopped	2
2	cloves garlic, minced	2
1	bay leaf	1
1 tsp	salt	5 mL
$^1/_2$ tsp	freshly ground black pepper	2 mL
$^1/_2$ cup	dry white wine, optional	125 mL

- Rinse peas well. In large soup kettle, cover peas with water. Bring to a rapid boil for 2 minutes, turn off heat and let stand for 1 hour. Skim top. Rinse and drain.
- Add ham bone, onions, carrots, celery, garlic, bay leaf, salt and pepper. Pour on 10 cups (2.5 L) water. Bring to a boil, reduce heat and simmer, uncovered, for about 2 hours or until peas are tender.
- Remove any ham from bone. Chop ham and set aside. Discard bone and bay leaf. (For a smooth soup, purée in blender or food processor.) Return chopped ham to soup. Heat to piping hot, stir in wine, if desired, season with more salt and pepper, to taste.

Makes 12 servings.

Variation

HEARTY BEAN SOUP

- In place of split peas, use small dry white beans; add 1 can (14 oz/ 398 mL) tomatoes.

BEEF, VEGETABLE AND NOODLE SOUP

The simmering that draws out the beefy flavor from the meat in this soup takes time, so while I'm at it I usually double the recipe.

♦

$^1/_2$ lb	oxtails, braising ribs or stewing beef	250 g
5 cups	water	1.25 L
1	bay leaf	1
2 tsp	salt	10 mL
$^1/_4$ tsp	whole black peppercorns	1 mL
2	stalks celery, diced	2
1	large carrot, diced	1
1	small onion, finely chopped	1
1 cup	thin egg noodles	250 mL
1	can (14 oz/398 mL) tomatoes, undrained	1

• In large soup pot or Dutch oven, combine oxtails, water, bay leaf, salt and peppercorns. Bring to a boil, reduce heat, cover and simmer for 1 $^1/_2$ hours. (Skim off froth occasionally.)

• Defat by spooning off fat. Strain mixture through sieve. Discard bay leaf and peppercorns. Trim fat from meat; discard fat with bones. Cut meat into small cubes; set aside.

• Place pot with broth over medium heat. Add celery, carrot and onion. Bring to a boil; cook for 15 minutes or until vegetables are tender.

• Meanwhile, in another saucepan, cook noodles in lightly salted boiling water for about 8 minutes or until al dente (tender but firm). Drain; add noodles to vegetable mixture.

• Stir in tomatoes, breaking up any large pieces, and reserved meat cubes. Bring to a boil again; cook for about 2 minutes longer.

Makes 6 servings.

BORSCHT

There are many, many versions of borscht, but I don't think there's one that can match the beet soup made by my Ukrainian "baba" years ago in tiny Radisson, Saskatchewan.

◆

8 cups	vegetable or beef broth	2 L
1	onion, finely chopped	1
1	clove garlic, minced	1
2	beets, peeled and cut into shoestring strips or coarsely grated	2
1	carrot, peeled and cut into shoestring strips	1
2	stalks celery, thinly sliced	2
1	potato, peeled and cubed	1
3 cups	shredded cabbage	750 mL
1 cup	tomato juice	250 mL
1 tbsp	lemon juice	15 mL
	Salt and pepper	
$^{1}/_{2}$ cup	commercial sour cream	125 mL
1 tbsp	chopped fresh dill or parsley	15 mL

• In large saucepan or soup kettle, combine broth, onion, garlic and beets; simmer for 15 to 20 minutes or until the beets are partly cooked.
• Add carrot, celery and potato; cook for 5 minutes.
• Add shredded cabbage and continue cooking until cabbage is tender but not overcooked. Stir in tomato and lemon juice. Season with salt and pepper, to taste. (Borscht develops a richer flavor after standing for a few hours. To reheat, bring to a simmer. Do not boil.)
• Stir in sour cream, just before serving. Garnish with chopped dill.

Makes 10 to 12 servings.

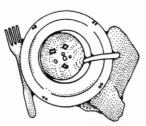

FRENCH ONION SOUP

The quality of the broth makes the soup. If it's weak, the soup will be too. Make strong broth by boiling regular broth to reduce it and make it more concentrated.

◆

¹/₄ cup	butter	50 mL
5	yellow onions, halved and sliced	5
2 tbsp	all-purpose flour	25 mL
3¹/₂ cups	strong beef broth	875 mL
¹/₂ cup	red wine	125 mL
1 tsp	Worcestershire sauce	5 mL
2	drops hot pepper sauce	5 mL
	Salt and freshly ground black pepper	
2 cups	Croutons (see page 42)	500 mL
¹/₄ cup	grated Parmesan cheese	50 mL
1 cup	shredded Gruyère cheese	250 mL

• In large saucepan, melt butter. Stir in sliced onions, cover and simmer for 30 minutes. Stir in flour and cook for 1 minute.

• Add beef broth, wine, Worcestershire sauce, hot pepper sauce, salt and pepper, to taste. Bring to a boil, reduce heat, cover and simmer for 5 minutes.

• Spoon hot soup into ovenproof bowls. Float croutons on top; sprinkle with Parmesan cheese then Gruyère cheese.

• Place under preheated broiler. Broil for about 1 minute or until cheese is bubbly and golden.

Makes 4 to 6 servings.

CHUNKY TOMATO SOUP

The canned vegetable I think of as a staple is the canned tomato. There is always a can of tomatoes right beside the canned corn and kidney beans in my staple cupboard.

◆

1 tbsp	olive oil	15 mL
1	small onion, chopped	1
1	clove garlic, minced	1
1 tbsp	all-purpose flour	15 mL
1	can (28 oz/796 mL) tomatoes, undrained or 6 large fresh tomatoes, peeled	1
2 cups	chicken broth	500 mL
1	bay leaf	1
1 tsp	crumbled dried sweet basil or 1 tbsp (15 mL) chopped fresh	5 mL
$\frac{1}{2}$ tsp	granulated sugar	2 mL
$\frac{1}{2}$ tsp	crumbled dried thyme	2 mL
$\frac{1}{2}$ tsp	salt	2 mL
$\frac{1}{4}$ tsp	baking soda	1 mL
Pinch	freshly ground black pepper	Pinch
$\frac{3}{4}$ cup	milk	175 mL

• In large saucepan, heat oil. Add onion and garlic; sauté for about 3 minutes or until tender. Stir in flour until smooth.
• Add tomatoes, breaking them into small pieces, chicken broth, bay leaf, basil, sugar, thyme, salt, baking soda and pepper. Bring to a boil, reduce heat, cover and simmer for 20 minutes for flavors to blend. Discard bay leaf.

• Stir about 1 cup (250 mL) tomato mixture into milk until well blended, then stir this mixture back into simmering soup. (If allowed to boil after milk is added, soup may curdle.) Ladle into soup bowls.

Makes 4 generous or 8 appetizer servings.

Variations

CHUNKY CLAMATO SOUP

• Add 1 can (5 oz/142 g) clams to tomato mixture after it has simmered for 20 minutes.

DUTCH TOMATO SOUP WITH GIN

• Add 6 juniper berries to simmering tomato mixture. Heat 2 tbsp (25 mL) to $1/4$ cup (50 mL) gin in a metal container, flame it; then stir it into soup before adding milk. Discard juniper berries.

HUNGARIAN TOMATO SOUP

• Stir 2 tsp (10 mL) paprika and $1/4$ cup (50 mL) dry white wine into simmering tomato mixture.

TOMATO BASIL SOUP

• Add an additional 1 tbsp (15 mL) chopped fresh or 1 tsp (5 mL) dried basil to tomato mixture.

CREAMY TOMATO SOUP

• Transfer any of the above soup mixtures to container of food processor or blender; process for 1 to 2 minutes or until puréed. Strain through a sieve into clean saucepan. For hot soup, heat just to simmering. Or chill thoroughly before serving. Drizzle 1 tsp (5 mL) low-fat yogurt or sour cream on each serving.

CHEESE SOUP

This rich soup calls for crunchy homemade Melba Toast (see page 30). Add a spinach salad and a crisp, juicy apple for dessert.

◆

1/4 cup	butter	50 mL
1	onion, minced	1
1/2 tsp	minced garlic	2 mL
1/4 cup	all-purpose flour	50 mL
1 1/2 cups	strong chicken broth	375 mL
2 cups	milk	500 mL
1 1/2 cups	shredded medium or aged Gouda or Cheddar cheese	375 mL

- In large saucepan, melt butter. Sauté onion and garlic for about 4 minutes or until onion is soft. Sprinkle with flour, stir in and cook for 2 to 3 minutes.
- Stir in chicken broth and milk. Cook over medium heat, stirring frequently, for about 3 minutes or until thickened and smooth.
- Over very low heat, stir in cheese just until it melts.
- After cheese is added, keep soup from boiling to prevent curdling.
- Keep warm over very low heat or hot water until serving time.

Makes 4 to 6 servings.

Variation

BROCCOLI CHEESE SOUP

- Add 2 cups (500 mL) chopped cooked broccoli to thickened broth and milk mixture.

Smooth No Name Soup

Our instructor at the Mexican cooking school in San Miguel Allende concocted a soup similar to this for us one day for a quick lunch. Although he had added only a few ounces of milk the soup was very creamy. The secret he said was the thickening quality of the potato.

◆

2	stalks celery	2
1	leek	1
1	small carrot	1
1	small white turnip	1
1	kohlrabi	1
1	potato	1
1 cup	green peas	250 mL
4 cups	chicken broth	1 L
1 tbsp	chopped fresh cilantro (fresh coriander) or parsley or 1 tsp (5 mL) dried parsley	15 mL

• Wash and slice celery and leek (use only white and light green part). Place in large saucepan.
• Wash, peel and chop carrot, turnip, kohlrabi and potato.
Add to saucepan. Stir in peas and chicken broth. Bring to a boil, then boil gently for 20 minutes until vegetables are tender. Add cilantro. Cook for 1 minute longer.
• Place about 2 cups (500 mL) at a time in container of blender or food processor. Process until puréed and smooth.
• Return to saucepan to reheat or refrigerate at this point to serve later. Serve hot or chilled garnished with chopped cilantro.

Makes 6 servings.

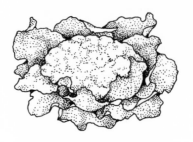

SMOOTH
CAULIFLOWER SOUP

I've discovered there is no end to variations of Smooth No Name Soup that work. This one and the following are ones I like and make regularly. For added pizzaz, I sprinkle croutons or swirl a little low-fat yogurt on top of each serving.

♦

1	medium head cauliflower, chopped (about 4 cups/1 L)	1
2	stalks celery, thinly sliced	2
1	potato, peeled and cubed	1
1	small onion, chopped	1
4 cups	chicken broth	1 L
1	bay leaf	1
$\frac{1}{2}$ tsp	salt	2 mL
$\frac{1}{8}$ tsp	white pepper	0.5 mL
Pinch	nutmeg	Pinch
$\frac{1}{2}$ cup	milk	125 mL

• In large saucepan, combine cauliflower, celery, potato, onion, chicken broth, bay leaf, salt, pepper and nutmeg. Bring to a boil. Reduce heat and simmer, covered, for 20 to 25 minutes or until cauliflower and potato are tender. Remove bay leaf.

• Transfer mixture to blender or food processor, in batches. Process for 1 to 2 minutes or until puréed and smooth.

• Pour back into saucepan. Stir in milk. Heat to simmering. Ladle into soup bowls.

Makes 4 generous or 6 appetizer servings.

Variations

SMOOTH ASPARAGUS SOUP

• In place of cauliflower, use 4 cups (1 L) chopped fresh or frozen asparagus.

SMOOTH BROCCOLI SOUP

• In place of cauliflower, use 4 cups (1 L) chopped fresh or frozen broccoli (1 bunch).

SMOOTH CUCUMBER SOUP

• In place of cauliflower, use 2 large English cucumbers, peeled and chopped; omit nutmeg and add 1 tsp (5 mL) dried dillweed or 1 tbsp (15 mL) chopped fresh dill. Garnish with plain yogurt and toasted chopped walnuts. Serve chilled, if you wish.

SMOOTH GREEN BEAN SOUP

• In place of cauliflower, use 4 cups (1 L) chopped green beans.

SMOOTH MUSHROOM SOUP

• In place of cauliflower, use 1 lb (500 g) mushrooms (reserving 3 or 4 to thinly slice for garnish).

SMOOTH PARSNIP OR CARROT SOUP

• In place of cauliflower use 4 cups (1 L) thinly sliced parsnips or carrots (or half and half). Add $^1/_4$ cup (50 mL) orange juice and 1 tsp (5 mL) grated orange rind.

SMOOTH PEAR SOUP

• In place of cauliflower, use 4 ripe pears, peeled, cored and chopped.

SMOOTH PUMPKIN OR SQUASH SOUP

• In place of cauliflower, use 3 cups (750 mL) cubed pumpkin or squash (butternut, acorn or hubbard). Add 1 tsp (5 mL) sugar and $^1/_2$ tsp (2 mL) cinnamon. Garnish with finely chopped toasted walnuts or pecans.

VICHYSSOISE

• In place of cauliflower, onion and milk use 5 leeks, white part only, sliced, 3 more potatoes, diced, $^1/_2$ cup light cream and dash Worcestershire sauce. Serve hot or chilled, garnished with chopped chives.

CROUTONS

♦

| 6 | slices lightly buttered bread, preferably French or Italian style | 6 |
| 2 tbsp | butter, melted | 25 mL |

• Cut bread into small to medium cubes. Spread on jelly-roll pan.
• Bake in 325 F (160 C) oven for 15 minutes.
• Turn and sprinkle melted butter over cubes. Turn again. Return to oven to bake for 15 minutes longer or until crisp and lightly browned.
• Cool before using.
• To store: Pack in airtight bags or containers. Keep in cool, dry place or refrigerator for up to 4 weeks.

Makes 4 to 5 cups (1 L to 1.25 L).

Variations

GARLIC CROUTONS

• Add 1 minced clove garlic to melted butter.

PARMESAN CROUTONS

• After drizzling on melted butter, sprinkle with $^1/_4$ cup (50 mL) grated Parmesan cheese.

SUMMER GAZPACHO

When speed is important the ingredients in this classic uncooked soup can be combined and puréed in a food processor. However, I still prefer to hand chop the celery, pepper and cucumber for a crunchy texture.

◆

12	plum tomatoes, peeled and chopped, or 6 regular	12
1	slice white bread	1
1	green onion, chopped	1
1	clove garlic	1
1 tbsp	chopped fresh basil or parsley	15 mL
1 tbsp	olive oil	15 mL
2 tsp	cider vinegar	10 mL
Dash	hot pepper sauce	Dash
1 cup	tomato juice	250 mL
1	sweet red or green pepper, diced	1
1 cup	finely chopped cucumber	250 mL
$^1/_2$ cup	finely chopped celery	125 mL
	Salt and pepper	

• In food processor or blender, purée tomatoes, bread, onion, garlic, basil, olive oil, vinegar and hot pepper sauce.
• Stir in tomato juice, red pepper, cucumber and celery. Season with salt and pepper, to taste. Chill for at least 1 hour before serving.
• To store: Keep in a covered container in refrigerator for up to 5 days. Always stir well before serving.

Makes 6 servings.

Variation

QUICK GAZPACHO

• In place of fresh tomatoes (when they are unavailable or too expensive), use 1 can (19 oz/540 mL) tomatoes.

SUMMER FRUIT SOUP

Both the color and flavor of this soup are more vibrant when you use fresh fruit. For exciting taste variations I mix several fruits.

◆

4 cups	fresh, frozen or canned fruit (strawberries, raspberries, cherries, sliced apricots, peaches, pears)	1 L
1 cup	fruit juice (orange, apple or cranberry)	250 mL
$^1/_3$ cup	granulated sugar	75 mL
$^1/_4$ cup	cornstarch or quick-cooking tapioca	50 mL
$^1/_2$ tsp	cinnamon	2 mL
$^1/_4$ tsp	salt	1 mL
2 cups	water	500 mL
$^1/_4$ cup	dry white wine	50 mL
	Plain yogurt, cream or commercial sour cream	

• In food processor or blender, combine fruit, juice, sugar, cornstarch, cinnamon and salt. Process for about 2 minutes until puréed.
• Pour into saucepan. Stir in water. Bring to a boil. Cook, stirring for about 2 minutes or until thickened. Stir in wine. Cook for 1 minute longer.
• For extra smooth soup, strain through a sieve.
• Serve hot or cold. Garnish with dollop or swirl of yogurt.

Makes 6 servings.

SALADS &
DRESSINGS

◆

When I lived with my parents, the season dictated what kind of side salad we had. In summer, it was tossed, using the lettuce, green onions and radishes that grew in our garden. In the winter, it was coleslaw, Waldorf, carrot and raisin or jellied salad made from vegetables, fruits and canned fruits stored in the cellar. There was no year round supply of salad greens except iceberg lettuce and celery. And after the vegetables travelled to Sakatchewan in the dead of winter they were pretty sad and limp.

The selection of greens at my fingertips today is almost unlimited. So is the assortment of salads I serve.

Dressings — vinaigrettes to creamy mayonnaise-types — make the salad. With the assortment of oils, vinegars, herbs and spices available, it's possible for every salad to be unique.

HELPFUL HINTS

Salad Greens
• Salad greens may include any of the following, on their own or in combination: lettuces — iceberg, Boston, green and red leaf, Napa, romaine, radicchio, mâche; chicory; endive; Belgian endive; dandelion greens; celery; spinach.

To Store Greens
• Wash and dry thoroughly. Place in a plastic bag with a piece of dry paper towel. Close loosely. Store in crisper in refrigerator for up to 6 days.

TOSSED GREEN SALAD

You could have a different tossed green salad every day for a month by varying both the greens and dressings.

———————————————————— ♦ ————————————————————

4 cups	bite-size pieces mixed salad greens	1 L
3 to 4	thinly sliced green onions	3 to 4
$^{1}/_{3}$ to $^{1}/_{2}$ cup	any oil and vinegar dressing (see pages 65 to 67) or Tangy Yogurt Dressing (see page 72) or Creamy Herb Dressing (see page 70)	75 to 125 mL

- In salad bowl, combine crisp and well-drained salad greens and green onions.
- Pour dressing over top. Toss lightly until all greens are coated.
- Serve immediately.

Makes 4 servings.

CAESAR SALAD

Some Caesar Salad lovers insist on making it with crisp bacon bits. I'm on the side of the ones who prefer anchovies.

◆

1	large head romaine lettuce	1
2 cups	Garlic Croutons (see page 42)	500 mL
Dressing:		
4	anchovy fillets, drained	4
1	clove garlic, minced	1
$^1/_2$ tsp	dry mustard	2 mL
	Juice of 1 lemon	
$^1/_2$ tsp	Worcestershire sauce	2 mL
1	coddled egg	1
$^1/_4$ cup	grated Parmesan cheese	50 mL
$^2/_3$ cup	olive oil	150 mL

• Wash and thoroughly dry romaine leaves. Fold leaves down the spine, cut off spine and discard. Tear leaves into bite-size pieces. Place in plastic bag with a piece of paper towel. Refrigerate.
• Prepare Garlic Croutons in advance.
• *Dressing:* In large wooden salad bowl, combine anchovy fillets, garlic and mustard. Mash with metal spoon into a smooth paste. Beat in lemon juice, Worcestershire sauce, coddled egg and 2 tbsp (25 mL) grated Parmesan.
• Beat very rapidly while pouring in oil in a steady stream until dressing is thick and creamy.
• (Alternatively, in food processor combine anchovy fillets, garlic, mustard, lemon juice, Worcestershire sauce, egg and 1 tbsp (15 mL) grated Parmesan cheese; process until thick and creamy. Add oil in a steady stream, processing until thick and creamy. Then place in salad bowl.)
• Add chilled romaine, croutons and remaining Parmesan cheese. Toss to mix thoroughly. Serve immediately.

Makes 6 servings.

Variation

CAESAR WITH BACON

• Add well-drained, crumbled, cooked side bacon (about 4 slices) to romaine in salad bowl.

HELPFUL HINT

To Coddle Egg
• Bring a small saucepan of water to simmering. Gently slip egg into water. Remove from heat. Let stand for 4 to 5 minutes. Remove to cold water to cool.

ASPARAGUS MIMOSA

Any food sprinkled with sieved egg yolk takes on the name *mimosa*.

---

1 lb	fresh asparagus	500 g
6	mushrooms, thinly sliced	6
2 tbsp	chopped sweet red pepper or pimiento (optional)	25 mL
$^1/_2$ cup	Herb Vinaigrette (see page 65) or Italian Dressing (see page 67)	125 mL
2	hard-cooked eggs	2

• In lightly salted boiling water, cook asparagus for about 4 minutes until tender-crisp. Do not cook until soft. Drain and chill.
• Arrange chilled asparagus spears in a shallow serving dish or on individual salad plates. Top with mushroom slices and red pepper.
• Drizzle vinaigrette dressing over all.
• Chop eggs, then press through a sieve over asparagus.

Makes 4 to 6 servings.

Gingered Napa Cabbage and Mandarin Salad

Napa is a curly leafed Chinese cabbage. Its crisp sweetness goes well with the subtle tartness of fresh oranges.

◆

3 cups	shredded Napa cabbage	750 mL
1 cup	clementine or mandarin orange sections*, cut in half lengthwise	250 mL
4	green onions, thinly sliced	4
2 tbsp	shredded fresh ginger root	25 mL
⅓ cup	Italian Dressing (see page 67)	75 mL
2 tbsp	toasted almond slices or sesame seeds	25 mL

- In salad bowl, combine Napa lettuce, orange sections, green onions and ginger root; toss well.
- Pour dressing over lettuce mixture; toss well.
- Sprinkle with almonds. Serve immediately.

Makes 4 servings.

* from 2 fresh clementine or mandarin oranges or 1 can (10 oz/ 284 mL) mandarin sections, drained.

Variation

Spinach Mandarin Salad

- In place of Napa cabbage, use 6 cups (1.5 L) torn spinach leaves (10 oz/300 g).

THREE-BEAN SALAD

Fresh green salad fixings weren't as plentiful out of season in the '50s and '60s as they are now. Many innovative salads such as this one using three different canned beans found their way into magazine advertisements. For my version I use fresh, frozen and canned beans which are available thoughout the year.

◆

1¹/₂ lb	green beans, cut into 1-inch (2.5 cm) pieces or 2 packages (10 oz/283 g) frozen cut green beans	750 mL
1	package (10 oz/300 g) frozen small lima beans	1
1	can (19 oz/540 mL) red kidney beans, drained	1
4	green onions, finely chopped	4
1	clove garlic, minced	1
¹/₂ cup	Special French Dressing (see page 66) or Italian Dressing (see page 67)	125 mL

• In saucepan of lightly salted boiling water, cook fresh beans for 5 to 8 minutes or frozen beans just until tender-crisp. Cook lima beans following package directions. Drain both and cool under cold running water.
• In large bowl, combine green beans, lima beans, kidney beans and onions; toss gently to mix.
• In small bowl, combine garlic and dressing; pour over bean mixture; toss gently to coat.
• Cover; chill for 4 hours or overnight to allow flavors to blend.
• To store: Cover and refrigerate for up to 4 days.

Makes 6 servings.

WALDORF SALAD

All through my high school days this was my favorite salad, especially when Mom made it with brand new McIntosh apples in the fall. But in the spring when the stored apples were old and mealy with no crunch the salad's rating dropped.

This old specialty may be altered by varying the fruit and/or nuts and even adding spinach or cabbage. Try banana and pecans or in the summer peaches and peanuts in place of the apples and walnuts. I use yogurt in the dressing because I like the tang it adds. Mom never used it. She didn't even know it existed.

◆

¹/₄ cup	Mom's Cooked Salad Dressing (see page 71) or Mayonnaise (see page 69)	50 mL
¹/₄ cup	low-fat plain yogurt or commercial sour cream	50 mL
2 tsps	granulated sugar	10 mL
2 tsps	lemon juice	10 mL
	Salt and pepper	
2	firm red apples	2
2	stalks celery	2
¹/₂ cup	chopped walnuts or unblanched almonds	125 mL

• In small salad bowl, combine salad dressing, yogurt, sugar, lemon juice and salt and pepper, to taste.
• Core apples; cut into bite-size cubes. Dice celery. Add both to salad bowl. Fold in nuts.
• Chill for up to 2 hours. Toss before serving.

Makes 4 servings.

CUCUMBERS WITH SOUR CREAM

The marinating seems to partly pickle the cucumbers and onions in this salad. They're sweet, sour and crisp, just right with curried dishes.

◆

4	cucumbers	4
	or 2 long English cucumbers	
2	onions	2
1/3 cup	vinegar	75 mL
1/4 cup	granulated sugar	50 mL
1/4 cup	water	50 mL
2 tsp	salt	10 mL
1/2 cup	commercial sour cream or low-fat plain yogurt	125 mL
2 tbsp	chopped fresh dill or 2 tsp (10 mL) dried dillweed	25 mL
1/2 tsp	Dijon-style mustard	2 mL
1/4 tsp	freshly ground white or black pepper	1 mL

• Cut ends from cucumbers and discard. Cut regular cucumbers lengthwise in half. With small spoon scrape out seeds and discard.
• Cut cucumbers and onions into even slices. Place in glass bowl.
• In another bowl, combine vinegar, sugar, water and salt. Stir to dissolve sugar.
• Pour over cucumber mixture. Toss well.
• With small plate weighting down mixture, let stand in refrigerator for about 4 hours. Drain well.
• In salad bowl, combine sour cream, dill, mustard and pepper. Fold in cucumber mixture.

Makes 6 to 8 servings.

COLESLAW

Mom relied on cabbage as the base for a whole array of salads. It's probably because other greens were not as readily available.

—————————————— ♦ ——————————————

$^1/_2$	small head cabbage (2 cups/500 mL shredded)	$^1/_2$
$^1/_2$	small onion, finely chopped	$^1/_2$
$^1/_4$ cup	Mom's Cooked Salad Dressing (see page 71) or Mayonnaise (see page 69)	50 mL
$^1/_4$ cup	commercial sour cream Salt and freshly ground black pepper	50 mL

• Cut cabbage in quarters. Place cut side down on board and with sharp knife cut into thin shreds. In salad bowl, combine cabbage and onion.
• Mix together dressing and sour cream. Mix into cabbage mixture.
• Serve immediately or chill before serving.

Makes 4 servings.

Variation
———————————

COLESLAW VARIATIONS

• Add any one or a combination of the following: $^1/_2$ cup (125 mL) shredded carrot; $^1/_2$ cup (125 mL) finely chopped celery; $^1/_2$ cup (125 mL) shredded red cabbage (or make half or all of coleslaw with red cabbage); $^1/_2$ cup (125 mL) green or red seedless grapes; 2 tbsp (25 mL) peanuts; 2 tbsp (25 mL) raisins or currants. Every additional cup (250 mL) makes 2 more servings.

SAUERKRAUT
PINEAPPLE SALAD

Here's another salad that improves with age. It's great with chili.

--- ◆ ---

$^1\!/_2$ cup	cider vinegar	125 mL
$^1\!/_2$ cup	granulated sugar	125 mL
$^1\!/_4$ cup	vegetable oil	50 mL
1 tsp	salt	5 mL
4	drops hot pepper sauce	4
4 cups	sauerkraut	1 L
2	onions, halved, thinly sliced	2
2	stalks celery, thinly sliced	2
1	carrot, halved, thinly sliced	1
1	can (14 oz/398 mL) pineapple chunks, drained	1
1 tsp	celery seeds	5 mL
	Freshly ground black pepper	

• In saucepan, combine vinegar, sugar, oil, salt and hot pepper sauce. Bring to a boil, stirring constantly, until sugar is dissolved. Set aside.
• In colander or sieve, drain sauerkraut. Rinse under cold running water. Drain well, for about 15 minutes.
• With scissors, cut into pieces, about 1 inch (2.5 cm) long.
• In large bowl, combine sauerkraut, onions, celery, carrot, pineapple chunks and celery seeds. Pour on vinegar mixture. Toss to thoroughly mix. Season with pepper, to taste.
• Refrigerate, covered, stirring occasionally, for 24 hours.
• To store: Keep refrigerated for up to 10 days.

Makes 10 to 12 servings.

BROWN RICE SALAD

♦

$^1/_2$ cup	uncooked brown rice	125 mL
1 $^1/_4$ cups	water	300 mL
$^1/_4$ tsp	salt	1 mL
4	green onions, finely chopped	4
2	tomatoes, seeded and coarsely chopped	2
$^1/_2$	English cucumber, coarsely chopped	$^1/_2$
6	medium, pitted black olives, sliced	6
1 cup	alfalfa sprouts	250 mL

Dressing:

$^1/_2$ cup	low-fat yogurt	125 mL
2 tsp	lemon juice	10 mL
1 tsp	sesame oil	5 mL
$^1/_4$ tsp	chili powder	1 mL
	Salt and pepper	
	Leaf lettuce leaves	

• In saucepan, combine rice, water and salt. Bring to a boil, reduce heat and simmer, stirring occasionally, for 35 minutes or until rice is tender. Set aside to cool for about 30 minutes.

• In salad bowl, combine rice, onions, tomatoes, cucumber, olives and alfalfa sprouts; toss well.

• *Dressing:* In small bowl, combine yogurt, lemon juice, sesame oil and chili powder. Season with salt and pepper, to taste. Pour over vegetables; toss to coat.

• Serve on lettuce leaves placed on chilled salad plates.

Makes 4 to 6 servings.

Variations

BROWN RICE AND TUNA SALAD

• Add 1 can (7 oz/198 g) tuna, drained and broken in pieces to vegetable mixture before pouring on the dressing.

BEST POTATO SALAD

You'll notice this salad is dressed twice. That's what makes it the best potato salad I know.

———————————— ♦ ————————————

8	large potatoes	8
2 tsp	salt	10 mL
1	bay leaf	1
$^1/_2$ cup	Special French Dressing (see page 66)	125 mL
12	red radishes, sliced (optional)	12
4	hard-cooked eggs, chopped	4
1	onion, minced or 5 green onions, thinly sliced	1
1 cup	Mayonnaise (see page 69)	250 mL
$^1/_2$ cup	commercial sour or whipped cream	125 mL
	Salt and freshly ground black pepper	
	Chopped fresh parsley or chives	

• In saucepan, just cover potatoes with water. Bring to a boil, add salt and bay leaf. Cook, covered, for 20 to 25 minutes or until tender. Discard bay leaf. Drain; shake in pan over heat for a few seconds to steam dry. Cool for 10 minutes. While warm, peel and coarsely chop potatoes; put them in salad bowl.
• Pour on dressing; toss to coat potato pieces. Cool.
• Add radishes, if desired, eggs and onion; mix well.
• Combine mayonnaise and cream. Stir into potato mixture. Season with salt and pepper, to taste. Sprinkle with parsley.
• Cover and refrigerate until serving time.
• To store: Cover and refrigerate for up to 4 days. Stir before serving.

Makes 8 servings.

Avocado, Cheese and Walnut Stuffed Pears

This type of arranged salad may be served as a starter before the soup at a dinner party or as a separate course after it.

———————————— ◆ ————————————

2	firm ripe pears	2
1 tbsp	lemon juice, divided	15 mL
1	small ripe avocado	1
$\frac{1}{4}$ cup	crumbled blue cheese	50 mL
1 tbsp	chopped walnuts	15 mL
4	small lettuce leaves	4
12	slivers sweet red pepper	12

• Rinse and dry pears, cut lengthwise in half and with spoon remove core. Sprinkle cut surfaces with 1 tsp (5 mL) lemon juice.
• Peel and pit avocado. In small bowl, mash avocado; blend in blue cheese and remaining lemon juice. Stir in walnuts.
• Place a lettuce leaf on each salad plate. Place pear, cut side up, on lettuce.
• Spoon avocado mixture into center cavity of each pear. Garnish with red pepper slivers. Chill until serving time.

Makes 4 servings.

———————————— ◆ ————————————

Helpful Hint

To Test Avocadoes For Ripeness
A ripe avocado always feels a little soft. An unripe one is as hard as a rock. To speed up ripening at home, place firm avocadoes in a paper bag and store them at room temperature. They will never ripen in the refrigerator.

TOMATO ASPIC

Jellied salads were popular when I was a teenager and I had my fill of them. However, I liked this one and Mom made several for my 1953 wedding buffet.

◆

2	envelopes unflavored gelatin	2
2¹/₂ cups	tomato juice	625 mL
¹/₂ cup	finely chopped celery	125 mL
2 tbsp	minced onion	25 mL
1 tbsp	granulated sugar	15 mL
1 tsp	red wine vinegar	5 mL
1 tsp	Worcestershire sauce	5 mL
2 tbsp	lemon juice	25 mL
	Salt	
	Lettuce leaves	

• In small dish or cup, sprinkle gelatin over ¹/₂-cup (125 mL) tomato juice; let stand for 5 minutes to soften.
• In saucepan, combine remaining tomato juice, celery, onion, sugar, vinegar, Worcestershire sauce and lemon juice. Heat to simmer and simmer for about 5 minutes. Stir in gelatin until it dissolves. Season with salt, to taste.
• Strain into rinsed 4-cup (1 L) mold or 8 small ¹/₂-cup (125 mL) custard cups.
• Refrigerate for about 4 hours until firm.
• Unmold on lettuce leaves on serving plate or individual salad plates.

Makes 8 servings.

Variations

ORANGE TOMATO ASPIC

- Replace 1 cup (250 mL) of the tomato juice with 1 cup (250 mL) orange juice.

ASPIC WITH PEAS

- Chill strained Tomato Aspic mixture for about 30 minutes or until slightly gelled and mixture mounds on a spoon. Fold in 1 cup (250 mL) cooked fresh or frozen green peas.

PERFECTION SALAD

The original recipe for this molded cabbage and carrot salad probably called for an orange gelatin dessert powder, but since I'm a "from scratch" cook, this is the version I prefer.

◆

2	envelopes unflavored gelatin	2
²/₃ cup	cold water	150 mL
1 cup	boiling water	250 mL
¹/₃ cup	granulated sugar	75 mL
¹/₄ cup	lemon juice	50 mL
2 tbsp	white vinegar	25 mL
¹/₂ tsp	salt	2 mL
1¹/₂ cups	finely chopped cabbage	375 mL
1 cup	shredded carrot	250 mL
¹/₂ cup	finely chopped celery	125 mL
2 tbsp	minced onion	25 mL
	Lettuce leaves	

- In small bowl, sprinkle gelatin over cold water; let stand for 5 minutes to soften.
- Add boiling water; stir until gelatin completely dissolves. Stir in sugar, lemon juice, vinegar and salt until sugar dissolves.
- Place in refrigerator to chill for about 15 minutes or until partially set and mixture mounds slightly on a spoon.
- In large bowl, combine cabbage, carrot, celery and onion.
- Add partially gelled mixture; stir until well combined.
- Pour into 4-cup (1 L) mold, 8-inch (20 cm) square baking dish or eight $1/2$-cup (125 mL) custard cups. Chill for 4 hours or until set.
- At serving time, unmold on bed of lettuce.
- To store: Cover and refrigerate for up to 4 days.

Makes 8 servings.

Variations

PINEAPPLE PERFECTION SALAD

- In place of water, use juice drained from 1 can (14 oz/398 mL) pineapple tidbits (if necessary, add water to make up difference) and fold pineapple pieces into cabbage and carrot mixture.

BEET AND CRANBERRY PERFECTION SALAD

- In place of carrots, use 1 cup (250 mL) shredded cooked beets. Cook $3/4$ cup (175 mL) fresh cranberries with $1/4$ cup (50 mL) granulated sugar and 2 tbsp (25 mL) water for about 4 minutes or until cranberries are tender. Stir into boiling water and gelatin mixture. Or use $3/4$ cup (175 mL) cooked cranberry sauce.

CARROT SALAD

The marinade of this make ahead winter salad is like a thick sauce and clings to the carrots.

— ◆ —

16	carrots	16
1	bay leaf	1
2	white onions	2
1	can (10 oz/284 mL) condensed tomato soup	1
$^1/_3$ cup	vegetable oil	75 mL
$^3/_4$ cup	granulated sugar	175 mL
$^2/_3$ cup	white vinegar	150 mL
1 tsp	dry mustard	5 mL
4 drops	hot pepper sauce	4
$^1/_2$ tsp	salt	2 mL
$^1/_4$ tsp	freshly ground black pepper	1 mL

• Cut carrots into 2-inch (5 cm) long sticks or $^1/_4$-inch (5 mm) slices. In saucepan of lightly salted boiling water, cook carrots and bay leaf for 8 minutes. Drain and discard bay leaf.
• Cut onions into $^1/_4$-inch (5 mm) slices. Separate into rings. Set aside.
• Meanwhile, in large bowl, combine tomato soup, oil, sugar, vinegar, mustard, hot pepper sauce, salt and pepper; mix well.
• Add hot carrots and onions to marinade. Cover and refrigerate, stirring occasionally, to marinate for at least 24 hours.
• To store: Keep covered in the refrigerator for up to 2 weeks.

Makes 8 to 10 servings.

Variation

CARROT RAISIN SALAD

• Add $^1/_2$ cup (125 mL) raisins to marinade to marinate with carrots.

Marinated Green Beans and Carrots

These partly cooked vegetables make a great winter salad.

◆

1 lb	fresh green beans	500 g
4	carrots, sliced	4
$\frac{1}{3}$ cup	olive oil or safflower oil	75 mL
$\frac{1}{4}$ cup	fresh lemon juice	50 mL
2 tbsp	chopped fresh parsley	25 mL
1 tbsp	chopped green pepper	15 mL
1 tsp	salt	5 mL
$\frac{1}{8}$ tsp	freshly ground black pepper	0.5 mL
1	onion, thinly sliced	1

• In saucepan of lightly salted boiling water, cook beans and carrots for about 5 minutes or until tender-crisp. Drain; cool immediately under cold running water. Drain well.
• In salad bowl, whisk together oil, lemon juice, parsley, green pepper, salt and black pepper.
• Add cooled vegetables and onion, separated into rings. Toss to coat with dressing.
• Cover and refrigerate, turning occasionally, for at least 4 hours.

Makes 6 servings.

Variations

Schnippled Salad

• Cut carrots into 2-inch (5 cm) long thin sticks. Cook 2 slices side bacon until crisp; drain, crumble and set aside.
• In place of oil and lemon juice mixture, combine $\frac{1}{2}$ cup (125 mL) commercial sour cream, 1 tbsp (15 mL) granulated sugar and 1 tbsp (15 mL) cider. Garnish with crumbled bacon.

DILLED BEANS AND CARROTS

- Instead of slicing carrots, cut them into 2-inch (5 cm) thin sticks.
- Add 1 tsp (5 mL) bruised dill seeds to the cooking water.

LIGHT TURKEY SALAD

You may substitute any lean meat or poultry for the roast turkey in this recipe. Just be sure any visible fat is removed.

◆

3	slices cooked turkey breast ($^1/_4$ lb/125 g), coarsely chopped	3
4	radishes, thinly sliced	4
1	carrot, thinly sliced	1
1	zucchini, thinly sliced	1
1	small clove garlic, minced	1
$^1/_2$	small white onion, thinly sliced	$^1/_2$
2 tbsp	low-fat plain yogurt	25 mL
1 tsp	prepared Dijon-style mustard or horseradish (for beef)	5 mL
1 tsp	soy sauce	5 mL
$^1/_2$ tsp	granulated sugar	2 mL
1 cup	shredded lettuce	250 mL
1 tbsp	sesame seeds, toasted	15 mL

- In salad bowl, combine turkey, radishes, carrot, zucchini, garlic and onion.
- In small bowl, combine yogurt, mustard, soy sauce and sugar. Pour over turkey mixture; toss gently.
- On 2 cold salad plates arrange lettuce. Divide salad evenly between the 2 plates. Sprinkle each with sesame seeds.

Makes 2 servings.

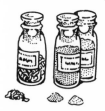

HERB VINAIGRETTE

The traditional formula for classic vinaigrettes has always been three parts oil to one part vinegar. However, the concern in the late '80s about reducing dietary fat has made many of us appreciate that an oil-rich dressing is anything but light. To reduce the fat content of these dressings, replace half the oil with chicken broth. Use homemade, if you can, because it is more gelatinous than broth made from bouillon cubes or a mix. It helps the dressing cling to the other salad ingredients.

◆

1	clove garlic, minced	1
1 tsp	salt	5 mL
1 tsp	crumbled dried sweet basil	5 mL
$^1/_2$ tsp	dry mustard	2 mL
$^1/_2$ tsp	dried thyme	2 mL
$^1/_2$ tsp	crumbled dried tarragon	2 mL
$^1/_4$ tsp	turmeric	1 mL
Pinch	ground cloves	Pinch
$^1/_3$ cup	white vinegar	75 mL
1 cup	vegetable oil	250 mL

• In jar or wide-mouthed bottle with tight-fitting lid, combine garlic, salt, basil, mustard, thyme, tarragon, turmeric and cloves.
• Add vinegar; swirl to moisten dry ingredients.
• Pour in oil. Cover tightly; shake vigorously. Always shake just before using.
• To store: Keep in covered container in refrigerator for up to 4 weeks.

Makes 1$^1/_3$ cups (325 mL).

SPECIAL FRENCH DRESSING

◆

2 tsp	salt	10 mL
1 tsp	granulated sugar	5 mL
$\frac{1}{2}$ tsp	paprika	2 mL
$\frac{1}{4}$ tsp	dry mustard	1 mL
$\frac{1}{8}$ tsp	freshly ground black pepper	0.5 mL
$\frac{1}{3}$ cup	white or cider vinegar	75 mL
1 cup	vegetable oil	250 mL

• In jar or wide-mouthed bottle with tight-fitting lid, combine salt, sugar, paprika, dry mustard and pepper.
• Add vinegar; swirl to moisten dry ingredients.
• Pour in oil. Cover tightly; shake vigorously. Always shake just before using.
• To store: Keep in covered container in refrigerator for up to 4 weeks.

Makes 1$\frac{1}{3}$ cups (325 mL).

Variations

BLUE CHEESE FRENCH

• Add $\frac{1}{3}$ cup (75 mL) crumbled blue cheese.

CHUTNEY FRENCH

• Add 2 tbsp (25 mL) finely chopped chutney and $\frac{1}{4}$ tsp (1 mL) curry powder.

HONEY FRENCH

- In place of sugar, use 1 tbsp (15 mL) liquid honey.

TOMATO FRENCH

- Add ¹/₄ cup (50 mL) tomato paste.

ITALIAN DRESSING

◆

1 tbsp	granulated sugar	15 mL
1 tsp	salt	5 mL
¹/₂ tsp	dry mustard	2 mL
¹/₂ tsp	paprika	2 mL
¹/₂ tsp	dried oregano	2 mL
¹/₂ tsp	dried thyme	2 mL
2	cloves garlic, minced	2
¹/₄ cup	minced onion	50 mL
¹/₃ cup	wine vinegar	75 mL
1 cup	vegetable oil	250 mL

- In jar or wide-mouthed bottle with tight-fitting lid, combine sugar, salt, mustard, paprika, oregano, thyme, garlic and onion.
- Add vinegar; swirl to moisten dry ingredients.
- Pour in oil; shake vigorously. Always shake just before using.
- To store: Keep in covered container in refrigerator for up to 4 weeks.

Makes about 1²/₃ cups (400 mL).

BLENDER
MAYONNAISE

Machines have taken the work out of making mayonnaise.

——————————————————— ♦ ———————————————————

2	eggs	2
1 tsp	salt	5 mL
$^1/_2$ tsp	dry mustard	2 mL
2 tbsp	lemon juice or white vinegar	25 mL
1$^3/_4$ to	canola, safflower or peanut oil	425 to
2 cups		500 mL

• In blender or food processor, combine eggs, salt, mustard and lemon juice. Process for 30 seconds or until well blended.
• With machine running, in a slow, thin, steady stream, gradually add oil, adding it more quickly as sauce emulsifies. Blend only until sauce is smooth and thick.
• To store: Keep in covered container in refrigerator for up to 4 weeks.

Makes 2 cups (500 mL).

Variations

—————————————

SOUR CREAM MAYONNAISE

• In bowl, mix equal amounts of mayonnaise and commercial sour cream. Use for seafood, chicken salads or coleslaw.

GREEN SAUCE

• To 1 cup (250 mL) mayonnaise, add 2 tbsp (25 mL) finely chopped fresh parsley, 2 tbsp (25 mL) finely chopped fresh basil or 1$^1/_2$ tsp (7 mL) dried basil. This is an excellent sauce for tomato slices, cold seafood or fish.

MAYONNAISE

This is the slower, traditional method of making mayonnaise.

◆

3	egg yolks	3
1 tsp	salt	5 mL
$^1/_2$ tsp	dry mustard	2 mL
$1^3/_4$ cups	canola, safflower or peanut oil	425 mL
2 tbsp	lemon juice or white vinegar	25 mL

• In mixing bowl, beat egg yolks for about 10 minutes or until thick and pale yellow. Add salt and mustard. Beat vigorously for 1 minute.
• Gradually whisk or beat in oil, drop by drop until $^1/_2$ cup (125 mL) oil has been added and mixture is thick.
• Beat in remaining oil, in a slow steady stream, until all oil has been added. Add lemon juice; mix well.
• To store: Store in jar with tight-fitting lid in refrigerator for up to 4 weeks.

Makes 2 cups (500 mL).

CREAMY HERB DRESSING

In the spring, as soon as I can gather a handful of fresh herbs, a bunch of leaf lettuce and a clutch of wee radishes from my garden, my favorite salad shows up on our table. It's simply leaf lettuce and slivered radishes lavishly dressed with this wonderful mixture.

◆

⅓ cup	light cream	75 mL
1 tbsp	lemon juice or white wine vinegar	15 mL
1 tbsp	each, chopped fresh tarragon, sweet basil, thyme and parsley or 1 tsp (5 mL) each, dried	15 mL
Pinch	granulated sugar	Pinch
	Salt and freshly ground black pepper	

• In small bowl, whisk together cream, lemon juice, tarragon, sweet basil, thyme, parsley and sugar until well blended. Season with salt and pepper, to taste. Let stand for about 15 minutes.
• Whisk again before tossing with salad greens.

Makes about ½ cup (125 mL), enough for 4 cups (1 L) salad greens.

MOM'S COOKED SALAD DRESSING

For fruit salads, add a little sugar or honey, a squeeze of lemon juice and fold in an equal amount of whipped cream. To make a mayonnaise-type dressing, I often drizzle about $^1/_2$ cup (125 mL) cooking oil into the cold basic cooked dressing while whirling it in the blender at high speed.

♦

2 tbsp	granulated sugar	25 mL
2 tbsp	all-purpose flour	25 mL
$1^1/_2$ tsp	dry mustard	7 mL
1 tsp	salt	5 mL
1	egg, beaten	1
1 cup	milk	250 mL
$^1/_4$ cup	vinegar	50 mL
2 tbsp	butter	25 mL

• Measure dry ingredients into top of double boiler. Add well-beaten egg and blend into a smooth paste. Pour in milk; stir until smooth. Gradually add vinegar.
• Cook over hot water, stirring constantly, for about 10 minutes or until thick.
• Remove from heat and stir in butter. Cool.
• Beat dressing before using for salad. If too thick, thin with a little milk.
• To store: Keep in refrigerator in covered jar for up to 4 weeks.

Makes about $1^1/_2$ cups (375 mL).

TANGY YOGURT DRESSING

If vegetable oil was used in this dressing in place of the low-fat yogurt there would be more than ten times as many calories from fat as there are in this low-fat salad dressing.

———————————————— ◆ ————————————————

1 cup	low-fat plain yogurt	250 mL
1 tsp	granulated sugar	5 mL
1 tsp	white vinegar	5 mL
1	small clove garlic, minced	1
1 tsp	Worcestershire sauce	5 mL
$^1/_2$ tsp	dried tarragon	2 mL
$^1/_2$ tsp	dry mustard	2 mL
$^1/_4$ tsp	celery seed	1 mL
$^1/_2$ tsp	salt	2 mL
$^1/_4$ tsp	ground white pepper	1 mL

• In a blender or food processor, combine yogurt, sugar, vinegar, garlic, Worcestershire sauce, tarragon, mustard, celery seed, salt and white pepper. Process for 15 seconds or until smooth. Or in bowl, whisk ingredients together until well blended. Pour into screw top jar. Always shake just before using.
To store: Keep in refrigerator for up to 3 weeks.

Makes 1 cup (250 mL).

SMALL MEALS

♦

Supper, not lunch, was the small meal when I was growing up. Dad always came home at noon and Mom cooked a bigger, heartier dinner for our mid-day meal.

She called Macaroni and Cheese, Spanish Rice and Spaghetti and Meat Balls "supper dishes." They are easy-to-prepare and she liked the convenience of preparing them in advance. I like them too and call them "slow fast-food." After tidying up the mess, you can walk away to do something else while they cook and before you know it they are ready to serve.

Cheese is the first ingredient I think of when it comes to planning a small lunch or supper. Cheese dishes range from the simple — foods dressed with a golden cheese sauce — to the more complicated — cheese incorporated in a soufflé. Included in this section are some of the hundreds of recipes I developed when I was assisting in the promotion of Holland Imported Cheese in Canada.

MOM'S MONDAY MACARONI

When I was a kid, Monday was wash day. In those days a wringer washer did the job and the clothes were hung outside on a strong galvanized line to dry even when it was below freezing. There was little time for cooking, but this supper dish saved the day for Mom. It still takes less time to prepare than packaged macaroni and cheese dinners. Granted it takes longer to cook but you can forget about it while it's in the oven.

◆

1 tbsp	butter or margarine	15 mL
1	onion, finely chopped	1
1½ cups	uncooked elbow macaroni	375 mL
1 cup	diced Cheddar cheese	250 mL
1	can (19 oz/540 mL) tomatoes, undrained	1
1 cup	water	250 mL
1 tsp	salt	5 mL
Pinch	pepper	Pinch
Topping:		
1 tsp	soft butter	5 mL
½ cup	soda cracker crumbs (8 crackers) Salt and pepper	125 mL

• In skillet over medium heat, melt butter. Add onion; sauté for 4 minutes or until limp. Transfer to buttered 8-cup (2 L) casserole.
• Add macaroni, cheese, tomatoes, water, salt and pepper. Stir well, breaking the tomatoes into small pieces.
• Bake covered, in 350 F (180 C) oven for 35 minutes or until macaroni is nearly tender.
• *Topping:* Combine butter and cracker crumbs; season with salt and pepper, to taste.
• Remove casserole from oven. Sprinkle topping evenly over top. Return to oven; bake, uncovered, for 20 minutes longer or until crumbs begin to brown and macaroni is tender.
Makes 4 to 6 servings.

Quick Macaroni and Cheese

In this recipe, the macaroni is precooked to shorten the baking time.

◆

2 cups	elbow macaroni (8 oz/250 g)	500 mL
2 tbsp	butter	25 mL
2 tbsp	all-purpose flour	25 mL
1/2 tsp	dry mustard	2 mL
2 cups	milk	500 mL
1/2 tsp	salt	2 mL
Pinch	white pepper	Pinch
2 cups	shredded medium or old Cheddar cheese (1/2 lb/250 g)	500 mL

Topping:

1/2 cup	bread crumbs	125 mL
2 tsp	soft butter	10 mL

- In 8 cups (2 L) lightly salted boiling water, cook macaroni for about 8 minutes or until al dente (tender but firm); drain.
- Meanwhile, in saucepan, melt butter; blend in flour and mustard.
- Gradually stir in milk. Heat to boiling. Cook, stirring constantly, for about 4 minutes or until thickened. Season with salt and pepper.
- Remove from heat, add 1 cup (250 mL) cheese and stir until cheese melts.
- In buttered 6-cup (1.5 L) casserole, layer half macaroni, 1/3 cup (75 mL) remaining shredded cheese and half the sauce. Repeat.
- Topping: Combine bread crumbs and butter; sprinkle over top.
- Bake in 350 F (180 C) oven for 25 minutes or until crumbs are golden.
- Remove from oven; sprinkle remaining cheese over top. Return to oven and bake for about 5 minutes longer or until cheese melts.

Makes 4 to 6 servings.

TUNA NOODLE CASSEROLE

After making its debut on the pot luck dinner circuit in the late '50s, the recipe for this creation spread quickly from household to household. One friend, leaning against a wall in a church cloakroom, scratched it out on the back of two grocery sales slips, while another called out the ingredients over the mountain of winter coats. The one doing the writing ended up losing one of the sales slips. As a result, she forgot about the chow mein noodles and didn't put them in. They make a difference. Make sure they are included when you put this casserole together.

◆

4 cups	medium egg noodles (8 oz/250 g)	1 L
1	can (10 oz/284 mL) condensed cream of mushroom soup	1
2 cups	milk	500 mL
1 tbsp	dry sherry, optional	15 mL
1 cup	thinly sliced celery	250 mL
1 cup	frozen chopped green beans or peas	250 mL
1 tbsp	minced onion	15 mL
$\frac{1}{4}$ tsp	salt	1 mL
$\frac{1}{4}$ tsp	freshly ground black pepper	1 mL
1	can (7 oz/198 g) tuna, chunk light or solid tuna	1
$\frac{1}{4}$ cup	sliced almonds, toasted	50 mL
1 cup	chow mein noodles or crumbled potato chips	250 mL

• In 8 cups (2 L) lightly salted boiling water, cook noodles for about 5 minutes or until al dente (tender but firm); drain.
• In 10-cup (2.5 L) casserole, mix together soup, milk and sherry, if desired, until smooth. Stir in cooked egg noodles, celery, green beans, onion, salt and pepper.

• Drain tuna; separate into chunks if it is solid. Fold into noodle mixture with almonds. Scatter chow mein noodles over top.
• Bake in 350 F (180 C) oven for 30 minutes or until hot and bubbly.

Makes 6 servings.

FETTUCCINE WITH HAM AND BROCCOLI

Classic fettuccine is gussied up here with vegetables and ham.

————————————— ♦ —————————————

1	package (200 g) fettuccine, spaghetti or egg noodles	1
2 tbsp	butter	25 mL
1	onion, finely chopped	1
1	clove garlic, minced	1
1$^1/_2$ cups	diced cooked ham	375 mL
2 cups	small broccoli florets ($^1/_2$ lb/250 g)	500 mL
1 tbsp	all-purpose flour	15 mL
$^3/_4$ cup	light cream	175 mL
$^1/_2$ tsp	salt	2 mL
	Freshly ground black pepper	
$^1/_2$ cup	grated Parmesan cheese	125 mL

• In pot of lightly salted boiling water, cook fettuccine following package directions until al dente (tender but firm).
• Meanwhile in large skillet, heat butter. Sauté onion and garlic for 2 minutes or until onion is nearly tender. Stir in ham and broccoli; cook for 4 minutes or until broccoli is tender but crisp.
• Push broccoli and ham aside. Stir in flour until blended. Stir cream in gradually and bring to a boil. Season with salt and pepper, to taste.
• Drain fettuccine then return to pot. Pour ham and broccoli mixture over fettucine. Sprinkle with Parmesan cheese. Toss to mix in cheese. Serve immediately.

Makes 4 servings.

BASIC SPAGHETTI SAUCE

Spaghetti and meat sauce were a rare treat from my Mom's kitchen because she was a fan of macaroni, not spaghetti. In my kitchen they had equal time. Now, spaghetti is preferred by my children.

◆

1 tbsp	olive oil	15 mL
2	onions, finely chopped	2
2	cloves garlic, minced	2
1 lb	lean ground beef	500 g
2 tbsp	chopped fresh basil or 2 tsp (10 mL) dried	25 mL
1	can (28 oz/796 mL) tomatoes (Italian plum, if possible)	1
1	can (5^1/$_2$ oz/156 mL) tomato paste	1
1 cup	beef broth	250 mL
^{1}/$_2$ cup	dry red wine	125 mL
1 tsp	granulated sugar	5 mL
1 tsp	salt	5 mL
1	bay leaf	1
1 tsp	dried thyme	5 mL
^{1}/$_2$ tsp	dried oregano	2 mL
^{1}/$_2$ tsp	pepper	5 mL

- In large saucepan or Dutch oven, heat oil. Add onions; sauté for about 5 minutes or until soft. Add garlic; cook for 1 minute longer.
- Crumble beef into saucepan; cook, stirring occasionally, for about 5 minutes or until no longer pink.
- Stir in basil, tomatoes, tomato paste, broth, wine, sugar, salt, bay leaf, thyme, oregano and pepper; bring to a boil. Reduce heat and simmer, uncovered, stirring occasionally, for 1 hour or until sauce is thick. Discard bay leaf.
- To store: Pour into containers with tight-fitting lids. Keep in refrigerator for up to 3 days; in the freezer for up to 3 months.

Makes 4 to 5 cups (1 to 1.25 L).

Variations

SPAGHETTI MEATBALL SAUCE

- Add 1 batch cooked Zesty Meatballs (see page 94) to Basic Spaghetti Sauce. Omit Zesty Sauce.

BASIC MEATLESS SPAGHETTI SAUCE

- Delete ground beef. In place of broth, use water. Increase olive oil to ¼ cup (50 mL). Add 1 additional onion, coarsely chopped.
- Add 1 cup (250 mL) each of diced carrot, zucchini and eggplant and 1 sweet red pepper, seeded and chopped, to the tomato mixture.
- Cook as directed in recipe.

♦

HELPFUL HINT

Cooking Pasta
To prevent any pasta (macaroni, spaghetti, noodles) from boiling over, drizzle a little vegetable or olive oil (about 2 tsp/10 mL) into the cooking water.

PYROHY

My "Baba's" table always had a big bowl of pyrohy on it for her Ukrainian Christmas Eve feast. For that occasion, the fillings were meatless — mashed potato with onion, sauerkraut, mushroom.

━━━━━━━━━━━━━━━━━━━━━━ ◆ ━━━━━━━━━━━━━━━━━━━━

1	egg	1
3/4 cup	warm water	175 mL
1/4 cup	canola or sunflower oil	50 mL
1 tsp	salt	5 mL
2 1/2 cups	all-purpose flour	625 mL

Filling:

2 tbsp	canola oil or butter	25 mL
1/2 cup	finely chopped onion	125 mL
2 cups	mashed potatoes	500 mL
1 cup	cottage cheese, preferably dry	250 mL
1 tsp	salt	5 mL
	Freshly ground black pepper	

Topping:

1/4 cup	butter	50 mL
1 cup	chopped onions	250 mL
	Salt and freshly ground black pepper	

• In large bowl, beat together egg, water, oil and salt. Gradually stir in flour until dough is smooth. With hands work in last bit of flour. Knead 10 to 12 times to smooth texture of dough.

• On lightly floured surface, with rolling pin, roll out to 1/8-inch (3 mm) thickness. Cut into 3-inch (8 cm) squares or circles (with cookie cutter).

• *Filling:* In skillet, heat oil. Sauté onion for 3 minute or until tender. In bowl, combine onions, mashed potato, cottage cheese and salt. Season with pepper, to taste.

- Place a generous teaspoonful (5 mL) of filling in center of each square of rolled dough; fold diagonally to form a triangle. Pinch edges together, making sure they are well sealed. Place on oiled plate and cover with plastic wrap to keep from drying.
- Into pot of lightly salted boiling water, drop in 6 to 8 pyrohy at a time. With wooden spoon, stir occasionally. Boil for about 10 minutes or until pyrohy float to the surface and dough is tender. Remove with slotted spoon; place in colander to drain.
- *Topping:* In skillet, heat butter. Sauté onions for about 5 minutes or until tender. Season with salt and pepper, to taste. In warm bowl, toss pyrohy with onions. Serve with sour cream.
- To store: Layer pyrohy, with waxed-paper between layers, in container with lid. Keep in refrigerator for up to 2 days; in freezer for up to 6 weeks.

Makes 24 to 36.

Variations

Cottage Cheese Filling

- In bowl, combine 1 cup (250 mL) cottage cheese (drained if cream style), 1 lightly beaten egg, 1 tbsp (15 mL) chopped fresh parsley or green onion, $\frac{1}{2}$ tsp (2 mL) salt and pinch of freshly ground black pepper. Makes enough for about 18 pyrohy.

Mushroom Filling

- In skillet, heat $\frac{1}{4}$ cup (50 mL) butter. Add $\frac{1}{2}$ cup (125 mL) finely chopped onion and 2 cups (500 mL) finely chopped mushroom. Cook, stirring, for about 10 minutes or until moisture has just evaporated. Makes enough for about 18 pyrohy.

LASAGNE

The recipe for this classic Italian casserole is one my Mom, sister and children copied to make up in their own kitchens.

———————————————————— ♦ ————————————————————

1	batch Basic Spaghetti Sauce	1
	(see page 78)	
9	lasagne noodles (about 8 oz/250 g)	9
1	egg	1
2 cups	ricotta or cottage cheese (1 lb/500 g)	500 mL
$^1/_2$ cup	grated Parmesan cheese	125 mL
$^1/_2$ lb	whole-milk mozzarella cheese slices	250 g

- Prepare Basic Spaghetti Sauce; set aside.
- In large pot of lightly salted boiling water, cook lasagne noodles for about 8 minutes or until al dente (tender but firm); rinse under cold water and drain.
- Lightly beat egg; stir in ricotta and half of the Parmesan.
- Cut mozzarella into thin strips.
- To assemble: Spread about 1 cup (250 mL) of the sauce over bottom of a 13 x 9 x 2-inch (33 x 23 x 5 cm/4 L) baking dish.
- Top with 3 noodles in a single layer, another cup of the sauce, $^1/_3$ of the ricotta mixture and $^1/_3$ of the mozzarella strips. Repeat layers twice, reserving about 1 cup (250 mL) meat sauce; spoon it over top. Sprinkle with remaining Parmesan.
- To store: At this point, lasagne can be covered and kept in the refrigerator for up to 3 days; in the freezer, well wrapped for up to 3 months. Defrost in refrigerator for 1 day before baking.
- Bake in 325 F (160 C) oven for about 35 minutes or until hot.
- Let stand for 10 minutes before cutting into squares to serve.

Makes 12 servings.

SPANISH RICE

Number two for Mom's busy day suppers when I was a child were rice casseroles. They are as comforting and easy to make as macaroni dishes.

◆

1 cup	converted long-grain rice	250 mL
1 tbsp	olive oil or butter	15 mL
1	onion, finely chopped	1
1	clove garlic, minced	1
$^1/_2$	sweet red or green pepper, finely chopped	$^1/_2$
1	can (14 oz/398 mL) tomato sauce	1
1 tsp	brown sugar	5 mL
Pinch	ground cloves	Pinch
Few grains	cayenne pepper	Few grains
$^1/_2$ cup	grated Parmesan cheese	125 mL

• Add rice to saucepan of $2^1/_2$ cups (625 mL) lightly salted boiling water; stir. Bring back to a boil, reduce heat, cover tightly and simmer for 20 minutes or until tender.

• Meanwhile, in small saucepan, heat oil. Sauté onion, garlic and sweet pepper for 4 minutes or until tender.

• Stir in tomato sauce, brown sugar, cloves and cayenne pepper. Bring to a boil, then turn off heat.

• Pour over cooked rice; mix well. Pour into oiled or buttered 6-cup (1.5 L) casserole. Sprinkle grated cheese over top.

• Bake in 350 F (180 C) oven for 30 minutes or until rice is very tender.

Makes 6 servings.

Variation

MEXICAN RICE WITH BEANS

- Chop 1 whole sweet pepper to sauté with onion and garlic.
- In place of tomato sauce, use 1 can (19 oz/540 mL) tomatoes (breaking up tomatoes if they are whole).
- Add 3 to 4 tsp (15 to 20 mL) chili powder, a few flakes of dried chili peppers and 1 can (19 oz/540 mL) red kidney beans, drained.
- In place of Parmesan cheese, sprinkle 1 cup (250 mL) shredded Monterey Jack or Cheddar cheese over top of rice.
- Serve with crisp corn chips.

CABBAGE ROLLS

The cabbage rolls (*Holubse*) made by Mom and my Ukrainian Baba were the best I've ever tasted. Mom told me that in the good old days they made theirs with sour cabbage, from the whole heads of cabbage Baba buried in the sauerkraut she put down every fall.

◆

1	large head cabbage	1
	Boiling water	
2 cups	long-grain rice	500 mL
1 tsp	salt	5 mL
4	strips side bacon	4
1	onion, finely chopped	1
1	clove garlic, minced	1
1/2 lb	ground pork or beef	250 g
1/4 tsp	freshly ground black pepper	1 mL
1	can (14 oz/398 mL) sauerkraut	1
1 1/2 cups	tomato juice	375 mL

- With sharp knife, remove core from cabbage. Place cabbage in deep bowl. Pour boiling water into hollow made from removing core and completely cover cabbage with boiling water. Let stand for about 15 minutes and leaves become soft and pliable; drain. Take the cabbage apart, one leaf at a time. With paring knife, trim center rib of each leaf to make leaf same thickness throughout, but do not remove rib. If leaves are very large, cut in half.
- In large saucepan, combine rice, 2 cups (500 mL) boiling water and salt. Bring to a boil. Cover, turn off heat and let stand for about 15 minutes or until rice absorbs all the water.
- Cut bacon into small pieces. In skillet, over medium heat, cook bacon until crisp. Remove from skillet. Crumble and reserve for garnish.
- In bacon drippings, sauté onion for 2 to 3 minutes or until tender. Add meat and continue to cook until meat is no longer pink. Stir into rice. Season with more salt, if desired and pepper, to taste. Cool until mixture is easy to handle.
- Rinse sauerkraut under cold running water; drain well. Spread about $^1/_3$ on bottom of deep casserole.
- Place a generous portion of rice mixture on each cabbage leaf. Roll up, tucking in sides to form neat parcels. Arrange seam side down on sauerkraut, layering with remaining sauerkraut, leaving enough sauerkraut for a thin top layer.
- Pour tomato juice over top. Place any remaining cabbage over top to prevent scorching. Cover.
- Bake in 315 F (160 C) over for $1^1/_2$ to 2 hours or until both cabbage and rice are tender.
- To store: At this point, layer in container with lid. Refrigerate for up to 3 days; freeze for up to 6 weeks.
- Serve garnished with reserved bacon.

Makes 24 (8 large, 8 medium, 8 small), 8 to 10 servings.

CHILI CON CARNE
WITH CORN

In our family chili has been the perennial favorite for toting to the cottage or ski hill. I've found it's worth making in large batches; first, because people usually eat far more than you expect, and secondly, because it keeps well and improves in storage.

◆

2 lb	ground beef	1 kg
2	onions, coarsely chopped	2
2	stalks celery, coarsely chopped	2
2	cloves garlic, minced	2
1	small green pepper, chopped	1
1	can (19 oz/540 mL) tomatoes, undrained	1
1 tbsp	chili powder	15 mL
1½ tsp	salt	7 mL
¼ tsp	crushed red pepper	1 mL
¼ tsp	cinnamon	1 mL
Pinch	cayenne pepper (optional)	Pinch
1	can (19 oz/540 mL) red kidney beans	1
1	can (14 oz/398 mL) tomato sauce	1
1	can (12 oz/341 mL) kernel corn	1

• In cold, large skillet, combine ground beef, onions, celery, garlic and green pepper. Place over medium high heat. Cook, stirring occasionally to break up beef, for about 15 minutes or until beef is no longer pink. (If desired, at this point, skim off any extra visible fat.)
• Stir in tomatoes, chili powder, salt, red pepper, cinnamon and cayenne pepper, if desired. (It's hot.) Cook for 5 minutes longer for flavors to mingle.
• Drain kidney beans, reserving liquid. Stir beans into beef mixture. Stir in tomato sauce and kernel corn.
• Simmer, covered, for about 1 hour, or transfer to 10-cup (2.5 L) casserole or two 6-cup (1.5 L) casseroles.
• Bake in 350 F (180 C) oven for 1 hour or until heated through.
• Stir in small amount of reserved bean liquid at any time, as required, if mixture seems too thick.

- To store: Pack portions of chili in covered containers. Keeps in refrigerator for up to 4 days; in freezer for 3 months.

Makes 10 to 12 servings.

TEX-MEX MACARONI CHILI

◆

¹/₂	batch Chili Con Carne (see page 86)	¹/₂
2 cups	uncooked macaroni	500 mL
2 cups	corn chips	500 mL

- Prepare Chili Con Carne.
- In 8 cups (2 L) lightly salted boiling water, cook macaroni for about 8 minutes or until al dente (tender but firm).
- Stir into Chili Con Carne. Transfer to two 8-cup (2 L) casseroles; cover with lids or foil.
- Bake in 350 F (180 C) oven for 35 minutes or until heated through.
- Ten minutes before casseroles are done, place corn chips in baking pan. Bake in the same oven for 10 minutes or until crisp.
- When casseroles are removed from oven, tuck corn chips in rows around outside of casseroles.

Makes 12 servings.

DOUBLE CHEESE STRATA

Wonderful for a late breakfast or brunch.

◆

1 tbsp	butter or margarine	15 mL
2 tbsp	minced onion	25 mL
6	slices whole wheat bread cut into bite-size cubes	6
1 cup	shredded Cheddar cheese ($^1/_4$ lb/125 g)	250 mL
1 cup	cottage cheese	250 mL
$^1/_2$ tsp	salt	2 mL
$^1/_4$ tsp	freshly ground black pepper	1 mL
3	eggs	3
2 cups	milk	500 mL
$^1/_2$ tsp	prepared mustard	2 mL

• In small skillet, melt butter. Add onion; sauté for about 2 minutes or until soft.
• Place half of bread cubes in buttered 6-cup (1.5 L) casserole or soufflé dish. Top with shredded cheese, cottage cheese, sautéed onion and remaining bread cubes. Sprinkle with salt and pepper.
• Beat together eggs, milk and mustard. Pour over bread mixture. Stir lightly once or twice to mix. (Can be prepared to this point the night before. Cover and keep refrigerated.)
• Bake in 350 F (180 C) oven for 40 to 45 minutes or until set.

Makes 4 servings.

Variations

FISH OR HAM AND CHEESE STRATA

• Add 1 cup (250 mL) flaked, cooked fish or ham.

CHEESE SOUFFLÉ

There is no added butter or oil in this recipe, making it possible for the soufflé to rise very high.

---◆---

1 cup	milk	250 mL
$^1/_4$ cup	all-purpose flour	50 mL
4	egg yolks	4
1$^1/_2$ cups	shredded Gouda, Edam or Swiss cheese (6 oz/185 g)	375 mL
6	egg whites	6
$^1/_2$ tsp	cream of tartar	2 mL

• In saucepan, whisk together milk and flour. Over medium-low heat, bring to a boil, stirring constantly, until mixture thickens.
• In small bowl, beat egg yolks. Stir small amount of hot milk sauce into beaten yolks. Then stir yolk mixture back into hot sauce. Cook, stirring, for 2 minutes longer. Stir in cheese; remove from heat and beat until cheese is melted.
• In large bowl, beat egg whites and cream of tartar until stiff peaks form. Stir about $^1/_2$ cup (125 mL) beaten egg whites into cheese sauce, then fold cheese sauce into remaining beaten egg whites.
• Pour into unbuttered 6-cup (1.5 L) soufflé or baking dish; place in large pan. Pour hot water into pan to reach about 2 inches (5 cm) up sides of soufflé dish.
• Bake in 325 F (160C) oven for about 45 minutes or until golden and firm to touch. (Do not open oven door until soufflé has baked, otherwise, it may deflate.) Serve immediately.

Makes 6 servings.

CHEESE RAREBIT OR WELSH RABBIT

Some cheese lovers, especially if their roots are British, call this robust sauce *rabbit* instead of *rarebit*. Apparently, according to a bit of folklore, a desperate cook created it one day when her husband came home from hunting without the rabbit she expected to cook for dinner.

◆

1 tbsp	butter	25 mL
2 tbsp	all-purpose flour	25 mL
$^1/_2$ tsp	dry mustard	2 mL
$^1/_4$ tsp	salt	1 mL
	White pepper	
1 cup	beer, ale, tomato juice or milk	250 mL
2 cups	shredded old Cheddar, Edam or Gouda cheese ($^1/_2$ lb/250 g)	500 mL
4	slices warm whole wheat toast	

• In heavy saucepan, melt butter. Blend in flour, mustard, salt and pepper, to taste.
• Add beer. Cook over medium heat, stirring constantly, for about 7 minutes or until sauce thickens. Remove from heat; blend in cheese. Stir until cheese is melted and mixture is smooth.
• Spoon over toast. Serve immediately.

Makes 4 servings.

Variation

ASPARAGUS RABBIT

• Top toast with hot cooked asparagus spears before spooning on the cheese sauce. For a more substantial dish, include wedges of hard-cooked eggs and tomato slices.

Sesame Cheese Log, Cheese Shortbread,
Seed and Nut Cheese Shortbread, Ham and Cheese Pinwheels

◆

Smooth Cucumber Soup, Melba Toasts

Tomato Aspic, Coleslaw

◆

Quick Macaroni and Cheese

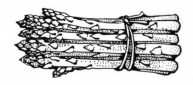

ASPARAGUS AND HAM ROLLS IN CHEESE SAUCE

Just add warm puffy biscuits and carrot sticks for a perfect spring lunch or supper. Cooked fresh green beans, broccoli or spinach may be used instead of asparagus in this dish.

◆

1	batch Best Cheese Sauce (see page 169)	1
1 lb	fresh asparagus	500 g
8	slices cooked ham, $^1/_8$ inch (3 mm) thick	8
$^1/_2$ cup	grated Parmesan cheese	125 mL

- Prepare Best Cheese Sauce.
- In large skillet or saucepan of lightly salted boiling water, cook asparagus for 4 to 7 minutes or until tender-crisp. Drain well.
- Place 2 or 3 asparagus spears in center of each slice of ham. Roll up tightly. Arrange seam side down in lightly buttered dish.
- Pour cheese sauce over ham rolls. Sprinkle with grated cheese.
- Bake in 400 F (200 C) oven for 10 to 12 minutes until hot and cheese melts and begins to turn golden brown.

Makes 4 servings.

PIZZA

There are perfectly good packaged frozen pizza crusts available today in several sizes. Some bakery shops also sell them fresh out of the oven. If you want pizza in a hurry, use one of those. Or you can prepare this crust, wrap it well and tuck it in the freezer until you fancy having a pizza.

◆

Crust:

1 tsp	granulated sugar	5 mL
1 cup	warm water	250 mL
1	envelope active dry yeast	1
1 tbsp	vegetable oil	15 mL
2¹/₂	all-purpose flour	625
to 3 cups		to 750 mL
1 tsp	salt	5 mL

Topping for 1 pizza crust:

1	can (7¹/₂ oz/213 mL) tomato sauce	1
¹/₄ lb	mozzarella cheese, thinly sliced and cut in pieces	125 g
2 oz	salami, sliced and cut in pieces	60 g
¹/₄ cup each	chopped onion, green pepper, sliced pitted green olives and mushrooms	50 mL
	Grated Parmesan cheese (optional)	

• *Crust:* In large bowl, dissolve sugar in warm water; add yeast and let stand for 10 minutes until frothy. Stir in oil, half the flour and salt; beat thoroughly. Stir in remaining flour. Turn out onto floured surface and knead for about 10 minutes or until smooth and elastic.

- Place in lightly oiled bowl, turning dough over to oil all sides. Cover and allow to rise in a warm place for 40 to 45 minutes or until doubled in bulk.
- Turn out onto floured surface. Knead briefly to force out large bubbles.
- For 1 thick, deep crust, use all of the dough; for 2 thin crusts, cut dough in half.
- Form dough into a ball; roll or press out, from the center, to form an 11-inch circle (27 cm). Lay on lightly oiled 12-inch (30 cm) pizza pan or baking sheet and form a rim around edge.
- To store: At this point, place in freezer for about 2 hours or until frozen firm. Remove from pan. Wrap in plastic or freezer wrap. Store in freezer for up to 4 weeks. When needed, unwrap and place on pizza pan to defrost. Or pizza crust can be covered with topping before freezing.
- *Topping:* With a rubber spatula, spread tomato sauce over crust. Scatter mozzarella and salami over sauce. Sprinkle onion, green pepper, olives and mushrooms evenly over top. Sprinkle with Parmesan cheese, if desired.
- Bake in 450 F (230 C) oven for about 20 minutes or until cheese is bubbly and crust is golden brown.
- With pizza cutter or sharp knife, cut into 8 wedges.

Makes 8 servings. (One thick deep pizza or one thin pizza plus one thin crust to freeze for another time.)

Variation

PIZZA TOPPINGS

- Toppings are unlimited; use sliced tomatoes or cooked artichokes, anchovy fillets or chopped or sliced ham or bacon and sprinkle with assorted herbs such as oregano, thyme, basil and garlic.

Zesty Meatballs

To make shaping meatballs quicker and easier, moisten hands before handling ground beef mixture.

◆

1 lb	medium ground beef	500 g
$^1/_2$ lb	bulk sausage	250 g
$^1/_2$ cup	soft bread crumbs	125 mL
1	egg	1
2 tbsp	vegetable oil	25 mL

Zesty Sauce:

1	can (14 oz/398 mL) tomato sauce	1
1	can (10 oz/284 mL) condensed onion soup	1
	Juice of 1 lemon	
1 tbsp	Worcestershire sauce	15 mL
3 tbsp	brown sugar	45 mL
2 tbsp	cornstarch	25 mL
2	cloves garlic, finely chopped	2

• In bowl, combine ground beef, sausage, bread crumbs and egg; mix well.
• With hands, shape meat mixture into 24 meatballs. (Meat can be refrigerated for 1 day or frozen, wrapped, for up to 2 months at this point, to use later.)
• In skillet, heat oil. Add meatballs. Cook over medium heat, turning occasionally, until brown.
• *Zesty Sauce:* In saucepan, combine tomato sauce, onion soup, lemon juice, Worcestershire sauce, brown sugar, cornstarch and garlic; mix well. Bring mixture to a boil, reduce heat, simmer for 5 minutes or until slightly thickened. Pour over meatballs in skillet.
• Cover and cook over low heat, stirring frequently, for 20 minutes or until meat is no longer pink inside.

Makes 6 main dish servings, or 12 to 18 appetizer servings.

SLOPPY JOES

This is a holdover from my bobby sox and saddle shoe high school days — long before McDonalds' take-out hamburgers and French fries. The ground beef isn't in a patty, instead it's cooked with sauce which may drip over the hamburger bun just like our Sloppy Joe sweaters used to droop over our pleated skirts.

◆

1 tbsp	butter	15 mL
1	clove garlic, minced (optional)	1
1/2 cup	finely chopped onion	125 mL
1/2 cup	finely chopped celery	125 mL
1 lb	medium ground beef	500 g
1/2 cup	chopped mushrooms	125 mL
1	can (7 1/2 oz/213 mL) tomato sauce	1
1 tsp	Worcestershire sauce	5 mL
	Salt and pepper	
4	toasted hamburger buns	4

• In skillet, heat butter. Add garlic, onion and celery; sauté for 4 minutes or until tender.
• Add ground beef, breaking up with a fork. Stir and cook for about 7 minutes or until meat is lightly browned. Spoon off any excess fat.
• Stir in mushrooms, tomato sauce and Worcestershire sauce. Cook for about 5 minutes or until liquid is reduced slightly. Season to taste with salt and pepper.
• Spoon into split buns. Or place toasted bun halves on serving plates and spoon saucy meat mixture over top.

Makes 4 servings.

BEEF STROGANOFF

As a young bride, I relied on this for company dinners with another couple. One pound of steak could be stretched a long way. Green beans and broiled tomato halves were the usual escorts for the stroganoff.

◆

1 lb	sirloin or strip loin beef steak	500 g
1/4 cup	butter	50 mL
8	mushrooms, sliced	8
1	onion, thinly sliced	1
1	clove garlic, minced, optional	1
1 cup	strong beef broth	250 mL
1 tsp	Worcestershire sauce	5 mL
1/2 tsp	salt	2 mL
1/2 tsp	dried thyme or dillweed	2 mL
Pinch	freshly ground black pepper	Pinch
1/4 cup	all-purpose flour	50 mL
1 cup	commercial sour cream	250 mL
	Hot cooked rice or egg noodles	
	Chopped fresh parsley	

• With sharp knife, cut beef across the grain into 2 x 1/4-inch (5 cm x 5 mm) strips.

• In large skillet, heat butter. Add mushrooms, onion and garlic, if desired. Sauté for 5 minutes or until tender; remove and set aside.

• In same skillet, stir-fry steak in 3 batches until lightly browned, adding each batch to onions as they brown. To the last batch, add reserved onion mixture and browned beef.

• Reserve 1/4 cup (50 mL) beef broth. Stir remainder into beef mixture with Worcestershire sauce, salt, thyme and pepper. Cook for 5 minutes or just until beef is no longer pink.

• Blend flour into reserved broth. Stir into beef mixture. Heat to boiling, stirring constantly for 1 1/2 minutes or until thickened. Stir in sour cream. Heat through and do not boil again (or sauce will curdle).

• Spoon over rice. Garnish with parsley.

Makes 4 servings.

BANGERS AND MASH

Sausages, mashed potatoes, peas and dill pickles were regular fare at Mom's table. For her they were quick and easy; for me they were pretty plain. That is until one day back in '43 when my new girl friend from England, a wartime refugee living with a family in Radisson, Saskatchewan, joined us for our noon-hour dinner. She called the sausages and potatoes "bangers and mash". I loved the name, and ever since, that combination has been more than an ordinary meal for me. Now I often add onions and celery or apples to the skillet when the sausages are cooking.

◆

1 tbsp	vegetable oil	15 mL
6 to 8	breakfast sausages	6 to 8
1	onion	1
1	stalk celery or apple, core removed	1
1 tbsp	brown sugar	15 mL
Pinch each	salt and pepper	Pinch each
1/4 cup	water	50 mL
	Mashed Potatoes (see page 162)	

• In medium skillet, heat oil over medium-high heat. Add sausages and cook for about 5 minutes or until sausages are lightly browned.
• Cut onion into quarters then into thick slices and celery into thin slices. Add to skillet. Cook, stirring occasionally, for about 4 minutes or until onion is translucent.
• Sprinkle brown sugar over top and season with salt and pepper.
• Pour water over top. Reduce heat to low, cover and simmer for 5 minutes or until sausages are no longer pink and celery is tender.
• Mound mashed potatoes in center of dinner plate. Surround with sausage mixture. (And please add the peas and dill pickles.)

Makes 2 servings.

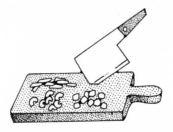

CHICKEN LIVER
SAUTÉ WITH HAM

Save the chicken livers from whole chickens in a plastic bag in the freezer until you have enough for a dish like this one, or buy them fresh and cook them on the day they are purchased.

♦

2 tbsp	butter	25 mL
1	clove garlic, minced	1
1 lb	chicken livers, cut into small pieces	500 g
1 tbsp	fresh summer savory, finely chopped, or $^1/_2$ tsp (2 mL) dried savory	15 mL
8	slices cooked ham, cut into thin strips	8
24	green seedless grapes	24
2 tbsp	dry white wine (optional)	25 mL
$^1/_2$ tsp	salt	2 mL
Pinch	freshly ground black pepper	Pinch
4	thin slices buttered toast	4

• In skillet, heat butter. Add garlic; sauté for 1 minute.
• Add chicken livers and savory; sauté for about 2 minutes or until liver loses its pink color. Stir in ham, grapes, wine, if desired, and salt and pepper. Cook over medium-low heat for 2 minutes or until heated through. Do not overcook livers as they will become tough.
• Serve on toast.

Makes 4 servings.

CHICKEN À LA KING

Of all the uses for leftover chicken from Sunday's roast, this is one of the tastiest. If you want to make it for a crowd, roast or simmer a whole chicken and claim all the cooked meat for double or triple batches of à la King. Or if you want it just for two, make up half the recipe.

◆

2 tbsp	butter	25 mL
1 cup	sliced mushrooms	250 mL
1 tbsp	all-purpose flour	15 mL
1 cup	chicken broth	250 mL
1/4 cup	dry sherry (optional)	50 mL
1/2 tsp	salt	2 mL
1/4 tsp	white pepper	1 mL
Pinch	cayenne pepper	Pinch
2	egg yolks, lightly beaten	2
2 cups	diced cooked chicken	500 mL
1/3 cup	diced pimientos or sweet red pepper	50 mL
	Basic Baking Powder Biscuits (see page 190) or Croustades (see pages 18-19)	
	Chopped fresh parsley	

• In medium skillet over medium heat, melt butter. Add mushrooms; stir-fry until moisture evaporates. Stir in flour until blended.

• Gradually add broth, stirring, for about 3 minutes or until sauce thickens.

• Stir in sherry, if desired, salt, pepper and cayenne. Stir a little of the sauce into eggs and then stir this mixture into rest of sauce.

• Add chicken. Continue to stir and cook for about 3 minutes or until sauce is thicker and chicken is hot. Stir in pimientos.

• Serve hot over split biscuits. Garnish with parsley.

Makes 4 servings.

SAVORY CRÊPES

More good things can be created with thin crêpes when they are wrapped around meaty or vegetable fillings, such as, cooked spinach or broccoli. A good sauce is all that's necessary for their finishing touch.

◆

8	Crêpes (see page 188)	8
1	batch any of the following fillings	1
2 cups	thin Flavored White Sauce (see page 169) or Cheese Sauce (see page 169)	500 mL
¹/₄ cup	grated Parmesan cheese	50 mL

Possible fillings: Cheesy Crab or Shrimp (see page 19)
Mushroom Oyster (see pages 18-19)
Chicken à la King (see page 99)
Sloppy Joes mixture (see page 95)

• Lay crepes out on work surface. Divide filling evenly among crêpes, placing it along lower half of each circle. Roll up and put crêpes seam-side down on lightly buttered shallow baking dish or in 4 individual ramekins or casseroles.
• Pour sauce over top. Sprinkle with grated Parmesan cheese. (Prepare to this point then cover and refrigerate for up to 6 hours before heating and serving.)
• Bake in 325 F (160 C) oven for about 15 minutes or until heated through and sauce just begins to be bubbly.

Makes 4 servings.

SUMMER FRITTATA

Mom used to make something like this. We called it farmer's omelet.

◆

¹/₂ lb	side bacon	250 g
1	onion, thinly sliced	1
1	clove garlic, minced	1
1	small green pepper, cored, seeded and cubed	1
1	tomato, seeded and chopped	1
2	small zucchini, diced	2
3	new potatoes, cooked and cubed	3
8	eggs	8
1 tsp	salt	5 mL
¹/₄ tsp	freshly ground black pepper	1 mL
2 tbsp	grated Parmesan cheese	25 mL

• Cut bacon into small pieces. In heavy, ovenproof skillet, cook until almost crisp. Remove to paper towels to drain; set aside.
• Discard all but 2 tbsp (25 mL) fat from skillet.
• Add onion and garlic; sauté for about 3 minutes or until onion is translucent but not browned. Add green pepper, tomato and zucchini. Cook, stirring occasionally, for about 4 minutes or until vegetables are nearly tender.
• Add potatoes and bacon. Stir lightly; cook for 1 minute longer.
• In large bowl, whisk eggs with salt and pepper until thoroughly blended. Pour egg mixture over mixture in skillet. Cook for about 3 minutes or until eggs are just set. Sprinkle with Parmesan cheese.
• Place skillet in 350 F (180 C) oven; bake for about 5 minutes or until eggs are set.
• Cut into wedges and serve from pan.

Makes 6 servings.

CREAMED SALMON

I was allowed to make this when I was about six. Mom must have chopped the vegetables. I remember how I loved Dad's compliments to "little cook, Kathleen."

♦

2 tbsp	butter or margarine	25 mL
1	onion, finely chopped	1
1	stalk celery, finely chopped	1
2 tbsp	all-purpose flour	25 mL
1/4 tsp	salt	1 mL
Pinch	freshly ground black pepper	Pinch
1 cup	milk	250 mL
1	can (7$^1/_2$ oz/213 g) salmon	1
1 cup	fresh or frozen peas	250 mL
1 tbsp	chopped fresh dill, parsley or sweet red pepper	15 mL
1 tsp	lemon juice	5 mL
	Buttered toast, hot rice or noodles	

• In medium skillet, heat butter. Add onion and celery; sauté for about 4 minutes or until just tender.
• Stir in flour, salt and pepper until well blended. Gradually stir in milk. Cook, stirring, for about 3 minutes or until mixture thickens.
• Stir in salmon and peas; mix well. Continue to cook, stirring occasionally, for about 4 minutes or until peas are tender. Stir in dill and lemon juice.
• Serve over toast or, as an alternative, over rice or noodles.

Makes 4 servings.

CLAMATO FISH STEW

If this stew had more liquid, it would be called soup. Its "clamato" broth is wonderful sopped up with hot French bread.

◆

3	potatoes, peeled, halved and sliced	3
2	stalks celery, chopped	2
1	can (14 oz/398 mL) tomatoes, undrained	1
1	can (5 oz/142 g) clams, undrained	1
1 lb	fish fillets (flounder, cod, haddock or halibut), fresh or frozen (thawed)	500 g
1 cup	frozen green peas	250 mL
	Salt and freshly ground black pepper	

- In large skillet or electric frypan, combine potatoes, celery, tomatoes and liquid from clams. Reserve clams for later. Bring to a boil, reduce heat and simmer for 15 to 18 minutes or until potatoes are tender.
- Cut fish into bite-size pieces. Add reserved clams and fish to potato mixture. Simmer for about 5 minutes then add peas. Continue to simmer for 3 to 4 minutes longer or until fish is opaque and flakes easily when tested with fork. (If cut-up fish is still frozen or has ice crystals, add about 5 more minutes.) Season with salt and pepper, to taste.
- To serve, ladle into deep plates or shallow soup bowls.

Makes about 4 servings.

GRILLED CHEESE SANDWICHES

This recipe is here to answer a special request from my son Bob, who said, "Mom, tell us how to make your crisp grilled cheese sandwiches without making a mess." He loved them made with process cheese and served with a mug of tomato soup. He'd have eaten them every day for lunch when he was little if I had permitted it.

The routine I use for making them guarantees the bread slices will fit each other and there won't be butter all over.

◆

4	slices 100% whole wheat bread	4
	Soft butter	
2	slices process or natural Cheddar cheese	2

- On board or counter, top a slice of bread with one cheese slice then cover with the second slice of bread. Repeat for each sandwich.
- Heat skillet, preferably nonstick, or griddle over medium heat.
- Butter top bread slice of each sandwich; place buttered side down on skillet. Top each with cheese slice. Now butter underside of single bread slices sitting on board; place on respective cheese slice buttered side up.
- Press in place with turner. Cook until browned on bottom. Flip over and brown on other side.
- Serve immediately.

Makes 2 sandwiches.

ENTRÉES

◆

Starting this section with Bob's requested roast duck recipe seems to give the bird a little more emphasis than it deserves. The truth is, I cook duck about once or twice a year. When I do, it is special — somewhat expensive but easy to enjoy.

Dad was certainly a meat and potatoes man. Roast pork or beef, chops, stews, meat loaves and chicken in every way imaginable were the featured items at our noon hour dinners every day when I was a child.

And it was chicken every Sunday at Mom's table. She loved chicken — roasted, fried, braised and stewed — and even canned it, processing it carefully for a long time. Even though her chicken dishes were marvelous, her touch with beef, except stew, left something to be desired.

My menu planning always starts with choosing an entrée — the main part of a meal. The ones that follow are great examples of real Mom-style fare that continue to please both my family and friends.

BOB'S ROAST DUCK
WITH APPLE GRAVY

This entire section begins with roast duck because plans for writing this cookbook started the night my son, Bob, called long distance for advice concerning his roasting duck. Here's how to do it in print, Bob; the recipe is dedicated to you.

Rare duck was promoted by some nouvelle cuisine chefs in the '80s, but I prefer a well-done duck with crisp skin. There is no stuffing because it would absorb too much of the fat and not be too appealing.

◆

1	domestic duck (5 lb/2.5 kg)	1
	Boiling water	
1	apple, cored	1
1	onion	1
1	clove garlic	1

Glaze:

2 tbsp	apple juice	25 mL
2 tbsp	soy sauce	25 mL
2 tbsp	corn syrup	25 mL

Gravy:

1/2 cup	apple juice	125 mL
2 tbsp	all-purpose flour	25 mL
1/2 cup	cold water	125 mL
	Salt and freshly ground black pepper	

• Preheat oven to 425 F (220 C).

• Remove neck and giblets from cavities. Rinse well. Place duck in large sieve or sink; quickly pour boiling water (that drains away immediately) over the bird. Cool and dry thoroughly.

• Fold flap of neck skin back. Gently twist wing tips back to hold skin in place against back of duck. Place duck breast side up on rack in shallow roasting pan.

- Cut apple, onion and garlic into quarters. Stuff into body cavity. Fold skin on either side of cavity over opening. With fork, prick skin all over. Sprinkle lightly with salt and pepper.
- Place in hot oven. Reduce oven temperature to 325 F (160 C). Roast for 2 hours, carefully removing from oven every 30 minutes to prick skin all over.
- *Glaze*: In small dish, combine apple juice, soy sauce and corn syrup; mix well. Brush all over duck. Continue to roast for 30 minutes longer, brushing with glaze 2 more times, until tender and skin is chestnut brown.
- Carefully remove duck to platter. Let stand 15 minutes before carving. (Discard apple, onion and garlic from cavity.)
- *Gravy*: Skim fat from pan juices, removing as much as possible. Place roasting pan over medium-low heat. Pour in apple juice and remaining glaze, if there is any. Stir to dissolve and scrape up brown bits. Mix flour into cold water until smooth. Stir into pan juices. Cook, stirring, for about 2 minutes or until gravy thickens and is smooth. Season with salt and pepper, to taste. Pour into warm gravy boat. Serve with roast duck.

Makes 2 to 3 servings.

HELPFUL HINT

To Make Pan Juices
Discard as much fat as possible from roasting pan. Place over low heat; add 1 cup (250 mL) water. With wooden spoon, stir to dissolve and scrape up any brown bits. Strain into gravy mixture.

Old-Fashioned Stuffing

This stuffing can be prepared the day before but must be stored covered in the refrigerator. Stuff the bird just before you put it into the oven. (Remember to allow time for this in the overall preparation plan for your meal.) An uncooked, stuffed bird should not be allowed to sit on the counter or even in the refrigerator.

◆

¼ cup	butter	50 mL
2	onions, finely chopped	2
2	stalks celery, finely chopped	2
1	clove garlic (optional)	1
2 tsp	crumbled dried sage	10 mL
2 tsp	dried summer savory	10 mL
1 tsp	salt	5 mL
¼ tsp	black pepper	1 mL
8 cups	day-old bread cubes	2 L
1 cup	strong chicken broth	250 mL

• In large skillet, melt butter. Sauté onions, celery and garlic, if desired, for about 8 minutes or until tender.
• Stir in sage, savory, salt and pepper. Add bread cubes; mix well. Stir in chicken broth to slightly moisten bread cubes.

Makes 9 to 10 cups, enough for one 12 to 16-lb (5 to 7 kg) turkey.

Variation

Sausage Stuffing

• Reduce butter to 2 tbsp (25 mL) and add 1 lb (500 g) sausage meat to skillet to cook with onion mixture. Stir occasionally and cook for 10 to 12 minutes or until sausage is no longer pink.

STUFFED ROAST
TURKEY

Turkeys ranging from 12 to 16 lb (5 to 7 kg) are the easiest to handle and roast. I always buy a fresh one if there's one available. Sometimes I select a butter-basted or oil-injected one, but I'm not convinced it's worth paying extra for that added feature.

———————————————   ♦   ———————————————

1	turkey (12 to 16 lb/5 to 7 kg)	1
1	batch Old-Fashioned Stuffing (see page 108).	
	Soft butter	

- Rinse turkey and its cavity; pat dry.
- Loosely stuff neck and body cavity with stuffing.
- Truss bird.
- Place breast side up on rack in large shallow roasting pan. (Roasting on a rack prevents bird from cooking in its own fat and juices.) Brush all over with butter. Cover with loose tent of foil, made by criss-crossing 2 strips of foil over bird. Tuck it in at the ends.
- Roast in 325 F (160 C) oven for 3 hours. Remove foil; baste with pan juices. Roast for 1 to 1$^1/_2$ hours longer or until golden brown, drumstick feels loose when wiggled, juices run clear when thigh is pierced and roast meat thermometer registers 185 F (85 C) internal temperature in the thickest part of the thigh and 165 F (74 C) in the stuffing.
- Let stand on platter 15 minutes before carving.

Makes about 14 servings.

MUSHROOM GRAVY

From the first time I made this gravy, it's become as much a part of our traditional Thanksgiving and Christmas dinners as roast turkey.

◆

1 lb	mushrooms, sliced	500 g
3 cups	water	750 mL
¼ cup	butter	50 mL
¼ cup	all-purpose flour	50 mL
1 cup	turkey or chicken pan juices	250 mL
1 tsp	salt	5 mL
2 drops	hot pepper sauce	2 drops
1 tbsp	dry sherry	15 mL

• In saucepan, simmer mushrooms in water for 10 minutes.
• In another saucepan, over medium-low heat, melt butter; stir in flour until well blended and foamy.
• Stir in pan juices, salt, pepper sauce, mushrooms and their liquid. Cook and stir constantly for about 5 minutes or until thickened and smooth. Stir in sherry. Pour into gravy boat.

Makes 5 cups (1.25 L).

◆

HELPFUL HINT

To Stuff and Truss Fowl
Stuff both cavities lightly with stuffing.
With bird on its breast, pull the skin over the stuffing in the neck cavity and along the back of the bird. Grasp the wing tip joints and, with a slight twist, fold them back to hold the neck skin in place. With poultry pins or skewers, close vent leading to the body cavity. Or, with darning or trussing needle and thin string, stitch opening closed.

With cotton string, tie around tail, criss-cross and tie around ends of drumsticks to hold legs close to the body.

ROAST CHICKEN

Perhaps our Sunday chicken was more trendy in the '80s when I stuffed it with Wild and Brown Rice Stuffing. Even so, I still find the aroma and taste or roasting chicken filled with Old-Fashioned Stuffing (see page 108) irresistible. (For a bird this size make up half the batch. If there is too much, bake the extra in a small casserole for the last 30 minutes of the roasting time.)

◆

1	batch Wild and Brown Rice Stuffing (see page 112)	1
1	roasting chicken, (4 lb/2 kg)	1
	Salt and pepper	
	Butter	

- Prepare stuffing.
- Meanwhile, remove neck and giblets from chicken. Rinse cavity; pat bird dry and season lightly with salt and pepper to taste.
- Fill body cavity and neck opening of bird with stuffing.
- With skewers or needle and thread, close openings; lightly rub all over with butter. Tie legs in place close to body.
- Place bird, breast side up, on rack in roasting pan. Cover loosely with foil. Roast in 350 F (180 C) oven for 1½ hours, basting frequently with pan juices.
- Remove foil and roast for 30 to 40 minutes longer or until browned and juices run clear when bird is pierced with skewer, or until meat thermometer registers 185 F (80 C).
- Remove to serving platter.
- Let stand for 15 minutes. Remove skewers before carving.

Makes 4 to 5 servings.

WILD AND BROWN RICE STUFFING

On its own, this stuffing makes a superb pilaf to serve with pork, lamb chops or roast lamb.

◆

¹/₂ cup	wild rice	125 mL
3 cups	chicken broth	750 mL
¹/₂ cup	brown rice	125 mL
	Salt	
¹/₄ cup	currants	50 mL
2 tbsp	butter	25 mL
1	onion, minced	1
¹/₂ tsp	salt	2 mL
Pinch	freshly ground black pepper	Pinch
¹/₂ cup	chopped cashews	125 mL
¹/₄ tsp	dried sage	1 mL
¹/₄ cup	dry white wine	50 mL

• In sieve, rinse wild rice under cold running water. Transfer to saucepan of boiling water; cook for 5 minutes, remove from heat, cover and let stand for 1 hour. Drain.

• Add broth; bring to boil; stir in brown rice and salt.

• Reduce heat, cover and simmer for 20 minutes. Stir in currants and simmer for 10 minutes longer or until rice is tender.

• In skillet, heat 1 tbsp (15 mL) of the butter; sauté onion for 4 minutes or until soft-tender. Stir in salt, pepper, cashews, sage and cooked rice. Moisten with wine.

Makes 4 cups (1 L), enough for one 2¹/₂ to 4 lb (1.25 to 2 kg) roasting chicken, guinea fowl or duck.

GIBLET GRAVY

Giblets make good broth and as far as Dad was concerned they were as important to good chicken or turkey gravy as the juices from the roasting pan.

———————————————— ♦ ————————————————

	Turkey or chicken neck and giblets, (neck, gizzard, heart and liver)	
3 cups	water	750 mL
1	onion, coarsely chopped	1
1	stalk celery, coarsely chopped	1
5	whole black peppercorns	5
1	bay leaf	1
1 tsp	salt	5 mL
1 cup	roast turkey or chicken pan juices	250 mL
1/4 cup	all-purpose flour	50 mL
2 tbsp	soft butter	25 mL
	Salt and pepper	

• Rinse giblets. In saucepan, pour water over giblets. Add onion, celery, peppercorns, bay leaf and salt. Bring to a boil, reduce heat and simmer for about 1 hour or until neck meat is very tender. Remove liver and discard or mash it with butter and season it with salt and pepper. Then spread it on a few crackers for a nibble before dinner. (The gravy is best without chopped liver in it.)
• Strain broth into clean saucepan. Finely chop bits of meat from neck and remaining giblets. Add to broth. Discard bones and vegetables. Strain pan juices into broth.
• In small skillet, heat flour until golden. Stir in butter to make paste (roux). Stir into hot broth over medium heat. Cook, stirring, until thickened and smooth. Season with salt and pepper, to taste. (For a thicker gravy, make and use more roux.)
• Pour into gravy boat.

Makes 4 cups (1 L).

POACHED CHICKEN

Whenever I need cooked chicken for salad or pot pie, this is the route I take. As well, I end up with good full-bodied broth for soup.

♦

2	chickens (about 3 lb/1.5 kg each)	2
1	onion stuck with 3 cloves	1
1	clove garlic, cut in half	1
1	stalk celery with leaves, chopped	1
1	carrot, thickly sliced	1
1 tbsp	salt	15 mL
$^1/_4$ tsp	whole black peppercorns	1 mL
2	bay leaves	2
12 cups	water	3 L

• Rinse chickens and their giblets. (Reserve livers for another dish, such as paté, and freeze until needed.) Cut chicken into pieces.
• In large stock pot or Dutch oven, combine chicken pieces, giblets, onion, garlic, celery, carrot, salt, peppercorns, bay leaves and water.
• Bring to a boil, reduce heat, cover and simmer for 1 hour.
• Set aside to cool to room temperature. Cover and refrigerate, as is, for 8 hours or overnight or until fat congeals on top. Remove congealed fat and discard. Heat pot until gel just melts.
• Remove chicken pieces to platter. Remove meat from bones, keeping dark meat separate, chicken breast meat in large pieces and small bits in a separate dish. Discard bones and skin.
• To store: Wrap in separate packages and refrigerate for up to 3 days or freeze for up to 2 months.
• Strain broth through cheesecloth-lined sieve into large saucepan. Discard vegetables in cheesecloth. Place broth over medium-high heat. Boil for about 8 minutes to reduce slightly.
• To store: Pour into containers with tight-fitting lids. Store in refrigerator for up to 1 week; in the freezer for up to 3 months.

Makes 2 cooked chicken breasts, 3 cups (750 mL) dark meat and 1 cup (250 mL) chicken bits; 8 cups (2L) chicken broth.

OLD-FASHIONED CHICKEN STEW

An old-time pot of chicken and veggies is a fine example of the prairie country cooking that is part of my heritage.

♦

2 tbsp	butter	25 mL
2	onions, coarsely chopped	2
2	stalks celery, thinly sliced	2
1	clove garlic, minced	1
1/2 lb	mushrooms, quartered	250 g
3	potatoes, peeled and diced	3
3	carrots, diced	3
4 cups	chicken broth	1 L
2	bay leaves	2
1 tsp	dried thyme	5 mL
1/2 tsp	salt	2 mL
1/4 tsp	freshly ground black pepper	1 mL
4 cups	cubed cooked chicken, (1 inch/2.5 cm pieces)	1 L
1 cup	fresh or frozen green peas	250 mL
1/2 cup	milk	125 mL
1/4 cup	all-purpose flour	50 mL

• In large saucepan, melt butter. Add onions, celery, garlic and mushrooms; sauté for about 5 minutes or until tender and liquid from mushrooms has evaporated.

• Stir in potatoes, carrots, chicken broth, bay leaves, thyme, salt and pepper. Bring to a boil, reduce heat and simmer for 15 minutes until nearly tender.

• Add chicken and peas. Cook for 4 minutes longer or until peas are tender and chicken heated through. Remove bay leaves.

• In bowl, combine milk and flour; mix until very smooth. Stir into chicken mixture. Cook, gently stirring, for about 2 minutes or until sauce thickens.

Makes 6 servings.

PORK STEW

• In place of cooked chicken, use 4 cups (1 L) cubed cooked pork.

OLD-FASHIONED CHICKEN POT PIE

My editor says, "This was one of my favorites as a child." Mine, too, and it rates in the top ten with my kids. (Half or double recipe, if you wish.)

— — — — — ♦ — — — —

1	batch Basic Baking Powder Biscuits (see page 190)	1
1	batch Old-Fashioned Chicken Stew (see page 115)	1

• After kneading biscuit dough, flatten it into a 9-inch (23 cm) round patty. Cut into 12 wedges.
• Pour hot Old-Fashioned Chicken Stew into shallow 10-cup (2.5 L) round or oblong casserole. Arrange biscuit wedges on top.
• Bake in 400 F (200 C) oven for about 15 minutes or until biscuits are golden brown. Or bake biscuits separately and serve on stew.

Makes 8 servings.

Variation

PORK POT PIE

• In place of Old-Fashioned Chicken Stew, use Pork Stew (see above).

CORONATION CHICKEN

Many years ago Sue Paterson served cold curry-sauced chicken at a lunch in her charming English country home. A similar creation was served to Queen Elizabeth II for lunch on the day of her coronation.

◆

Poached Chicken (see page 114)
Rice Salad (see page 56)

Sauce:

1 tbsp	olive oil	15 mL
1	small onion, finely chopped	1
1	small clove garlic, chopped	1
1 tbsp	curry powder	15 mL
1/4 cup	dry red or white wine	50 mL
1/4 cup	chicken broth or water	50 mL
2 tbsp	lemon juice	25 mL
2	dried apricots, chopped	2
1	bay leaf	1
2 tbsp	granulated sugar	15 mL
1 tsp	tomato paste	5 mL
1 1/2 cups	mayonnaise	375 mL
1/2 cup	whipping cream	125 mL

• Prepare and cook chicken at least 8 hours ahead to allow it to thoroughly cool. Prepare Rice Salad and refrigerate.

• *Sauce:* In small saucepan, heat oil. Add onion and garlic; sauté for 4 minutes or until tender. Stir in curry powder; cook for 1 minute.

• Add wine, broth, lemon juice, apricots, bay leaf, sugar and tomato paste; mix well. Simmer for about 8 minutes or until apricots are soft. Discard bay leaf. In food processor, process mixture until puréed. Stir into mayonnaise.

• Whip cream. Fold into flavored mayonnaise.

• Cut chicken into even pieces. Reserve about 1 cup (250 mL) mayonnaise sauce; mix remainder with chicken.

• Arrange chicken in center of serving dish. Coat with reserved sauce. Surround with Rice Salad. Garnish with watercress.

Makes 8 servings.

CURRIED CHICKEN

Thinking of curried chicken, I can see myself spooning it out onto warm plates on cool, crisp Labor Day weekends at the cottage. I make it in the city and warm it in the country where its spicy aroma helps the glowing fire keep out chilly drafts.

♦

1 tsp	vegetable oil	15 mL
1 tbsp	butter	15 mL
1	broiler chicken (about 3 lbs/1.5 kg), cut into serving pieces	1
2	stalks celery, thinly sliced	2
1	onion, finely chopped	1
1	clove garlic, minced	1
1 tbsp	curry powder (or more, if you wish)	15 mL
1 tsp	paprika	5 mL
$^1/_2$ tsp	dried basil	2 mL
1 tsp	salt	2 mL
$^1/_4$ tsp	freshly ground black pepper	1 mL
$^1/_4$ cup	all-purpose flour	50 mL
1 cup	chicken broth	250 mL
1 cup	coconut milk	250 mL
$^1/_2$ cup	raisins	125 mL
$^1/_2$ cup	chopped peanuts	125 mL
	Hot cooked rice	

• In skillet or flameproof casserole, heat vegetable oil and butter. Brown chicken pieces and remove to warm dish.
• Sauté celery, onion and garlic in remaining fat for about 4 minutes. Stir in curry powder, paprika, basil, salt and pepper. Blend flour into fat in skillet. Add broth and coconut milk. Stir and cook until mixture thickens. Stir in raisins and peanuts.
• Place reserved chicken pieces in sauce. (Transfer from skillet to casserole, if necessary.)
• Cover and bake in 350 F (180 C) oven for 1 hour or until tender.
• Serve over hot rice.
Makes 4 servings.

OVEN-CRISP CHICKEN

Far less fat clings to pieces of this breaded chicken than clings to deep-fried chicken.

◆

1	frying chicken (about 3 lbs/1.5 kg) cut into serving pieces	1
	Salt and pepper	
²/₃ cup	all-purpose flour	150 mL
2	eggs, well beaten	2
1 tbsp	water	15 mL
3 cups	soda cracker crumbs	750 mL
¹/₄ cup	grated Parmesan cheese	50 mL
¹/₃ cup	melted butter	75 mL

• Wash chicken pieces and pat dry. Season lightly with salt and pepper. Dredge chicken in flour.

• In bowl, combine eggs and water; mix well.

• Dip each chicken piece into egg mixture then into crumbs. Place in shallow buttered baking dish. Drizzle butter over chicken.

• Bake in 350 F (180 C) oven for 1 hour, turning chicken once during baking time, until chicken is golden and juices run clear. Serve hot or cold.

Makes 4 servings.

CHICKEN AND
PEACHES

My daughter, Patti, tells me this is her all-time favorite, standby meal. While it's baking, she cooks wild or brown rice, sometimes in the oven with the chicken dish. Close to serving time, she steams green beans and slices a few garden tomatoes. She says, "It's so convenient, Mom, and it waits if we're not ready to eat when it's cooked."

♦

8	broiler chicken pieces, (breasts, cut in half or thighs and drumsticks, disjointed)	8
¼ cup	all-purpose flour	50 mL
2 tbsp	butter	25 mL
1	large onion, thickly sliced	1
1	clove garlic, minced	1
1	can (14 oz/398 mL) peach halves, or 3 fresh peaches, peeled and halved	1
¼ cup	white wine	50 mL
	Freshly ground black pepper and salt	

• In plastic bag, shake together chicken pieces and flour to coat chicken with flour.
• In nonstick skillet, heat butter. Lightly brown chicken pieces. Arrange in buttered 9-inch (23 cm) baking dish or casserole.
• Layer onion slices, garlic and peaches evenly over top. Pour wine over all. Season with pepper and a little salt, to taste.
• Cover and bake in 350 F (160 C) oven for 20 minutes. Remove cover; continue to bake for 35 minutes longer or until top is lightly browned, juices are slightly thickened and chicken is fork-tender. Reduce heat to hold until serving time.

Makes 4 servings.

HERBED RACKS OF LAMB

It took Dad some time to discover that the lamb I purchased wasn't like the mutton he had had as a child. This roast proved it to him.

◆

4	racks of lamb with chine bones removed (4 lb/2 kg)	4
1 cup	dry bread crumbs	250 mL
$\frac{1}{2}$ cup	chopped fresh parsley	125 mL
$\frac{1}{4}$ cup	dried dillweed	50 mL
2 tbsp	dried sweet basil	25 mL
$\frac{1}{2}$ tsp	salt	2 mL
$\frac{1}{4}$ tsp	dry mustard	1 mL
	Freshly ground black pepper	
$\frac{1}{4}$ cup	water	50 mL
$\frac{1}{4}$ cup	butter, melted	50 mL

• Remove fat and trim meat from ends of rib bone, exposing about 1 inch (2.5 cm) bone.

• In bowl, combine bread crumbs, parsley, dillweed, sweet basil, salt, mustard, pepper, to taste, water and butter; mix well until mixture is moist.

• Press crumb mixture evenly onto fat surface of racks of lamb. Place lamb racks bone side down on rack in a shallow roasting pan.

• Roast in 325 F (160 C) oven for about 45 minutes to 1 hour until lamb is pink or longer for well done.

• Place racks on serving platter interlacing ribs to form arch, if desired. Let stand for 5 minutes before carving between bones to serve.

Makes 8 servings.

BEEF AND MUSHROOM POT ROAST

The long, slow cooking tenderizes the beef.

◆

1/3 cup	all-purpose flour	75 mL
1 1/2 tsp	salt	7 mL
1/4 tsp	freshly ground black pepper	1 mL
2 1/2 lb	beef pot roast (round, rump or brisket)	1.25 kg
2 tbsp	vegetable oil	25 mL
1 lb	mushrooms, sliced	500 g
2 cups	beef broth	500 mL
2	medium onion, thinly sliced	2
	Water	
3	medium-sized tomatoes, cut into wedges	3

• In large bowl, combine 2 tbsp (25 mL) flour, salt and pepper; mix well. Using rim of saucer or mallet, pound flour into both sides of meat.

• In heavy skillet or Dutch oven, heat oil. Add meat; cook over medium heat for 10 to 15 minutes or until brown on both sides. Remove to plate.

• To skillet, add mushroom slices; sauté for 5 minutes or until golden.

• Return meat to pan, add broth and onions; mix well. Bring to a boil; cover, reduce heat and simmer for 2 hours or until meat is tender.

• Or bake in 350 F (180 C) oven for 2 hours or until tender. Skim off excess fat.

• In bowl, combine remaining flour and enough water to make a smooth paste; mix well. Stir into skillet. Bring back to a boil, reduce heat, stirring constantly, for about 5 minutes or until thickened. Add tomatoes. Cover and cook, just until tomatoes are heated.

Makes 6 servings.

ROAST BEEF AU JUS WITH YORKSHIRE PUDDING

As far as my son Bob is concerned, roast beef and Yorkshire go together just like ham and eggs. For him, the only Yorkshire Pudding worth noting is the individual puffs I've been serving with roast beef since he was about three. I can still hear the "wow" he exclaimed when he saw one on his plate for the first time.

◆

4 to 5 lb	sirloin or prime rib roast	2 to 2.5 kg
1	clove garlic, cut in half	1
2 tsp	Worcestershire sauce	10 mL
1 tsp	dry mustard	5 mL
½ tsp	dried rosemary	2 mL
	Freshly ground black pepper	
	Salt	
	Yorkshire Pudding (recipe follows)	

• Rub outside of roast with cut side of garlic halves, Worcestershire sauce, mustard, rosemary and pepper.
• Place roast, fat side up, on rack in shallow roasting pan.
• Insert roast meat thermometer (if you have one) into thickest part of roast, making sure tip does not rest on bone or in fat.
• Roast, uncovered, in 325 F (160 C) oven for 20 minutes per lb (45 minutes per kg) for rare; 25 minutes per lb (55 minutes per kg) for medium and 30 minutes per lb (65 to 75 minutes per kg) for well done.
• Season with salt, to taste. Cover loosely with tent of foil; keep warm for 15 minutes to allow juices to settle and roast to firm before carving or for 30 minutes if making Yorkshire Pudding.

- To make au jus: Pour $^1/_2$ cup (125 mL) water in roasting pan; scrape up and dissolve any brown bits. Pour into small saucepan. Skim off and discard fat. Add 1 cup (250 mL) boiling water and 1 beef bouillon cube. Bring to a boil, reduce heat and simmer for about 5 minutes to reduce slightly. Taste; season with salt and pepper, to taste.
- Just before serving, stir in any juice collected in the meat platter. Pour into gravy boat.
- Serve roast with au jus and Yorkshire Pudding.

Makes about 10 to 12 servings.

YORKSHIRE PUDDING

If you'd rather have one large Yorkshire Pudding, heat 1 to 2 tbsp (15 to 25 mL) fat and drippings from roast in an 8-inch (20 cm) baking pan; pour in all the popover batter and bake for about 30 minutes or until golden. (This version will collapse after cooling for a few minutes. The outside will be crisp, the center soft and custardy.)

♦

| 1 | batch Popover batter (see page 209) | 1 |

- Prepare Popover batter; refrigerate for about 1 hour.
- Increase oven heat to 450 F (230 C).
- Place about 1 tsp (5 mL) beef dripping and fat (before making au jus) into each of 12 large muffin cups.
- Place in oven for about 2 minutes or until piping hot.
- Pour Popover batter into muffin cups filling them $^2/_3$ full.
- Bake for about 25 minutes or until golden brown.
- Serve hot with Roast Beef au Jus.

Makes 12 servings.

MOM'S MEATLOAF

As soon as I was old enough to skip to main street Radisson on my own, Mom sent me off to the butcher shop to buy 15 cents worth of hamburger, enough for a meatloaf. By the time I got home, she had all the other fixings ready. She'd add the hamburger and pop it into the oven in minutes.

In restaurant language, meatloaf is bistro fare. Sometimes chefs, like many home cooks, gussy it up with lots of ketchup. But Mom wasn't big on ketchup (neither am I), so ours is a straightforward mixture that I vary by adding herbs and spices.

♦

1 1/2 lb	ground beef	750 g
2/3 cup	fine cracker or bread crumbs	150 mL
1	onion, minced	1
1	stalk celery, minced	1
1	clove garlic, minced (optional)	1
2/3 cup	evaporated or regular milk	150 mL
2 tbsp	tomato paste	25 mL
1/2 tsp	Dijon-style mustard	2 mL
1	egg, lightly beaten	1
1 tsp	salt	5 mL
1/4 tsp	freshly ground black pepper	1 mL

• In mixing bowl, combine ground beef, crumbs, onion, celery, garlic, if desired, milk, tomato paste and mustard. Mix well with a fork, breaking meat into small pieces, until well blended. Stir in egg, salt and pepper; mix until well blended.
• Pack into 8 1/2 x 4 1/2-inch (22 x 11 cm/1.5 L) loaf pan; smooth top. Or shape mixture into a mound on a lightly buttered or non-stick baking pan if you like the browned crusty surface of meatloaf.
• Bake in 350 F (180 C) oven for 45 to 50 minutes or until meat is no longer pink. Allow to set for 10 minutes before serving.
• To store: Wrap any leftover meatloaf in plastic wrap. Refrigerate for up to 3 days; freeze for up to 6 weeks.

Makes 6 servings.

HERB-SCENTED MEATLOAF

• To the raw ground beef mixture, add 1 tbsp (15 mL) each chopped fresh parsley and thyme (or 1 tsp/5 mL dried) and 1 tsp (5 mL) chopped fresh oregano or rosemary (or $^1/_2$ tsp /2 mL dried).

POTATO FROSTED MEATLOAF

Meatloaf variations are unlimited. Sometimes I mix other ground meats — pork, veal or ham — with the beef. The following presentation is one of the nicest.

--- ◆ ---

1	batch Mom's Meatloaf mixture (see page 125)	1
8	potatoes	8
1	bay leaf	1
$^1/_4$ cup	commercial sour cream or milk	50 mL
1 tbsp	butter	15 mL
1 cup	shredded Cheddar cheese ($^1/_4$ lb/125 g)	250 mL

• Press meat mixture into 9-inch (23 cm) baking dish or casserole.
• Bake in 350 F (180 C) oven for 35 minutes.
• Meanwhile, in lightly salted boiling water, cook peeled and chopped potatoes and bay leaf for about 12 minutes or until tender. Discard bay leaf. Drain and mash potatoes with sour cream, butter and $^1/_2$ cup (125 mL) of the shredded cheese.
• Frost meatloaf with mashed potato mixture. Sprinkle with remaining cheese. Return to oven; bake for 15 minutes longer or until cheese melts and meat is no longer pink.

Makes 6 servings.

Beef and Chick Pea Stew

Legumes, such as these chick peas, are as good in a stew as other vegetables.

♦

1¹/₂ lb	boneless stewing beef, cut in 1-inch (2.5 cm) cubes	750 g
¹/₄ cup	all-purpose flour	50 mL
2 tbsp	vegetable oil	25 mL
1	medium onion, coarsely chopped	1
2	stalks celery, thinly sliced	2
¹/₂ cup	Italian-style salad dressing	125 mL
1 cup	beef broth	250 mL
1	can (19 oz/540 mL) chick peas, drained	1
1	can (14 oz/398 mL) tomatoes, undrained	1
1 tsp	granulated sugar	5 mL
¹/₂ tsp	salt	2 mL
¹/₄ tsp	dried oregano	1 mL
¹/₈ tsp	ground cloves	0.5 mL
¹/₈ tsp	freshly ground black pepper	0.5 mL

• In bag, dredge beef cubes in flour.
• In skillet, heat oil. Add beef cubes; cook over medium heat for 10 minutes or until brown on all sides.
• Add onion; sauté for 5 minutes or until tender.
• Add celery, Italian dressing, broth, chick peas, tomatoes, sugar, salt, oregano, cloves and pepper; mix well.
• Reduce heat, simmer, covered, 1¹/₂ to 2 hours or until meat is tender. Or place in covered casserole. Bake in 350 F (180 C) oven for 1¹/₂ to 2 hours.

Makes 6 servings.

OLD-FASHIONED STEW

Stew has been a leader in the comfy food category for years. However, the name in magazines and cookbooks has often been disguised as "ragout", "carbonnade", "oven-cooked beef" or "beef braised in wine."

Mom's recipe for good old-fashioned stew was in her head. Until I sat down to write this, so was mine. Now here's the best of both.

♦

2 lb	boneless brisket or stewing beef	1 kg
$^1/_4$ cup	all-purpose flour	50 mL
$^1/_2$ tsp	salt	2 mL
Pinch	black pepper	Pinch
$^1/_4$ cup	butter or oil	50 mL
3	onions, thickly sliced	3
4	potatoes, peeled, and cubed	4
4	carrots, thickly sliced	4
2	stalks celery, thickly sliced	2
2 cups	hot water	500 mL
2	beef bouillon cubes	2
1 tsp	Worcestershire sauce	5 mL
2 tbsp	dry sherry (optional)	25 mL
1	bouquet garni	1
	Salt and freshly ground black pepper	

- Cut beef into 1-inch (2.5 cm) cubes.
- In plastic bag, combine flour, salt and pepper. Add beef cubes, a few at a time; shake to coat beef with flour mixture. Set aside.
- In large skillet or Dutch oven, melt butter. Add beef cubes, about $^1/_4$ at a time. Cook quickly, turning until all sides begin to brown. Set aside.
- Add onions, cook, stirring for about 3 minutes or until soft. Stir in any flour that remains after coating meat.
- Return beef to Dutch oven, if using, or combine beef and onion in large 8-cup (2 L) casserole.
- Stir in potatoes, carrots and celery.
- In measuring cup, combine hot water, bouillon cubes, Worcestershire sauce and sherry, if desired; stir well until bouillon dissolves. Pour over meat and vegetables.
- Add bouquet garni to Dutch oven or casserole.
- Cover. Simmer very gently, on top burner or element if using Dutch oven. Stir occasionally.
- Or bake in 325 F (160 C) oven for $2^1/_2$ to 3 hours or until meat is tender. Discard bouquet garni.
- To store: Place meal-size portions in covered containers. Keep in refrigerator for up to 3 days; in freezer for up to 3 months.

Makes 8 servings.

Variation

OLD-FASHIONED STEW WITH TURNIP

- Add 1 small turnip or rutabaga cut into $^1/_2$-inch (2.5 cm) cubes.

BEEF BOURGUIGNON

When it comes to stews, this classic French one receives top marks. It's an old standby for entertaining at the cottage. I take pots of it from the city to reheat, or stash the ingredients in a big basket so I can cook it there. For accompaniments I serve chunks of crusty French stick, pan-browned or mashed potatoes and crisp greens tossed with a simple vinaigrette. A good, robust Burgundy is wonderful with it.

◆

¼ lb	salt pork, diced	125 g
2 tbsp	butter	25 mL
2	cloves garlic, minced	2
2 lb	stewing beef, cut in 1-inch (2.5 cm) cubes	1 kg
½ tsp	salt	2 mL
¼ tsp	freshly ground black pepper	1 mL
18	small cooking onions	18
18	button mushrooms, halved	18
¼ cup	brandy	50 mL
1 cup	dry red wine (Burgundy)	250 mL
1 cup	strong beef broth	250 mL
¼ cup	all-purpose flour	50 mL
2 tbsp	tomato paste	25 mL
1 tbsp	red wine vinegar	15 mL
2 cups	1-inch (2.5 cm) carrot slices	500 mL
2	bay leaves	2
½ tsp	dried thyme	2 mL

- In large heavy skillet or Dutch oven, over medium-high heat, melt butter. Add salt pork and garlic; sauté for about 2 minutes.
- Add half of beef and cook until well browned on all sides. Transfer to bowl. Repeat with remaining beef.
- Remove skillet from heat and pour off all but 2 tbsp (25 mL) of the fat. Stir in salt and pepper, onions, mushrooms and browned beef. Cook for 1 minute or until heated through. Pour brandy over meat mixture and flame.
- In measuring cup, combine wine, broth, flour, tomato paste and vinegar; mix until smooth. Stir into beef mixture, scraping up any brown bits in skillet.
- Add carrots, bay leaves and thyme. Stir well. Bring mixture to a boil then reduce heat, cover skillet and simmer for about 2 hours or until meat is tender. Or transfer to 10-cup (2.5 L) casserole, cover and bake in 350 F (180 C) oven for about 2 hours.
- Cool to room temperature. Refrigerate overnight. Lift and discard any congealed fat from top.
- To store: Cover and refrigerate for up to 4 days; or cover, wrap and freeze for up to 3 months.
- To serve, defrost if frozen, then rewarm over medium heat; warm in 350 F (180 C) oven for 40 minutes; in microwave oven at Medium-High (70% power), stirring once or twice, for 8 to 10 minutes or until heated through.

Makes 6 servings.

♦

HELPFUL HINT

To Turn Meat, Poultry or Fish
Always use tongs, lifters or even two wooden spoons. Forks pierce meat, allowing the juices to run out.

TOURTIÈRE

I first tasted a version of this savory, French Canadian meat pie during the first winter I spent in Ontario. When I praised the cook, she gave me an idea of what was in it but added that nearly every cook in Quebec uses his or her own secret combination of herbs and spices. A week later I created this variation and every Christmas season I make as many as five or six. Since Tourtières freeze beautifully, I make them ahead before the rush of the festive season overwhelms me.

◆

	Flaky Pastry (see page 271) for double crust 9-inch (23 cm/1 L) pie	
2 lb	lean ground pork	1 kg
2	cloves garlic, minced	2
1	onion, minced	1
1½ tsp	salt	7 mL
1 tsp	crumbled sage	5 mL
¼ tsp	nutmeg	1 mL
¼ tsp	black pepper	1 mL
Pinch	each ground cloves and allspice	Pinch
1 cup	chicken broth	250 mL
3	potatoes	3

- Prepare Flaky Pastry; set aside.
- In large heavy saucepan, combine ground pork, garlic, onion, salt, sage, nutmeg, pepper, cloves and allspice. Stir in chicken broth. Cook over low heat, stirring and breaking up ground pork for about 15 minutes or until meat loses its pink color and half liquid is evaporated. Reduce heat; simmer for 15 minutes longer.
- Meanwhile, boil and mash potatoes (see page 162).
- Stir into meat mixture until very well mixed. Set aside to cool for about 30 minutes.
- Roll out half pastry to line 9-inch (23 cm/1 L) pie plate with bottom crust. Trim off at edge of pie plate.
- Fill with cooled meat mixture, pressing it firmly into the lined pie plate.
- Roll out remaining pastry to fit top of pie and allowing for $1/2$-inch (1 cm) overhang. Place on top of filling. Tuck overhang under edge of bottom crust. Seal, form rim around pie and flute. Cut slashes in top for steam vents.
- Bake in 425 F (225 C) oven for 10 minutes. Reduce heat to 350 F (180 C); bake for about 35 minutes longer or until golden brown.
- To store: Wrap and refrigerate for up to 3 days; freeze for up to 3 months.

Makes 8 servings.

◆

HELPFUL HINT

To Use Ground Meats
Fresh ground meats should be cooked within 2 days of purchase. Always store loosely covered in refrigerator. If not using immediately, freeze for up to 2 months.

Oriental Roast Pork

If Mom didn't have a chicken on Sunday, she served roast pork. Cuts of pork have become leaner over the years, but a loin of pork is still one of the tastiest because it self-bastes as it roasts.

◆

1	boned pork loin roast, tied (5 to 6 lb/2.5 to 3 kg)	1
¹/₂ cup	soy sauce	125 mL
¹/₂ cup	dry sherry	125 mL
2	cloves garlic, minced	2
1 tbsp	dry mustard	25 mL
1 tbsp	grated fresh ginger root	25 mL
1 tsp	dried thyme	5 mL
Tangy Sauce:		
1 cup	black or red currant jelly	250 mL
2 tbsp	dry sherry	25 mL
1 tbsp	soy sauce	15 mL
1 tbsp	grated fresh ginger root or 1 tsp (5 mL) ground ginger	

- Place roast in double plastic bag.
- In bowl, combine soy sauce, sherry, garlic, mustard, ginger root and thyme; mix well. Pour over meat in bag, press out air, secure with twist tie and set in bowl in refrigerator. Let stand for 4 to 6 hours to marinate. Remove roast, reserving marinade. Place roast on rack in shallow roasting pan.
- Roast in 325 F (160 C) oven for 3 hours or until meat thermometer registers 170 F (75 C) and juice is no longer pink. Let stand for 15 minutes before carving.
- *Tangy Sauce:* In small saucepan, combine jelly, sherry, soy sauce and ginger root; mix well. Heat until jelly melts. Serve with pork.

Makes 10 to 12 servings.

BAKED HAM "STEAK"

Since a whole ham seems to last forever, I'm delighted when I find a nice thick slice in the meat section that's enough for one meal.

———————————— ♦ ————————————

1	1$\frac{1}{2}$ inch (4 cm) thick ham slice (about 2 lb/1 kg)	1
8	whole cloves	8
$\frac{1}{2}$ tsp	dry mustard	2 mL
$\frac{1}{2}$ tsp	cinnamon	2 mL
1 cup	apple cider or apple juice	250 mL
$\frac{1}{4}$ cup	maple syrup or maple-flavored syrup	50 mL

• Push whole cloves at even intervals around outside of ham slice. Place ham in shallow baking dish just large enough to hold slice.
• Sprinkle with mustard and cinnamon. In bowl, combine cider and syrup; pour over ham.
• Bake in 325 F (160 C) oven, basting 2 to 3 times during last half hour, for 1 hour or until ham is tender and most of the liquid has evaporated.
• To serve: Cut diagonally across steak in thick or thin slices.

Makes 6 servings.

STIR-FRY PORK AND VEGETABLES

Cutting the vegetables takes time, but the cooking is speedy.

1 lb	lean pork	500 g
2 tbsp	vegetable oil	25 mL
1	clove garlic, minced	1
1 cup	celery slices, cut diagonally	250 mL
1 cup	thin carrot slices	250 mL
1 lb	green beans, cut diagonally in 2 inch (5 cm) lengths	500 g
1	small head Chinese cabbage or regular cabbage, shredded	1
1 cup	strong chicken broth	250 mL
2 tbsp	soy sauce	25 mL
1 tbsp	cornstarch	15 mL
$^{1}/_{4}$ cup	cold water	50 mL

• Cut pork across the grain in thin strips about 2 inches (5 cm) long.
• In heavy skillet or wok, heat oil. Cook garlic until brown; discard.
• Add pork; stir-fry for about 4 minutes or until no longer pink. Add celery, carrots, beans and cabbage; stir-fry for about 6 minutes or until vegetables are tender-crisp. Add chicken broth and soy sauce.
• In small bowl, mix cornstarch and cold water until smooth. Add slowly, stirring for about 1 minute or until liquid thickens and becomes clear. Serve immediately with rice.

Makes 6 servings.

Variation

STIR-FRY CHICKEN OR BEEF AND VEGETABLES

• In place of pork, use boneless chicken, or sirloin steak.

PORK AND SHRIMP MARILYN

These appear to be unlikely partners, but they are delicious together.

♦

1½ lb	pork tenderloin	750 g
¼ cup	all-purpose flour	50 mL
1 tsp	paprika	5 mL
½ tsp	pepper	2 mL
1 tbsp	sunflower oil	15 mL
1 tbsp	sesame oil	15 mL
1	clove garlic, minced	1
1 tbsp	finely chopped fresh ginger root	15 mL
½ lb	fresh or frozen, peeled and cleaned raw shrimp	250 g
1 cup	fish or beef broth	250 mL
6	green onions with tops, thinly sliced	6

• Cut pork into 1-inch (2.5 cm) cubes. Mix flour, paprika and pepper in bag. Add pork cubes. Shake to coat well, then shake off excess.
• In heavy skillet or wok, over medium heat, heat oils. Add garlic, ginger and pork. Stir-fry for about 7 minutes. Add shrimp and broth. Cover and simmer for 5 minutes. Stir in green onions. (Thicken with 2 tsp (10 mL) cornstarch stirred into 2 tbsp (25 mL) cold water, if desired.) Stir and cook about 2 minutes.

Makes 4 servings.

JAMBALAYA

When I discovered this casserole in the '60s, I thought it was wonderful and I still think it is one of the best.

◆

4	slices side bacon, chopped	4
3	onions, coarsely chopped	3
2	clover garlic, minced	2
1	stalk celery, thinly sliced	1
1	green pepper, coarsely chopped	1
2 cups	long-grain rice	500 mL
1 lb	cooked ham, cubed	500 g
2 cups	chicken broth	500 mL
1	can (28 oz/796 mL) tomatoes,	1
1 tsp	crumbled dried thyme	5 mL
$^1/_2$ tsp	salt	2 mL
$^1/_4$ tsp	pepper	1 mL
Pinch	crushed red pepper	Pinch
1 lb	cleaned fresh or defrosted frozen raw shrimp	500 g
2 tbsp	chopped fresh parsley	25 mL

• In large saucepan or Dutch oven, over medium heat, cook bacon until crisp. Remove bacon pieces; drain on paper towels.
• Add onions, garlic and celery to bacon drippings. Sauté for about 5 minutes or until just tender. Add green pepper and rice. Cook, stirring constantly for about 3 minutes longer.
• Add bacon, ham, chicken broth, tomatoes, thyme, salt, pepper and red pepper. Bring to a boil. At this point, transfer mixture from saucepan to a large 10-cup (2.5 L) casserole.
• Cover and bake in 350 F (180 C) oven for 20 minutes. Stir in shrimp. Continue baking for 20 minutes longer or until liquid is absorbed and rice is tender.
• Garnish with parsley.

Makes 8 to 10 servings.

VEAL MARENGO IN CASSEROLE

When I was first married and our dining room was small, it was dishes such as this one that made entertaining, buffet-style, possible.

◆

$^1/_3$ cup	butter, divided	75 mL
3 lb	boneless breast or shoulder veal, cut in 2-inch (5 cm) pieces	1.5 kg
1 tsp	salt	5 mL
$^1/_4$ tsp	freshly ground black pepper	1 mL
$^1/_2$ cup	dry white wine	125 mL
2 cups	chicken stock	500 mL
2 tbsp	finely chopped onion	25 mL
2	carrots, peeled and thinly sliced	2
1 tsp	salt	5 mL
$^1/_2$ tsp	dried savory	2 mL
$^1/_8$ tsp	cayenne pepper	0.5 mL
2 tbsp	all-purpose flour	25 mL
1	can ($5^1/_2$ oz/156 mL) tomato paste	1

• In large skillet, heat 2 tbsp (25 mL) butter; sauté veal for 7 minutes, turning once, until golden. Season with salt and pepper. Transfer veal to medium casserole.
• Add wine to skillet, scaping down sides and bottom of pan to deglaze and remove brown bits. Add chicken stock; mix well.
• In another skillet, heat remaining butter. Add onion, carrots, salt, savory and cayenne. Sauté for 5 minutes or until nearly tender.
• Stir in flour; mix until smooth paste forms. Stir in wine mixture and tomato paste. Bring mixture to a boil, reduce heat and simmer for 5 minutes or until slighly thickened. Pour wine mixture over veal.
• Cover and bake in 300 F (150 C) oven for 3 hours or until meat is tender.

Makes 8 to 10 servings.

SALMON LOAF

Dad talked about the sturgeon he and his brothers caught in the northern Saskatchewan River when he was a kid. But the only fish I ever tasted on the prairies when I was a kid came in a can — salmon, finnan haddie and sardines.

I often double this recipe then bake the mixture in an 8½ x 4½-inch (22 x 11 cm) loaf pan, just like Mom, or in a copper fish mold.

$\blacklozenge$

1	can (7.5 oz/213 g) salmon	1
½ cup	milk	125 mL
1	egg	1
¼ tsp	salt	1 mL
¼ tsp	Worcestershire sauce	1 mL
Pinch	pepper	Pinch
¾ cup	dry soda cracker or bread crumbs	175 mL
2 tbsp	finely chopped celery	25 mL
2 tsp	minced onion	10 mL
1½ tsp	finely chopped fresh parsley	7 mL
½ tsp	dried dillweed	2 mL
	Egg Sauce (see page 144)	

• In bowl, flake salmon with its bones and juice. Stir in milk, egg, salt, Worcestershire sauce and pepper until well combined.
• Add crumbs, celery, onion, parsley and dillweed; stir well.
• Pack into well-buttered 4-cup (1 L) ovenproof bowl.
• Bake in 350 F (180 C) oven for 45 minutes or until tester inserted near center comes out clean. Unmold onto serving platter.
• Serve hot with Egg Sauce.

Makes 4 servings.

Variations

TUNA LOAF

- In place of salmon, use 1 can (7 oz/198 g) chunk light tuna.

SALMON OR TUNA CAKES

- In place of cracker crumbs in Salmon or Tuna Loaf, use 1 cup (250 mL) mashed potatoes. (This is a great way to use leftover potatoes.) Shape mixture into patties.

- Coat them with dry cracker or bread crumbs.
- In nonstick skillet, sauté patties in a little butter or oil.

Makes 8 patties, 4 servings.

◆

HELPFUL HINT

Fish Tips
Any cooked fish (1 cup/ 250 mL flaked) can be used in place of salmon or tuna for fish loaves or cakes. Accentuate the flavor, if you wish, by adding 1 to 2 tsp (5 to 10 mL) lemon juice to the mixture before it is cooked.

BAKED OR
BARBECUED WHOLE
SALMON

The barbecued salmon served to a group of food writers on a visit to a salmon hatchery in British Columbia in the late '70s was so wonderful we had to have the recipe. The technician who prepared it shared his simple trick — the mayonnaise — with us.

◆

1	whole salmon, fresh or frozen, thawed	1
1	onion, sliced or chopped	1
1	stalk celery with leaves	1
	Parsley sprigs	
$^{1}/_{2}$ to 1 cup	mayonnaise	125 to 250 mL
	Egg Sauce (see page 144)	

• Rinse salmon and pat dry. (I always leave the head and tail intact. If you prefer to serve it without, I find it is easier to remove them after cooking.)
• Lay onion, celery and parsley sprigs in open cavity.
• Place fish in center of large piece of heavy-duty foil or 2 layers of regular foil cut about 8-inches (20 cm) longer than fish. Generously rub or brush mayonnaise all over outside of fish, including head and tail.
• Cover with piece of foil same size as first piece. Double fold on all sides to encase the fish leaving some space for steam expansion. (If fish is small or long and narrow a single piece of foil may work. Place fish lengthwise on lower half; fold top half over fish and double fold the long edges and ends to seal.) Place on large baking sheet or jelly roll pan if baking in oven.

- Bake in 450 F (230 C) oven, or place foil package on barbecue grill to cook over high heat, for 10 minutes per inch (2.5 cm) thickness or until fish just flakes or feels fairly firm. When barbecuing, turn halfway through cooking time.
- Let stand for 10 minutes to set juices.
- To serve hot: Open foil and remove all but the strip under fish. With knife, carefully remove exposed skin and discard. (Remove head and tail, if you wish.) Using spatulas, carefully slide fish onto serving platter and at the same time take foil from under fish.
- Garnish fish, if and as desired, with thin cucumber, zucchini, carrot and/or lemon slices and sprigs of parsley or dill.
- Starting at the head end, lift serving size pieces of fish from the backbone and bones. Once the top layer is completely removed, lift tail end and backbone away from the flesh that remains on platter and discard. The bottom layer of salmon is now ready to serve. Serve with Egg Sauce.
- To serve cold: Leave cooked fish wrapped in foil. Place in refrigerator to chill thoroughly in its own juice for at least 6 hours or until cold and very firm to touch.
- At serving time, remove foil and skin as if serving it hot. Place on platter whole and garnish.

One 4¹/₂ lb (2.25 kg) salmon makes 6 to 8 servings.

HELPFUL HINT

Salmon Tip
When choosing a frozen whole salmon, select one with a thin layer of ice all around it to ensure there is no freezer burn. Also, a quick frozen salmon, such as this, is not as expensive but just as moist and tender as a fresh one once it is cooked.

EGG SAUCE

My family would think hot baked salmon was missing something if there was no creamy egg sauce to go with it.

◆

¼ cup	butter	50 mL
½ cup	finely chopped onion	125 mL
½ cup	finely chopped celery	125 mL
½ cup	all-purpose flour	125 mL
2 cups	chicken or fish broth	500 mL
½ cup	milk	125 mL
½ tsp	salt	2 mL
Pinch	white pepper or curry powder	Pinch
3	hard-cooked eggs, coarsely chopped	3
¼ cup	chopped fresh parsley or dill	50 mL

• In 4-cup (1 L) heavy saucepan, melt butter. Add onion and celery; sauté for about 4 minutes or until tender. Stir in flour until well blended.

• Gradually stir in broth. Cook, stirring, for about 4 minutes or until mixture thickens and is smooth. Blend in milk. Season with salt and pepper.

• Fold in chopped eggs and parsley. Pour into sauce boat to serve hot with salmon.

Makes about 3 cups (750 mL).

VEGETABLES

◆

There seemed to be three kinds of vegetables when I was a child; fresh ones from the garden; stored ones in the cellar; and preserved ones in cans or jars. This was before the days of the frozen food locker and home freezers.

Today there are far more varieties of fresh vegetables available throughout the year. Still, I tend to cook what is in season. In summer and early fall, I use the amazing selection of produce from my garden and the local farmer's market. In winter, it's potatoes, other root vegetables and cabbages — the sorts Mom kept in her dark cold cupboard. There is nothing that beats the honest taste of just-cooked, al dente (tender but firm) vegetables. I steer away from gussying them up too much with sauces that might obscure rather than complement their real flavor.

HOT OR CHILLED COOKED ASPARAGUS

Very little preparation is necessary if the asparagus spears are farm fresh and picked the same day. That's when the texture, flavor and color of asparagus are at their best.

———————————— ♦ ————————————

| 2 lb | fresh asparagus | 1 kg |

- Wash stalks in cold water to remove any sand. Rinse under the bracts or scales if necessary. They don't have to be peeled as some cookbooks suggest unless the stalks seem very tough at the lower end. Snap the stalks at the point where they break easily. (No cutting is necessary.) Save the butt ends for soup. You can cook them then strain their purée through a sieve for soup.
- Put spears in lightly salted boiling water just to cover. A large skillet is ideal for this. Bring water back to a boil and boil gently, uncovered, for 5 to 7 minutes or until tender-crisp. Time will depend on the thickness of stalks. (Overcooking makes asparagus mushy.)
- Lift asparagus out with tongs to warm serving platter.
- If asparagus is to be served cold or in a salad, cool it immediately under cold running water. Drain.
- To store: Wrap and keep in refrigerator for up to 3 days.

Makes 4 to 6 servings.

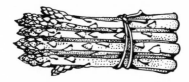

ASPARAGUS WITH WINE-BUTTER SAUCE

I have such a passion for asparagus every spring that I like to eat it without the interference of meat and other vegetables. This dish on its own is heavenly. I often serve it as the starter for a springtime sit-down dinner.

◆

2 lb	just cooked fresh asparagus (see page 146) or frozen, cooked following package directions	1 kg
1/3 cup	dry white wine	75 mL
2 tbsp	butter	25 mL
1 tbsp	chopped fresh parsley	15 mL
1 to 2	hard-cooked eggs, finely chopped	1 to 2

• In small saucepan, combine wine, butter and parsley. Heat until butter melts.
• Lift cooked asparagus onto heated serving platter or serving plates.
• Spoon hot wine-butter sauce over asparagus.
• Sprinkle with finely chopped egg.
• Serve immediately.

Makes 4 servings.

BAKED STUFFED TOMATOES

Tomatoes used for baking should not be too ripe. If they are, they may collapse in the oven.

◆

6	large ripe firm tomatoes	6
$^1/_4$ tsp	salt	1 mL
$1^1/_2$ cups	small bread cubes	375 mL
1	clove garlic, minced	1
1 tbsp	minced onion	15 mL
2 tsp	chopped fresh basil	10 mL
	or $^1/_2$ tsp (2 mL) dried	
$^1/_4$ tsp	dried oregano	1 mL
Pinch	freshly grated black pepper	Pinch
1 cup	dry pressed cottage cheese	250 mL
2 tbsp	grated Parmesan cheese	25 mL

• Cut tops off tomatoes, scoop out pulp. Chop and reserve $^1/_2$ cup (125 mL) firm pulp. (Save remainder to use for a fresh or cooked sauce.)

• Sprinkle inside of tomatoes with salt. Invert and place over paper towels for 20 minutes to drain.

• In bowl, combine bread cubes, garlic, onion, basil, oregano and pepper. Stir in cottage cheese and reserved tomato pulp. Divide evenly and spoon into tomatoes. Sprinkle Parmesan on top of each one.

• Place upright in shallow baking pan. Pour $^1/_4$ inch (5 mm) of water in pan.

• Bake in 350 F (180 C) oven for 12 to 15 minutes or until tomatoes are just tender and bread and Parmesan is golden.

Makes 6 servings.

SCALLOPED
TOMATOES

Dad's favorite dish was this canned tomato one. He always knew if Mom forgot to put in the bit of sugar.

———————————————— ♦ ————————————————

2 tbsp	melted butter	25 mL
1½ cups	day-old bread cubes	375 mL
1	can (14 oz/398 mL) tomatoes, undrained	1
1 tsp	granulated sugar	5 mL
	Salt and freshly ground black pepper	

• In bowl, stir bread cubes in melted butter until mixed.
• In 4-cup (1 L) casserole or baking dish, arrange ⅓ of tomatoes; sprinkle lightly with sugar and salt; generously with pepper. Repeat layers ending with bread cubes on top.
• Bake in 375 F (190 C) oven for 25 minutes or until top is golden.

Makes 4 servings.

Variations

SCALLOPED TOMATOES AND CORN

• Add 1 can (12 oz/341 mL) whole kernel corn, drained. Arrange ⅓ of corn over each layer of tomatoes.

SCALLOPED TOMATOES AND ONIONS

• Add 1 onion. Cover each layer of tomatoes with thinly sliced onion. Bake in 375 F (190 C) oven for about 30 minutes or until onion is tender and top golden.

PARSNIPS AND TOMATOES

This was the parsnip medley I made from the first bunch of parsnips I grew in my garden. Mom often did them this way, for a change from the plain boiled parsnips she prepared for us from the bushels that Dad's garden produced.

◆

1 lb	parsnips, sliced (3 cups/750 mL)	500 g
1	can (14 oz/398 mL) tomatoes, undrained	1
$^1/_2$ tsp	dried crumbled basil	2 mL
	Salt and fresh ground black pepper	

• In saucepan of lightly boiling water, cook parsnips, covered, for 10 minutes. Drain well.

• Add tomatoes to saucepan with parsnips. Bring to a boil; reduce heat and simmer, uncovered, for 10 to 12 minutes or until parsnips are tender and juice from tomatoes is slightly reduced. Stir in basil. Season with salt and pepper, to taste.

Makes 4 to 6 servings.

TOMATOES AND SUCCOTASH

This canned vegetable combination was a regular on Mom's table.

◆

1	can (19 oz/540 mL) tomatoes	1
1	can (19 oz/540 mL) green lima beans, drained	1
1	can (12 oz/341 mL) whole kernel corn, drained	1
2 tsp	all-purpose flour	10 mL
1 tbsp	soft butter	15 mL
	Salt and freshly ground pepper	

• In saucepan, combine tomatoes, drained lima beans and drained corn. Stir well, breaking tomatoes into pieces if they are whole.
• Bring to a boil, reduce heat, simmer for about 2 minutes to reduce slightly.
• Blend flour into butter until very smooth. Stir into vegetables. Continue to cook for about 1$^1/_2$ minutes or until thickened.
• Season with salt and pepper, to taste.

Makes 6 to 8 servings.

TURNIP AND SQUASH PURÉE

When I was a youngster, mashed turnips (that's what we called those big yellowy-orange roots now known as rutabagas) were always served at Christmas dinner. Through experimenting over the years, I've come up with this delicious variation.

♦

2 tbsp	butter	25 mL
1	onion, minced	1
2	butternut squash (4 lb/2 kg) peeled, seeded and cubed	2
2	rutabaga (4 lb/2 kg) peeled and cubed	2
4 cups	chicken broth	1 L
1/4 cup	whipping or commercial sour cream	50 mL
1/2 tsp	ground ginger	2 mL
1/2 tsp	salt	2 mL
1/4 tsp	white pepper	1 mL
1/4 cup	finely chopped raisins (optional)	50 mL

• In large saucepan, melt butter; sauté onion for about 7 minutes or until tender. Add squash, rutabaga and broth. Bring to a boil, reduce heat, cover and simmer for about 25 minutes or until vegetables are tender. Drain; reserve cooking liquid.

• In food processor or by hand, purée or mash vegetables in batches until smooth. Blend in cream, ginger, salt and pepper. If too thick, add some of the reserved cooking liquid.

• To store: Purée can be prepared ahead, covered and refrigerated for 1 day; reheat just before serving.

• Spoon into warm serving dish. Garnish with raisins, if desired.

Makes 12 servings.

Variation

Turnip and Apple Purée

• In place of squash, use 1 more turnip; add 2 to 4 chopped, unpeeled or peeled, firm apples to saucepan after turnips have cooked for about 15 minutes.

Apple Stuffed Squash

What a pair! The two flavors mingle beautifully.

◆

3	acorn squash	3
2 cups	applesauce	2
1/4 cup	raisins	50 mL
2 tbsp	butter, melted	25 mL
2 tbsp	dry bread crumbs	25 mL
1/2 tsp	cinnamon	2 mL

• Cut squash in halves; remove seeds and place cut side down in jelly-roll pan. Pour in enough boiling water to cover bottom of pan.
• Bake in 350 F (180 C) oven for 45 minutes. Remove from oven; turn squash over on pan.
• In bowl, mix together applesauce and raisins. Spoon into squash cavities.
• Combine butter, bread crumbs and cinnamon; mix thoroughly. Sprinkle over applesauce.
• Return to oven and bake for 20 minutes longer or until squash is tender.

Makes 6 servings.

HARVARD BEETS

Although buttered beets are great, these have a little more pizazz.

─────────────── ♦ ───────────────

2 cups	Cooked Beets, whole or cubed (see page 155)	500 mL
Sauce:		
2 tbsp	butter	25 mL
1 tbsp	cornstarch	15 mL
1 tbsp	granulated sugar	15 mL
$^1/_4$ cup	vinegar	50 mL
$^1/_4$ cup	water	50 mL
$^1/_4$ tsp	salt	1 mL

• Cook and peel beets.
• *Sauce:* In saucepan, melt butter. Stir in cornstarch and sugar until smooth. Add vinegar, water and salt. Cook, stirring, for about $1^1/_2$ minutes until thickened and cooked. Stir in beets; keep warm, stirring occasionally, until sauce is ruby red.

Makes 4 servings.

Variation

───────────────

HARVARD CARROTS

• In place of beets, use 2 cups (500 mL) cooked sliced carrots.

Roast Chicken, Wild and Brown Rice Stuffing

Potato Frosted Meatloaf

Scalloped Tomatoes and Corn, Apple Stuffed Squash

Cloverleaf Rolls, Parkerhouse Rolls, French Stick,
Cinnamon Rolls, Speedy Brown Bread

◆

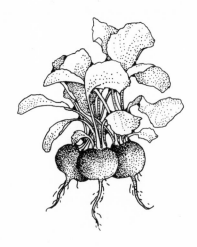

COOKED BEETS

Slipping the skin off cooked beets stains the hands. Wearing rubber gloves to do the job will prevent that from happening.

---◆---

| 1 lb | beets, unpeeled | 500 g |

- Cut off beet stems but leave root as it is. Wash well.
- In saucepan, cook beets in lightly salted boiling water for 30 to 50 minutes for new beets; 1 to 1½ hours for old beets. (Test the largest by piercing with a fork and continue cooking if it is not tender.)
- Drain well then place pan under cold running water to cool beets so they can be handled.
- With fingers, slip skins off beets. Leave small beets whole; slice, cube or chop large ones.
- Reheat in saucepan with a little water over low heat.

Makes 2 cups (500 mL).

RATATOUILLE

The best time to make this is in late summer when vegetables can be picked up at a roadside farmers' market.

—————————————— ◆ ——————————————

2 tbsp	olive oil	25 mL
2	onions, coarsely chopped	2
2	cloves garlic, minced	2
2	zucchini, cut in $\frac{1}{4}$-inch (5 mm) slices	2
1	eggplant, cubed	1
1	green pepper, seeded and diced	1
$\frac{1}{4}$ lb	mushrooms, quartered (about 12)	125 g
1	bay leaf	1
1 tbsp	chopped fresh basil or 1 tsp (5 mL) dried	5 mL
1 tsp	salt	5 mL
1 tsp	granulated sugar	5 mL
$\frac{1}{2}$ tsp	crumbled dried thyme	2 mL
$\frac{1}{4}$ tsp	freshly ground black pepper	1 mL
3	tomatoes, peeled and quartered	3
2 tbsp	capers (optional)	25 mL
	Chopped fresh parsley	

• In large skillet, heat oil. Sauté onions and garlic for about 4 minutes or until just tender.
• Add zucchini, eggplant, green pepper, mushrooms, bay leaf, basil, salt, sugar, thyme and pepper. Cook over medium heat, stirring occasionally, for 10 minutes or until some moisture evaporates.
• Stir in tomatoes. Simmer, stirring occasionally, for about 50 to 60 minutes or until eggplant is tender and mixture is fairly thick. Stir in capers, if desired. Discard bay leaf.
• Garnish with chopped parsley.

Makes 8 servings.

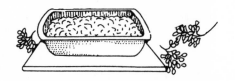

OVEN-CREAMED
ONIONS

These are wonderful with roasts. Have them ready to pop in the oven to cook as the meat finishes cooking.

◆

6 to 8	yellow onions, thickly sliced	6 to 8
2 tbsp	butter	25 mL
2 tbsp	all-purpose flour	25 mL
$^1/_2$ tsp	salt	2 mL
Pinch	white pepper	Pinch
1 cup	milk	250 mL

• In large saucepan of lightly salted boiling water, cook onions for 15 minutes. Drain and transfer to 6-cup (1.5 L) casserole.
• In small saucepan, melt butter; stir in flour, salt and pepper until well mixed. Slowly add milk; cook, stirring constantly, until sauce thickens. Pour over onions.
• Bake in 350 F (160 C) oven for 25 minutes or until bubbly and top is lightly golden.

Makes 6 servings.

STIR-FRY VEGGIES

Stir-frying quickly cooks vegetables, keeping them tender crisp.

♦

Sauce:

2 tbsp	cold water	25 mL
1 tbsp	dry sherry	15 mL
2 tsp	soy sauce	10 mL
1 tsp	cornstarch	5 mL
$^1/_2$ tsp	granulated sugar	2 mL

Vegetables:

1 tbsp	butter	15 mL
1 tbsp	olive oil	15 mL
1	onion, coarsely chopped	1
2	stalks celery, diagonally sliced	2
1 cup	fresh cauliflower florets ($^1/_2$ lb/250 g)	250 mL
1 cup	fresh broccoli florets ($^1/_3$ lb/175 g)	250 mL
$^1/_2$ cup	chicken broth or water	125 mL
2 tbsp	finely chopped sweet red pepper or fresh parsley	25 mL
	Salt and freshly ground black pepper	

• *Sauce:* In small dish or cup, combine water, sherry, soy sauce, cornstarch and sugar; mix well.
• *Vegetables:* In large skillet or wok, heat butter and oil. Add onion and celery; stir-fry for 4 minutes. Add cauliflower and broccoli; continue to stir-fry for 4 minutes longer. Stir in broth, cover, and allow to steam for 1 to 2 minutes.
• Push vegetables to one side. Stir sauce mixture into pan juices. Cook, stirring, for about 1 minute or until thickened. Fold into vegetables to lightly coat them with sauce. Stir in red pepper. Season with salt and pepper, to taste.
• Serve immediately.

Makes 4 to 6 servings.

Variations

MORE STIR-FRY COMBINATIONS

Other combinations that work (in all have about 4 cups (1 L) vegetables ready):

- Carrots, celery, cauliflower or broccoli and snow peas.
- Carrots, celery, diagonally cut green beans, mushrooms.
- Carrots, celery, onion, cabbage or bok choy.
- Celery, onion, zucchini, mushroom and sweet red pepper slices.

For an added touch of flavor, to the first vegetables in the pan, add:

- 1 tbsp (15 mL) grated fresh ginger root.
- 1 tbsp (15 mL) shredded lemon or orange rind.
- A few grains cayenne or crushed hot chili peppers.

Just before serving, add one of the following and stir in to heat through:

- 1 to 2 tomatoes, cut into thin wedges.
- 1 tbsp (15 mL) toasted sesame seeds.
- 1 to 2 tbsp (15 to 25 mL) toasted slivered almonds or chopped walnuts.
- 1 to 2 tbsp toasted pinenuts.

HELPFUL HINT

To Give An Added Polish To Stir-Fry Vegetables
Stir in about 2 tsp (10 mL) vegetable oil just before serving.

GLAZED PEAS, CARROTS AND ONIONS

The light sugar glaze makes the veggies glisten.

◆

4	carrots	4
2 cups	pearl onions	500 mL
2 cups	fresh or frozen peas	500 mL
1 tbsp	butter	15 mL
1 tbsp	grated fresh ginger root or $^1/_2$ tsp ground ginger	15 mL
2 tbsp	brown sugar Freshly ground black pepper	25 mL

- Cut carrots into $^1/_2$-inch (1 cm) slices.
- Pour boiling water over onions then cool under cold running water. Slip off skins.
- In saucepan of lightly salted water, cook carrots and onions for about 12 minutes or until nearly tender.
- Add peas; cook for 4 minutes longer or until vegetables are tender. Drain.
- Add butter, ginger root and brown sugar. Shake vegetables in pan over medium-low heat until sugar melts and coats carrots. Season with pepper, to taste.

Makes 6 servings.

Variation

GLAZED CARROTS

- Omit the onions and peas. In place of them, use 4 more carrots.

CORN PUFF

Corn is another canned vegetable I always keep on hand. I still prefer it to frozen corn.

——————————————— ◆ ———————————————

1 tbsp	butter	15 mL
1 tbsp	finely chopped onion	15 mL
¹/₂ cup	soft bread crumbs (1 slice bread)	125 mL
¹/₂ tsp	salt	5 mL
Pinch	white pepper	Pinch
Few grains	cayenne pepper	Few grains
2	eggs	2
1 cup	milk	250 mL
1	can (14 oz/398 mL) creamed corn	1
1	can (12 oz/341 mL) kernel corn	1

- Butter 6-cup (1.5 L) casserole.
- In small skillet, heat butter. Add onion; sauté for 1 minute. Stir in bread crumbs, salt, pepper and cayenne.
- In bowl, beat together eggs and milk. Stir in onion mixture, creamed corn and kernel corn.
- Pour into buttered casserole.
- Bake in 350 F (180 C) oven for 30 minutes or until tester inserted near center comes out clean.

Makes 6 servings.

Variation

———————————

CORN AND ASPARAGUS PUFF

- Add 2 cups (500 mL) cut-up (2 inch/5 cm lengths) fresh or frozen asparagus or 1 can (14 oz/398 mL) asparagus, drained and cut up.

BOILED POTATOES

Plain boiled, mashed, baked or scalloped, potatoes were as popular as our daily bread when I was a child. They are still the starchy staple for most of our meals planned around roasts, chops, or steak. But I'm sure I don't use half the quantity Mom did.

◆

Potatoes, scrubbed clean

• Peel potatoes, usually 1 to $1\frac{1}{2}$ per person depending on size.
• Cut into halves or quarters. Rinse well with cold water to remove excess starch. Drain.
• In saucepan, cover potatoes with lightly salted water (1 tsp/5 mL for 4 cups/1 L water). Add 1 bay leaf to water, especially if the potatoes are going to be used in potato salad.
• Bring to a boil, cook, covered, for about 20 minutes or until tender. Drain well; discard bay leaf.
• Return pan with potatoes to medium heat. Shake to let steam escape. Serve immediately with butter and chopped fresh parsley.

Variation

MASHED POTATOES

Allow 1 to $1\frac{1}{2}$ potatoes for each serving.

• Peel potatoes. Boil and drain well.
• With potato masher, mash the fresh boiled potatoes in the pan in which they were boiled until smooth and not lumpy. They may also be mashed with the electric mixer or in the food processor. Warm bowl and container before using them. One caution: Overbeating or overprocessing may make some potatoes a bit gummy.
• Add about 1 tbsp (15 mL) milk or cream or sour cream and 1 tsp (5 mL) butter for each potato. Mash or whisk into mashed potato. Work with saucepan over low-medium heat so potatoes will not become cold.

CREAMED NEW PEAS
AND POTATOES

Although Dad balked a bit when Mom wanted a hill or two of potatoes dug before they were mature, he always raved about the small ones once they were set before him. They were so good he'd say, "They're a sign we'll have the best potatoes ever."

◆

8 to 12	new potatoes	8 to 12
8	green onions	8
2 cups	new peas	500 mL
1¹/₂ cups	Thin White Sauce (see page 168)	375 mL
	Freshly ground black pepper	
¹/₄ cup	grated Parmesan cheese (optional)	50 mL

• In saucepan of lightly salted boiling water, cook potatoes for 15 minutes or until nearly tender.

• Cut onions into 1-inch (2.5 cm) pieces. Add with peas to saucepan of potatoes; continue cooking for about 8 minutes or until vegetables are tender. Drain, using the liquid for white sauce.

• Stir vegetables into white sauce or pour sauce over vegetables; stir to coat. Season with pepper, to taste. Serve immediately.

• OR arrange vegetables in 6-cup (1.5 L) casserole. Add white sauce; gently mix. Sprinkle with cheese, if desired. Bake in 375 F (190 C) oven for about 10 minutes or until cheese browns.

Makes 4 servings.

JIM'S SCALLOPED POTATOES

The first time Jim invited me to dinner at his place, I watched him meticulously layer potatoes, onions, butter, flour, salt and pepper in a casserole. Although he filled it too full, I didn't say a word. The potatoes were outstanding but his oven was a mess. Now, he's my husband and the Scalloped Potato expert in our family, but we make sure he uses a deep casserole so that the potatoes don't boil over.

◆

5	medium potatoes	5
1	yellow onion, thinly sliced	1
2 tbsp	butter	25 mL
2 tbsp	flour	25 mL
	Salt and pepper	
2 cups	milk (approx.)	500 mL

• Peel potatoes and cut in thin, crosswise slices. Reserve about $^1/_4$ potatoes for a top layer. Spread $^1/_4$ potatoes evenly in buttered baking dish; cover with $^1/_3$ the onions, $^1/_3$ the butter cut into tiny bits and $^1/_3$ the flour.
• Repeat above layers twice, adding salt and pepper, to taste, to each layer.
• Top the dish with balance of potatoes reserved for the purpose. Add milk until it can be seen between the pieces of potato.
• Cover and bake in 350 F (180 C) oven for 45 minutes. Uncover and bake for about 45 minutes longer or until tender and brown on top.

Makes 4 to 6 servings.

BAKED POTATOES

This is the standard way I serve Baked Potatoes to my family. For company I often go the extra step and stuff them.

◆

4	large baking potatoes	4
2 tsp	soft butter or oil	10 mL

Topping:

3/4 cup	commercial sour cream, light sour cream or low-fat yogurt	175 mL
2 tbsp	chopped chives or green onions Salt and freshly ground black pepper	25 mL
2 tbsp	crumbled crisp bacon pieces (optional)	25 mL

• Wash potatoes, dry and rub lightly with a bit of butter. Pierce skins in one or two places with knife tip to prevent splitting or exploding in oven.

• Bake in 400 F (200 C) oven 50 to 60 minutes or until center is tender when pierced with fork or thin knife.

• With oven mitt-covered hands, gently squeeze potatoes to soften inside. With fork or knife, pierce or cut large X through skin on top. Gently squeeze to push cooked potato through X. Serve plain with butter, if desired, or with topping.

• *Topping:* In small bowl, combine sour cream and chives. Season with salt and pepper, to taste.

• Spoon dollop of sour cream mixture on top of each potato. Garnish with crumbled bacon, if desired.

Makes 4 servings.

PARSLEY RICE

For a change from potatoes, try this rice dish.

◆

1 cup	long-grain white rice or brown rice	250 mL
2 cups	chicken broth	500 mL
¹/₂ tsp	salt	2 mL
1 tbsp	butter	15 mL
¹/₄ cup	chopped fresh parsley	50 mL
2 tsp	Worcestershire sauce	10 mL
	Freshly ground black pepper	

• In saucepan, combine rice, broth and salt. Bring to a boil, reduce heat, cover tightly and simmer for 20 minutes or until tender.
• Remove from heat. Let stand for 5 minutes. With a fork fluff rice.
• Fold in butter, parsley and Worcestershire sauce. Season with pepper, to taste.

Makes 6 servings.

Variation

RICE PILAF

The lemon and hot pepper sauce add a zesty touch that goes nicely with fish or pork.

• Before adding rice and broth to saucepan, sauté 1 chopped onion, 1 chopped stalk of celery and 1 minced clove garlic in 2 tbsp (25 mL) butter. In place of Worcestershire sauce, add 1 tsp (5 mL) grated lemon rind and 4 drops hot pepper sauce.

Herb-Scented Orzo

Orzo is one of the many different pasta shapes available in our markets today. It is shaped like a grain of barley or rice. After it is cooked, it is denser than most pasta.

♦

2 cups	water	500 mL
2 cups	chicken broth	500 mL
1 cup	orzo	250 mL
1 tsp	olive oil	5 mL
2	shallots or $^1/_2$ onion, finely chopped	2
1 tbsp	finely chopped fresh parsley or 1 tsp (5 mL) dried	15 mL
$^1/_2$ tsp	crumbled dried thyme	2 mL
$^1/_2$ tsp	dried oregano	2 mL
Pinch	freshly ground black pepper	Pinch
1 tbsp	low-fat plain yogurt	15 mL
1 tbsp	skim milk	15 mL

• In saucepan, bring water and broth to a boil. Add orzo; cook for about 10 minutes or until tender but firm. Drain; set aside.
• In skillet, heat oil. Add shallots, parsley, thyme, oregano and pepper; sauté for about 4 minutes until shallots are tender. Stir in drained orzo.
• Combine yogurt and milk. Stir into hot orzo just before serving.

Makes 4 servings.

WHITE SAUCE

In 1949 I learned to make smooth, lump-free white sauce in one of our first-year home economics cooking classes at the University of Saskatchewan. I'm glad I did because it's a sauce I've made countless times to use on its own or as the mother sauce for others. Too bad the name makes it sound so uninteresting. French chefs add flavoring — a bit of nutmeg, half a bay leaf or an onion stuck with a clove — and call it Bechamel. Now that sounds more inviting, doesn't it? Make the creamy sauce thin, medium or thick as its use dictates.

◆

	Thin	Medium	Thick
Butter	1 tbsp (15 mL)	2 tbsp (25 mL)	$\frac{1}{4}$ cup (50 mL)
All-purpose flour	1 tbsp (15 mL)	2 tbsp (25 mL)	$\frac{1}{4}$ cup (50 mL)
Nutmeg	Pinch	$\frac{1}{8}$ tsp (0.5 mL)	$\frac{1}{4}$ tsp (1 mL)
Milk	1 cup (250 mL)	1 cup (250 mL)	1 cup (250 mL)
Salt and pepper			

• In small heavy saucepan, melt butter over medium heat. Thoroughly blend in flour and nutmeg for 1 to 2 minutes. (For a smooth, lump-free sauce, every bit of flour must be coated with fat. This butter-flour blend is called roux.)
• Gradually whisk in milk, stirring as mixture comes to a boil; cook for $1\frac{1}{2}$ to 2 minutes or until thickened and there is no taste of raw flour. Season with salt and pepper, to taste.
• Remove from heat or keep warm over very low heat or pan of simmering water. (Cover surface with waxed paper or plastic wrap if

sauce is used immediately. This prevents a skin from forming on the surface.)

Makes about 1 cup (250 mL).

Variations

FLAVORED WHITE SAUCE

Add any of the following to vary the flavor:

- 1 tsp (5 mL) vinegar, lemon or lime juice.
- $^1/_2$ tsp (2 mL) barbecue or Worcestershire sauce.
- 1 to 2 tsp (5 to 10 mL) dry white wine or sherry.
- 1 tbsp (15 mL) chopped fresh parsley, chives, sweet basil or thyme or 1 tsp (5 mL) dried.

BEST CHEESE SAUCE

- Once White Sauce is cooked and thickened, vigorously stir in 1 cup (250 mL) shredded medium or aged Cheddar or Gouda cheese, or Gruyère or Havarti. Stir just until cheese melts and immediately remove from heat. (Continuing to cook and boil a cheese sauce causes it to break up and curdle.) Keep warm over hot water.

VELOUTÉ SAUCE

- In place of milk, use chicken, beef or fish broth.

ONION OR CELERY SAUCE

- Cook $^1/_4$ cup (50 mL) finely chopped onion or celery (or half of each) in butter before blending in the flour.

EASY HOLLANDAISE SAUCE

Be warned, this sauce is buttery-rich, but it's wonderful with cooked asparagus, broccoli, cauliflower and green beans.

◆

3	egg yolks	3
2 tbsp	lemon juice	25 mL
$^1/_4$ tsp	salt	1 mL
$^1/_2$ cup	butter	125 mL

• In blender or food processor, combine egg yolks, lemon juice and salt. Process at high speed for about 5 seconds.

• In saucepan, heat butter until it is hot and bubbly but do not allow it to brown. Turn blender on high and drizzle butter in a steady slow stream into egg mixture until mixture emulsifies and thickens.

• To hold: Place this blender-type of hollandaise over hot water to hold for several hours.

Makes 1 cup (250 mL).

BREAD & ROLLS

◆

One of my fondest childhood memories is the heady aroma of Mom's freshly baked bread or her wonderful cinnamon buns. For a great after-school treat, we'd spread butter on warm slices of the white bread then drizzle corn syrup on top.

There's a knack to kneading yeast breads. I learned it from Mom as I watched her punch, push and roll big pillows of bread dough on the kitchen table. She was an artist at forming it into loaf and roll shapes.

White bread was her specialty. It was much better than the loaves she'd buy when she wasn't in the mood to bake.

Breadmaking is a nice activity to plan for an evening or weekend. It takes a few hours from start to finish but not all of that is working time. Your first loaves may be a bit stodgy but don't give up. Mastering the art takes a bit of practice.

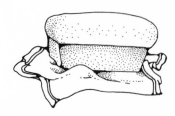

WHITE BREAD

Mom often saved potato water from boiled potatoes and used it in place of the water in her bread.

◆

1 tsp	granulated sugar	5 mL
¹/₂ cup	warm water	125 mL
1	envelope active dry yeast or 1 tbsp (15 mL)	1
1¹/₂ cups	lukewarm water	375 mL
1 tbsp	granulated sugar	15 mL
2 tsp	salt	10 mL
5¹/₂ cups	all-purpose flour	to 1.35 L
	Soft butter	

• In large mixing bowl, dissolve 1 tsp (5 mL) sugar in warm water; stir in yeast and let stand for 10 minutes. Stir well.
• Add lukewarm water, 1 tbsp (15 mL) sugar and salt. Beat in 2 cups (500 mL) flour until smooth. Gradually stir in remaining flour, using hands if necessary, until dough comes away from sides of bowl. (It may take 5 minutes mixing by hand). Only use the last ¹/₂ cup (125 mL) flour if dough seems too sticky.
• Turn out onto lightly floured surface using no more than ¹/₄ cup (50 mL) flour, less if possible. Let dough stand for 8 to 10 minutes; it will be easier to handle.
• With floured hands, knead dough for 5 to 10 minutes or until dough no longer sticks to board, feels smooth and elastic. Form into a ball. Return to buttered bowl; cover with buttered waxed paper and light cloth.
• Set in a warm place to rise for at least 45 minutes or until doubled in bulk. Punch down to remove some of the air bubbles.

- Let rise a second time, if you wish. (The final grain or texture will be finer.) Turn out onto very lightly floured surface. Knead for 2 to 3 minutes. Cut dough in half.
- Shape each part into a smooth roll to fit into buttered $8^1/_2$ x $4^1/_2$ inch (22 x 11 cm/1.5 L) loaf pan. Pans should be half full. With palm of hand, flatten dough in center to push it gently into the corners. Lightly butter tops with soft butter. Cover with buttered waxed paper.
- Let rise in warm place for 45 minutes to 1 hour or until doubled in bulk.
- Bake in 400 F (200 C) oven for 10 minutes or until tops begin to brown. Reduce heat to 350 F (180 C) and continue to bake for 45 to 50 minutes or until loaves are golden brown and sound hollow when tapped.
- Cool for 10 minutes. Remove from pans; cool on wire racks.

Makes 2 medium loaves.

Variations

WHOLE WHEAT OR GRAHAM BREAD

- In place of 2 cups (500 mL) of the all-purpose flour, beat $2^1/_2$ cups (625 mL) whole wheat or graham flour into the yeast mixture. Then work in the remaining 3 to $3^1/_2$ cups (750 to 875 mL) all-purpose flour.

RAISIN BREAD

- Knead 1 cup (250 mL) raisins and $^1/_2$ tsp (2 mL) ground nutmeg into dough when the White, Whole Wheat or Graham Bread dough is being kneaded prior to being shaped into loaves.

FINNISH RYE BREAD

- In place of 1 tbsp (15 mL) sugar, use 1 tbsp (15 mL) molasses and in place of $1^1/_2$ cups (375 mL) of the all-purpose flour, use $1^1/_2$ cups (375 mL) rye flour. In place of water, try to use potato water if at all possible.

CHEESE BREAD

• Beat 2 cups (500 mL) shredded firm cheese — Cheddar, Gouda, Edam or Swiss — with the first addition of flour to the yeast mixture when making White, Whole Wheat or Graham Bread.

FRENCH STICK

The secrets for making crusty loaves, such as French bread, are to always use hard wheat flour like our Canadian all-purpose flour and to make sure the dough is completely fat-free.

——————————————————— ♦ ———————————————————

2 tsp	granulated sugar	10 mL
$^1/_2$ cup	warm water	125 mL
2	envelopes active dry yeast or 2 tbsp (25 mL)	2
$1^1/_2$ cups	lukewarm water	250 mL
1 tbsp	granulated sugar	15 mL
2 tsp	salt	10 mL
5 to	all-purpose flour	1.25
$5^1/_2$ cups		to 1.37 L
	Cornmeal	

- In large mixing bowl, dissolve 2 tsp (10 mL) sugar in warm water; stir in yeast and let stand for 10 minutes. Stir well.
- Add lukewarm water, 1 tbsp (15 mL) sugar and salt. Beat in 2 cups (500 mL) flour until smooth. Gradually stir in remaining flour, using hands if necessary, until dough comes away from sides of bowl. (It may take 5 minutes mixing by hand.) Only use the additional $\frac{1}{2}$ cup (125 mL) if dough seems too sticky.
- Turn out onto lightly floured surface using no more than $\frac{1}{4}$ cup (50 mL) flour, less if possible. Let dough stand for 8 to 10 minutes; it will be easier to handle.
- With floured hands, knead dough for 5 to 10 minutes or until dough no longer sticks to board and feels smooth and elastic. Form into a ball. Return to unbuttered bowl; cover with light cloth.
- Set in a warm place to rise for at least 45 minutes or until doubled in bulk. Punch down to remove some of the air bubbles.
- Let rise a second time, if you wish. Turn out onto very lightly floured surface. Knead for 2 to 3 minutes.
- To shape loaves: Divide dough into 3 parts. Knead and then shape each part into a long sausage-shaped loaf about $2\frac{1}{2}$ to 3 inches (6 to 8 cm) in diameter.
- Sprinkle baking sheets with cornmeal; place loaves on cornmeal.
- With sharp knife, diagonally cut 4 to 5 slashes, about $\frac{1}{2}$ inch (1 cm) deep, along length of loaves.
- Cover with damp cloth supported by 2 or 3 glasses to prevent cloth from touching loaves. Let rise for about 1 hour or until doubled in bulk. Brush loaves with water.
- Place small pan of hot water on bottom of 400 F (200 C) oven.
- Bake in preheated oven for about 30 minutes or until golden brown and loaves sound hollow when tapped.

Makes 3 French sticks.

Variation

CRUSTY ROLLS

All of our big dinners and formals were held at the Bessborough Hotel during my four years in residence at the University of Saskatchewan. At every one the crusty rolls were fabulous. I remember promising myself then that I'd try to make them one day. These are close but not nearly as crusty as the ones baked in the hotel's oven.

◆

- When French Stick dough is ready to shape into loaves, roll it into a long sausage shape instead. Cut evenly into 24 pieces. Shape each one into a roll about 4 inches (10 cm) long and slightly pointed at each end. Place shaped rolls on unbuttered baking sheet sprinkled sparingly with cornmeal.
- With sharp knife, cut a lengthwise slash about $1/4$ inch (5 mm) deep in each roll.
- Set aside in warm place. Cover with damp cloth, supported by glasses so it will not touch rolls. Let rise for about 1 hour or until doubled in bulk.
- Brush each roll with water.
- Place small pan of hot water on bottom of 400 F (200 C) oven.
- Bake in preheated oven for about 15 minutes or until golden brown and rolls feel hard when touched.

Makes 2 dozen rolls.

◆

HELPFUL HINT

To Recrisp Crust of French Stick or Crusty Rolls
Warm loaves in 350 F (180 C) oven for 5 to 8 minutes or until crust is very hot.

No-Knead Oatmeal Bread

In the preparation of no-knead bread, the batter is thinner than in regular bread. The kneading is replaced by extra beating which develops the gluten in the all-purpose flour.

───────────────── ♦ ─────────────────

1¹/₂ cups	boiling water	375 mL
1¹/₂ cups	quick rolled oats	375 mL
1 tsp	salt	5 mL
1 tsp	granulated sugar	5 mL
¹/₂ cup	warm water	125 mL
1	envelope active dry yeast or 1 tbsp (15 mL)	1
¹/₄ cup	butter or shortening	50 mL
¹/₂ cup	molasses	125 mL
4 cups	all-purpose flour	1 L

• In bowl, combine boiling water, rolled oats and salt. Set aside for about 10 minutes to cool to lukewarm.
• In large mixing bowl, dissolve sugar in warm water; stir in yeast and let stand for 10 minutes. Stir well.
• Stir oatmeal mixture, butter and molasses into yeast mixture. Beat in 2 cups (500 mL) flour and then stir in remaining flour. Beat well until dough is stretchy, elastic and smooth but not too sticky.
• Cover with buttered waxed paper. Let rise in warm place for about 45 minutes or until doubled in bulk. Beat again for 3 to 4 minutes.
• Spoon into 3 buttered 8¹/₂ x 4¹/₂ inch (22 x 11 cm/1.5 L) loaf pans or 4 buttered coffee cans (369 g).
• Let rise in warm place for about 45 minutes or until doubled in bulk.
• Bake in 375 F (190 C) oven for about 50 minutes or until loaves are golden brown and sound hollow when tapped.
• Cool for 10 minutes. Remove from pans; cool on wire racks.

Makes 3 loaves or 4 tall round loaves.

SPEEDY BROWN BREAD

Without some all-purpose flour in it, whole wheat bread can be heavy and stodgy.

◆

2 tsp	granulated sugar	10 mL
1 cup	warm water	250 mL
2	envelopes active dry yeast or 2 tbsp (25 mL)	2
4 cups	all-purpose flour	1 L
3 cups	whole wheat flour	750 mL
1 tbsp	baking powder	15 mL
1 tsp	salt	5 mL
2$^1/_2$ cups	milk	625 mL
$^1/_4$ cup	liquid honey	50 mL
$^1/_2$ cup	butter or margarine, melted	125 mL

• In small bowl, dissolve sugar in warm water. Sprinkle yeast over top; let stand for 10 minutes or until foamy; stir well.
• In large bowl, stir together flours, baking powder and salt.
• In electric mixer bowl or food processor fitted with dough hook, combine milk, honey and melted butter. Beat in yeast mixture. Or, alternatively, whisk together by hand in mixing bowl.
• Gradually add flour mixture 1 cup (250 mL) at a time. Beat until smooth and no butter can be seen.
• When dough forms a smooth ball, turn out onto lightly floured board. Knead for about 8 minutes or until smooth and elastic.
• Divide dough into 4 equal pieces. Shape into small loaves tucking ends underneath. Place loaves into 4 well-buttered 8$^1/_2$ x 4$^1/_2$ inch (22 x 11 cm/1.5 L) loaf pans. Brush with butter or margarine. Cover with buttered waxed paper and damp light cloth.
• Set aside in warm place; let rise for about 1 hour or until doubled in bulk.
• Bake in 375 F (190 C) oven for about 40 minutes or until golden brown and loaves sound hollow when tapped. Remove from pans to wire racks to cool.

Makes 4 loaves.

BATTER BUNS

In the '40s, long before the days of machine cuisine, Mom sat with her big pottery mixing bowl in her lap to beat this batter.

---◆---

1 tbsp	granulated sugar	15 mL
1/2 cup	warm water	125 mL
1	envelope active dry yeast or 1 tbsp (15 mL)	1
1 cup	milk or water	250 mL
2 tbsp	soft butter, margarine or vegetable oil	25 mL
1 1/2 tsp	salt	7 mL
3 1/2 cups	all-purpose flour	875 mL

• Lightly butter medium muffin cups.
• In electric mixer bowl or food processor fit with plastic blade, dissolve 1 tsp (5 mL) sugar in warm water. Sprinkle yeast over top; let stand for 10 minutes or until foamy.
• Beat in milk, butter, remaining sugar and salt.
• Add half the flour; beat for 2 minutes, scraping down bowl once or twice. Stir in remaining flour and beat for 2 minutes longer. Set aside for 20 minutes to rise slightly.
• Beat dough for 1 minute longer. Drop by spoonfuls to fill each muffin cup half full. Batter will be sticky. Cover pans with buttered waxed paper.
• Let rise 1 hour or until doubled in bulk.
• Bake in 375 F (190 C) oven for 20 minutes or until golden brown. Cool in pans for 5 minutes. Remove and cool on cake racks.

Makes 24 buns.

Variation

QUICK BATTER BREAD

• Spread batter in one 6-cup (1.5 L) buttered casserole. Let rise until doubled in bulk. Bake in 350 F (180 C) oven for 40 minutes or until golden brown and loaf sounds hollow when tapped. Makes 1 loaf.

PECAN STICKY BUNS

I have seen batches of these disappear in less time than it takes to bake them.

◆

1	batch Batter Buns dough (see page 179)	1

Sticky Topping:

1 cup	packed brown sugar	250 mL
¹/₂ cup	butter	125 mL
¹/₄ cup	water	50 mL
1 cup	coarsely chopped pecans	250 mL

• Prepare Batter Buns dough.
• *Sticky Topping:* In small saucepan, combine brown sugar, butter and water; mix well. Bring to a boil.
• Place 1 tbsp (15 mL) of mixture in bottom of each buttered muffin cup. Divide chopped pecans evenly among muffin cups.
• Beat dough for 1 minute. Drop 1 heaping tbsp (15 mL) into each muffin cup. Cover pans with buttered waxed paper.
• Let rise in warm place for about 1 hour or until doubled in bulk.
• Bake in 375 F (190 C) oven for 20 minutes or until golden brown.
• Immediately invert pans onto waxed paper. Let stand for 5 minutes. Remove pans. Serve buns bottoms up.

Makes 24 buns.

Sweet Rolls

The food processor offers one quick way to make bread dough. You can also use a heavy electric mixer or mix the dough by hand.

♦

1 tsp	granulated sugar	5 mL
¹/₂ cup	warm water	125 mL
1	envelope active dry yeast or 1 tbsp (15 mL)	1
4 cups	all-purpose flour	1 L
2 tbsp	granulated sugar	25 mL
1 tsp	salt	5 mL
¹/₂ cup	butter, softened	125 mL
2	eggs	2
³/₄ cup	milk	175 mL

• Dissolve 1 tsp (5 mL) sugar in warm water. Sprinkle yeast over top; let stand for 10 minutes or until frothy.
• In food processor fitted with plastic blade and using the dome top or in heavy electric mixer fitted with dough hook, combine flour, 2 tbsp (25 mL) sugar, salt and butter; process until well mixed.
• In mixing bowl, beat together butter, eggs, milk and yeast mixture. With the machine running, pour into flour mixture through feed tube. Process for about 1 minute or until dough forms a smooth ball.
• Turn out onto floured surface. Knead for 3 to 4 minutes. Form into a ball. Transfer to lightly buttered large bowl; turn to butter all over. Cover with buttered waxed paper.
• Refrigerate for 4 hours or overnight until dough has doubled in bulk. Punch down dough.
• Cut dough into 18 equal pieces. Knead and form each one into a small ball. Place on buttered baking sheets.
• Cover with buttered waxed paper and damp light cloth. Set aside in warm place; let rise for about 1 hour or until doubled in bulk.
• Bake in 375 F (190 C) oven for 20 minutes or until golden brown and firm to the touch.

Makes 18 rolls.

Variations

BUTTERFLAKE ROLLS

• Roll punched down Sweet Rolls dough into an oblong $\frac{1}{8}$ inch (3 mm) thick; brush with melted butter. Cut into 1 to $1\frac{1}{2}$-inch (2.5 to 4 cm) strips, depending on size of muffin cups. Stack 5 to 7 strips, one on top of the other, depending on size of muffin cups. Cut each pile into 1-inch (2.5 cm) portions; place cut side down in buttered muffin cups. Let rise for about 1 hour or until very light. Bake in 375 F (190 C) oven for 15 to 20 minutes or until golden brown. Makes 12 to 18.

CLOVERLEAF ROLLS

• Have $\frac{1}{4}$ cup (50 mL) melted butter ready. Cut punched down Sweet Rolls dough into 36 to 54 equal pieces, depending on size of muffin cups. Roll each piece in the palm of the hand to form a smooth ball. Dip one-half of each ball in melted butter. Place 3 balls, with buttered side touching, in buttered muffin cups. Cover. Let rise for about 1 hour or until very light. Bake in 375 F (190 C) oven for 15 to 20 minutes or until golden brown. Makes 12 to 18.

PARKERHOUSE ROLLS

• Have ready $\frac{1}{4}$ cup (50 mL) melted butter. Roll out punched down Sweet Rolls dough $\frac{1}{2}$ inch (1 cm) thick. With floured round biscuit cutter, cut into rounds. With the floured handle of a wooden spoon, form a deep depression across the center of each round of dough; slightly flatten one-half of each round. Lightly brush melted butter on each round; fold the thicker half over the thinner half. Place 2 inches (5 cm) apart on buttered baking sheet. Cover with buttered waxed paper. Let rise for about 1 hour or until very light. Bake in 375 F (190 C) oven for 15 to 20 minutes or until golden brown. Makes 12 to 18.

HOT CROSS BUNS

Easter baking always includes making Hot Cross Buns. In our home, both Good Friday and Easter breakfast time wouldn't be right without them.

———————————— ♦ ————————————

1	batch Sweet Rolls dough (see page 181)	1
2 tsp	cinnamon	10 mL
$^1/_2$ tsp	nutmeg	2 mL
1 cup	raisins, currants or candied fruit or a mixture	250 mL
	Melted butter	
	Butter Cream Frosting (see page 262), optional	

• When preparing Sweet Rolls dough, stir cinnamon and nutmeg into the flour.
• Knead raisins into dough.
• Cut into 18 equal pieces. Knead and form each one into a ball, tucking ends underneath. Place on buttered baking sheet. With fingers, flatten each ball to 1-inch (2.5 cm) thickness.
• Cover with buttered waxed paper and damp light cloth.
• Set aside in warm place; let rise for about 1 hour or until doubled in bulk.
• With very sharp knife or razor blade, cut 2 shallow slashes to form a cross on top of each roll. Let stand for about 5 minutes.
• Bake in 375 F (190 C) oven for 20 to 25 minutes or until deep golden brown. Brush tops with melted butter.
• When buns are cool, if desired, using Butter Cream Frosting in pastry bag, pipe cross on each bun or spread it on with thin knife blade.

Makes 18 buns.

BUTTER PECAN RING

This proves how versatile a good yeast dough can be.

———————————— ◆ ————————————

1	batch Sweet Rolls dough (see page 181)	1
Filling:		
1 cup	brown sugar	250 mL
¹/₂ cup	butter	125 mL
2 tbsp	cinnamon	10 mL
1 cup	toasted pecans, coarsely chopped	250 mL
Glaze:		
¹/₂ cup	icing sugar	125 mL
2 tbsp	milk	25 mL
1 tsp	dark rum	5 mL

• Prepare Sweet Rolls dough.
• *Filling:* In bowl, cream together brown sugar, butter and cinnamon.
• On lightly floured surface, with floured rolling pin, roll dough into 22 x 10-inch (55 x 25 cm) rectangle.
• Spread creamed mixture over dough to within ¹/₂ inch (1 cm) of one long side. Evenly sprinkle nuts over top.
• Starting at long side (with creamed mixture), roll up tightly jelly-roll style; pinch the edge not spread with creamed mixture to seal.
• Transfer roll to buttered baking sheet. With sharp knife or scissors, cut 16 evenly placed slashes from the top to within ¹/₄ inch (5 mm) of the bottom. Form into a ring. Turn one slice to the center, the other to the outside and continue until all sections are turned. Cover with buttered waxed paper and damp light cloth.
• Set in warm place; let rise for 45 minutes or until doubled.
• Bake in 375 F (190 C) oven for 20 to 25 minutes or until golden brown and firm to touch. Remove to cake rack to cool for 20 minutes.
• *Glaze:* In small bowl, combine icing sugar, milk and rum; mix well until smooth. Brush over pecan ring.

Makes one 12-inch (30 cm) ring.

POPPY SEED BREAD

As a child I thought Aunt Mary was an artist because she baked a dark pinwheel design into every slice of her Poppy Seed Bread. This bread seemed to be her specialty and one that Mom didn't make.

◆

1	batch Sweet Rolls dough (see page 181)	1
Filling:		
1 cup	boiling water	250 mL
1 cup	poppy seeds	250 mL
1/4 cup	packed brown sugar	50 mL
1 tbsp	cornstarch	15 mL
1 tbsp	butter	15 mL
1/2 cup	finely chopped walnuts	125 mL
1	egg white	1

- Prepare Sweet Rolls dough.
- Meanwhile, prepare filling. Pour boiling water over poppy seeds. Let stand for 1 hour. Drain well. In bowl, combine with brown sugar, cornstarch and butter; mix well. Stir in walnuts. In another bowl, beat egg white until stiff; fold into poppy seed mixture.
- Divide dough evenly into 2 pieces.
- On lightly buttered surface, roll each piece into square about 1/2 inch (1 cm) thick.
- Spread half of poppy seed mixture on each piece to 1/2 inch (1 cm) of edges. Beginning at one end, roll up jelly-roll style. Pinch ends together. Place seam side down on buttered baking sheet. Or place in buttered 8 1/2 x 4 1/2-inch (22 x 11 cm/1.5 L) loaf pan.
- Cover with buttered waxed paper. Set aside and let rise in warm place for about 1 hour or until doubled in bulk.
- Bake in 375 F (190 C) oven for about 40 minutes or until golden brown and loaves sound hollow when tapped.

Makes 2 loaves.

ALMOND BRAID

You could call this a cake-bread, if you wish. It makes a scrumptious snack with a cup of coffee.

——————————— ◆ ———————————

1	batch Sweet Rolls dough (see page 181)	1
1 cup	finely chopped toasted almonds	250 mL
1	egg	1
1 tbsp	whipping cream or milk	15 mL
$^1/_2$ cup	coarsely chopped almonds	125 mL
$^1/_4$ cup	granulated sugar	50 mL

• Prepare Sweet Rolls dough.
• Knead toasted almonds into dough.
• Divide dough into 3 equal parts.
• Roll each portion into 18-inch (45 cm) long rope. Place ropes side by side, diagonally across buttered baking sheet. Braid ropes together, starting from the center, taking care not to stretch the dough. Pinch ends together and tuck them under. Cover with buttered waxed paper and light damp cloth.
• Set aside in warm place; let rise for 1 to $1^1/_2$ hours or until doubled in bulk.
• In bowl, beat together egg and cream with fork. Carefully brush over top of braid. Combine almonds and sugar; sprinkle over braid.
• Bake in 375 F (190 C) oven for 40 to 45 minutes or until golden brown and firm to touch.

Makes 1 braided loaf, about 16 inches (40 cm) long.

QUICK BREADS

◆

I love making pancakes, biscuits, muffins, scones and tea breads. They're classified as quick breads and are much faster to make and bake than yeast breads.

Their leavening comes from the air bubbles created in the soft doughs by baking soda in the presence of acid, baking powder or steam. It's yeast that provides this leavening action and lightness in regular bread and rolls.

Not only are quick breads easy to make, the doughs are versatile. Take baking powder biscuit dough, for example. By replacing some of the all-purpose flour with whole wheat flour, adding other ingredients, such as nuts, dried fruits, cheese, herbs and or spices and giving the dough a different twist, I can turn out all sorts of different creations.

I demonstrate this in the following recipes where the basic one acts as the starting point for others.

CRÊPES
(THIN PANCAKES)

Crêpes are so versatile I've used them rolled around savory fillings and topped with sauce (see page 100) for exciting appetizers and entrées. They also make exquisite desserts. Fill them with fruit and/or ice cream and garnish them with dollops of whipped cream and a dusting of icing sugar or cocoa.

◆

1 cup	all-purpose flour	250 mL
1 tsp	granulated sugar	5 mL
$^1/_4$ tsp	salt	1 mL
3	eggs	3
1 cup	milk	250 mL
1 tbsp	butter	15 mL

• In mixing bowl, combine flour, sugar and salt.
• In another bowl, beat together eggs and milk. Stir in dry ingredients and beat until smooth. OR place flour, sugar, salt, eggs and milk in container of blender or food processor and process until smooth.
• Cover; refrigerate for 1 hour to allow batter to rest.
• Melt butter, 1 tsp (5 mL) at a time, in 8-inch (20 cm), preferably nonstick, crêpe or omelet pan. Add more butter to pan as required.
• Pour about $^1/_4$ cup (50 mL) batter in preheated pan, swirl to just coat bottom of pan with thin layer. Cook for about 1 minute or until top looks dry and bottom is faintly golden. Loosen edges with spatula, slip onto plate.
• Repeat to make remaining crêpes.
• To store: Wrap and refrigerate for up to 2 days; freeze up to 2 months.

Makes 12 to 16 crêpes.

COUNTRY STYLE PANCAKES

There's no tally of the number of pancake breakfasts we've had at the cottage on Wood Lake. When every chair around our old oak table is taken, we work in shifts flipping these on the big electric griddle.

◆

1 cup	all-purpose flour	250 mL
1 cup	whole wheat or buckwheat flour	250 mL
1 tbsp	granulated sugar	25 mL
4 tsp	baking powder	20 mL
$\frac{1}{2}$ tsp	salt	2 mL
2	eggs	2
2 cups	milk	500 mL
2 tbsp	butter or margarine, melted	25 mL

- In mixing bowl, combine flours, sugar, baking powder and salt.
- In another bowl, beat together egg and milk. Quickly stir into dry ingredients until just mixed (batter will be lumpy). Fold in butter. If thinner pancakes are desired, stir a little more milk into batter.
- Pour about $\frac{1}{3}$ cup (75 mL) batter at a time onto hot, lightly buttered, preferably nonstick, griddle or skillet.
- Cook until puffy and bubbly on top. Turn when bubbles begin to break. Continue to cook until golden brown on both sides.

Makes 12 large pancakes, 6 servings.

Variations

BLUEBERRY PANCAKES

- Fold 1 cup (250 mL) blueberries into batter.

OAT BRAN PANCAKES

- In place of whole wheat flour, use 1 cup (250 mL) oat bran.

BAKING POWDER BISCUITS

This is the most versatile recipe in this collection. It's helped me out numerous times when there has been very little to serve with coffee to unexpected company. I can whip up biscuit dough in no time right in front of guests.

These biscuits are best if the batter is mixed and kneaded quickly. It will seem wet, but try not to incorporate much flour from the lightly floured surface into it. Added flour makes heavier biscuits.

———————————— ◆ ————————————

$2^1/_2$ cups	all-purpose flour	625 mL
2 tbsp	baking powder	25 mL
1 tbsp	granulated sugar	15 mL
$^1/_2$ tsp	salt	15 mL
$^1/_2$ cup	butter or margarine	25 mL
1 cup	milk	250 mL

• In mixing bowl, combine flour, baking powder, sugar and salt.
• With pastry blender or two knives, cut in butter until mixture looks like a combination of coarse and fine crumbs.
• Quickly stir in milk to make a light soft dough — not too sticky. Turn out onto lightly floured surface; sprinkle lightly with flour (about 2 tsp (10 mL)).
• With lightly floured hands, knead 8 to 10 times or for about 20 seconds until dough feels puffy and surface is smooth.
• With floured rolling pin and more flour on board, roll out, or with hands pat, to thickness of $^1/_2$ to $^3/_4$ inch (1 to 2 cm).
• With floured cookie cutter, cut out rounds (2 to $2^1/_2$ inches/5 to 6 cm in diameter) or cut into squares, triangles or rectangles.
• Place on lightly buttered baking sheets or shallow baking pan, 1 inch (2.5 cm) apart for crusty biscuits; touching for soft ones. Set aside for 10 minutes to allow to rise slightly.
• Bake in a 400 F (200 C) oven for 12 to 15 minutes or until golden brown.

Makes 16 to 24 biscuits.

Variations

BASIC WHOLE WHEAT BAKING POWDER BISCUITS

• In place of 1 cup (250 mL) of the all-purpose flour use 1 cup (250 mL) whole wheat or graham flour.

DROPPED BISCUITS

• Increase milk to $1^1/_3$ cups (325 mL). Stir milk into crumbly mixture to make a thick batter and omit kneading and rolling. Drop by heaping tablespoonfuls (15 mL) onto buttered baking sheet.

CHEESE BISCUITS

• Stir 1 cup (250 mL) shredded Cheddar, Edam or Monterey Jack cheese into crumbly mixture before adding milk.

NUTTY BISCUITS

• Add 1 cup (250 mL) finely chopped walnuts, almonds, filberts or pecans into the flour mixture before cutting in butter.

BUTTERSCOTCH PINWHEELS

• On lightly floured board, with floured rolling pin, roll prepared Basic Baking Powder Biscuit dough into an oblong about $^1/_3$ inch (7 mm) thick. Spread with about 2 tbsp (25 mL) soft butter.
• Evenly sprinkle $^2/_3$ cup (150 mL) brown sugar over butter. Starting at a wide side, roll up jelly-roll style into long cylinder.
• With sharp knife cut into 1-inch (2.5 cm) slices. Place 2 inches (5 cm) apart on buttered cookie sheet. Bake in 400 F (200 C) oven for about 20 minutes or until golden brown.

QUICK CINNAMON ROLLS

• In the Butterscotch Pinwheels recipe, instead of using brown sugar sprinkle the buttered dough with a mixture of $^2/_3$ cup (150 mL) granulated sugar and 1 tbsp (15 mL) cinnamon.

CHRISTMAS WREATH

Christmas morning would seem strange without this biscuit wreath
or tree included in our breakfast.

———————————— ◆ ————————————

1	batch Basic Baking Powder Biscuits dough (see page 190) or Sweet Rolls dough (see page 181)	1

Filling:

1¹/₂ cups	coarsely chopped almonds, divided	375 mL
¹/₂ cup	icing sugar	125 mL
1 tsp	grated lemon rind	5 mL
1	egg white	1
1 cup	currants	250 mL
¹/₂ cup	chopped candied fruit	125 mL

Glaze:

1	egg yolk	1
1 tbsp	milk	15 mL
1 tbsp	icing sugar	15 mL

• Make Basic Baking Powder Biscuits dough or Sweet Rolls dough.
• *Filling:* In food processor, combine 1 cup (250 mL) almonds, icing
sugar, lemon rind and egg white. Process until well puréed and
mixture forms a paste; set aside.
• In bowl, combine currants, candied fruit and remaining almonds.
• *Glaze:* In small bowl, beat egg yolk, milk and icing sugar. Cover and
set aside.
• On lightly floured surface, with floured rolling pin, roll dough into
25 x 13-inch (63 x 33 cm) rectangle.

- Spread thin layer of almond mixture to within 1 inch (2.5 cm) of wide sides. Evenly sprinkle fruit and nut mixture over top.
- Starting at a wide side, roll up jelly-roll style into long cylinder.
- Place on buttered pizza pan or baking sheet; forming roll into a wide ring and join ends. (Cut small bits off ends to make them straight and easy to stick together.)
- With sharp knife, cut slashes, halfway through ring at $1\frac{1}{4}$-inch (3 cm) intervals. Spread slightly open, turning every other slice away from the centre and the others towards the center. Let stand for 10 minutes.
- Bake in 375 F (190 C) oven for 30 to 35 minutes or until golden brown.
- Remove from oven. Generously brush top with glaze.
- Return to oven and bake for 2 minutes longer. Serve warm.
- To store: Cover tightly with plastic wrap or plastic bag. Keep in cold, dry, dark place for up to 2 days; in freezer for up to 4 weeks.
- To rewarm, place in 325 F (160 C) oven for 5 to 10 minutes.

Makes 10 to 12 servings.

Variation

CHRISTMAS TREE

- Cut long cylinder for Christmas Wreath into 18 slices.
- On large baking sheet, arrange slices in the shape of a Christmas tree, starting at the top with 1 slice. Add 2 slices underneath slightly overlapping the top slice and each other. Add 1 more slice to each row until there are 5 slices forming the bottom of the tree. Use the remaining 3 slices to form a triangle base for the tree.
- Press red candied cherry halves in place here and there to look like tree ornaments.
- Glaze and bake as directed for Christmas Wreath.

DANISH PASTRIES

Bakery "Danishes" are made with yeast dough. However, I find these made from Basic Baking Powder Biscuit dough are just as good, especially when they are fresh out of the oven.

◆

1	batch Basic Baking Powder Biscuits dough (see page 190)	1
1½ tsp	ground cardamom	7 mL
¼ cup	soft butter, divided	50 mL
1	egg	1
1 tsp	water	5 mL
¼ cup	finely chopped almonds	50 mL
½ cup	fruit jam or jelly	125 mL

Almond Glaze:

2 tbsp	soft butter or margarine	25 mL
1 cup	icing sugar	250 mL
½ tsp	almond flavoring	2 mL
2 tsp	water	10 mL

• Add ground cardamom to the flour mixture in the Basic Baking Powder Biscuits recipe then prepare dough as directed.
• After kneading dough, on lightly floured surface, with floured rolling pin, roll it out into a rectangle ¼ inch (5 mm) thick. Spread lightly with half the butter. Fold over twice; roll out into rectangle 10 x 24 inches (25 x 60 cm).
• Lightly spread again with butter. Starting at a wide side, roll up jelly-roll fashion. Cut into 1-inch (2.5 cm) thick slices.
• With floured hands, flatten to ½ inch (1 cm) thickness.
• In bowl, beat egg and water. Brush on flattened biscuits. Lightly sprinkle tops with finely chopped almonds.
• With finger or thumb, make an indentation in the center of each. Drop a teaspoonful (5 mL) of jam in each hole.
• Place on lightly buttered baking sheets. Let stand for about 10 minutes to rise slightly.
• Bake in 400 F (200 C) oven for about 14 minutes or until golden brown.

Almond Glaze: In small bowl, cream butter and icing sugar. Stir in almond flavoring and water until mixture is smooth and the consistency of a thick sauce. While warm, brush pastries with Almond Glaze, if desired.

Makes 24.

WHOLE WHEAT CREAM SCONES

A scone using a high percentage of whole wheat flour is finer textured and more tender than one made with only all-purpose flour because whole wheat flour is softer than all-purpose flour.

——————————————— ◆ ———————————————

2 cups	whole wheat flour	500 mL
1 cup	all-purpose flour	250 mL
4 tsp	baking powder	20 mL
2 tsp	granulated sugar	10 mL
$^1/_2$ cup	cold butter	125 mL
$^3/_4$ to 1 cup	light cream (half and half)	175 to 250 mL

- In mixing bowl, combine flours, baking powder and sugar.
- With pastry blender or 2 knives, cut in butter until mixture looks like small peas.
- In another bowl, beat together cream and egg. With fork, stir cream into flour mixture. Form into a ball. (It should be light and not too sticky.)
- Turn out onto floured surface. Dust lightly with flour. Knead 10 to 12 times.
- With floured rolling pin or hands, roll or pat out to $^1/_2$ inch (1 cm) thickness.
- Cut into rounds with floured 2-inch (5 cm) cookie cutter.
- Place on lightly buttered baking sheet.
- Bake in 400 F (200 C) oven for about 12 minutes or until tops and sesame seeds are golden brown.

Makes 12 to 16 biscuits.

SOUR CREAM SCONES

The addition of an egg or two makes scones richer than biscuits and gives them a muffin-like texture rather than a flaky one.

◆

2 cups	all-purpose flour	500 mL
2 tbsp	granulated sugar	25 mL
2 tsp	baking powder	10 mL
1 tsp	baking soda	5 mL
$^1/_2$ tsp	salt	2 mL
$^1/_3$ cup	cold butter	75 mL
1	egg	1
$^2/_3$ cup	commercial sour cream	150 mL
Glaze:		
2 tbsp	dairy sour cream	25 mL
2 tbsp	granulated sugar	25 mL

• In mixing bowl, combine flour, sugar, baking powder, baking soda and salt.
• With pastry blender or 2 knives, cut in butter until mixture is crumbly.
• In another bowl, beat egg lightly with sour cream; pour over crumbly mixture. With fork, quickly stir to make a soft dough. Form into a ball.
• Turn out onto floured surface. Dust lightly with flour. Knead 10 to 12 times. With floured rolling pin, roll out to $^3/_4$ inch (1 cm) thickness.
• With floured 2 to $2^1/_2$-inch (5 to 6 cm) cookie cutter, cut out 10 to 12 biscuits.
• Place on lightly buttered baking sheet.
• *Glaze:* Brush tops with sour cream. Sprinkle with sugar.
• Bake in 425 F (220 C) oven for about 15 minutes or until lightly browned.

Makes 10 to 12 biscuits.

Variation

CURRANT OR RAISIN SCONES

• Add 1 cup (250 mL) currants or raisins to dry ingredients before stirring in egg-sour cream mixture.

IRISH SODA BREAD

A rugged loaf like this one is perfect with chowders and other meal-in-a-pot soups or stews. I put it on the table on its own cutting board with a bread knife to slice as it's needed.

♦

2 cups	all-purpose flour	500 mL
2 cups	whole wheat flour	500 mL
2 tbsp	granulated sugar	25 mL
1¹/₂ tsp	salt	7 mL
1¹/₂ tsp	baking soda	7 mL
1 tsp	baking powder	5 mL
¹/₄ cup	butter	50 mL
2 cups	buttermilk	500 mL

• In mixing bowl, combine all-purpose and whole wheat flours, sugar, salt, baking soda and baking powder. With pastry blender or 2 knives, cut in butter until mixture resembles fine crumbs.
• Stir in buttermilk, all at once, to make a soft dough (a little sticky).
• Turn out on to floured surface. Knead about 10 times. Form into ball. Place on buttered baking sheet. Flatten into 3 inch (7.5 cm) thick round. With sharp knife, cut a large "X" about ¹/₄ inch (5 mm) deep.
• Bake in 375 F (190 C) oven for about 45 minutes and tester inserted in center comes out clean.

Makes 1 large loaf.

PLAIN MUFFINS

The mania for muffins took off in the '80s, and muffin shops with dozens of varieties seemed to pop up everywhere. Homemade muffins are easiest of all baked things to put together. Besides, if you make them yourself, you'll know how much sugar and fat they contain; unfortunately some of the tastiest take-out ones are richer and sweeter than cupcakes.

♦

2 cups	all-purpose flour	500 mL
1/3 cup	granulated sugar	75 mL
1 tbsp	baking powder	15 mL
1/2 tsp	salt	2 mL
1	egg	1
1 1/4 cup	milk	300 mL
1/4 cup	butter or margarine, melted or vegetable oil	50 mL

• In mixing bowl, combine flour, sugar, baking powder and salt. Make well in the center.
• In another bowl, beat together egg, milk and melted butter. Add, all at once, to dry ingredients. Quickly stir just until flour disappears and dry ingredients are just moistened. Do not overmix or beat.
• Spoon batter into buttered or paper-lined muffin cups, filling each 2/3 full.

- Bake in 400 F (200 C) oven for 20 to 30 minutes, depending on size, until golden brown and tops feel firm when lightly touched. Remove from pan to wire rack to cool.

Makes 12 to 16 muffins depending on size.

Variations

GRAHAM (OR WHOLE WHEAT) MUFFINS

- In place of 1 cup (250 mL) of the all-purpose flour, use 1 cup (250 mL) graham or whole wheat flour.

OAT BRAN MUFFINS

- In place of $^1/_2$ cup (125 mL) of the all-purpose flour, use $^3/_4$ cup (175 mL) oat bran.

CORNMEAL MUFFINS

- In place of 1 cup (250 mL) of the all-purpose flour, use 1 cup (250 mL) cornmeal. Combine it with the milk (to soften it slightly). Beat the butter and egg into milk mixture before stirring it into the dry ingredients.

JOHNNY CAKE

- Pour Cornmeal Muffins batter into buttered or oiled 9-inch (23 cm) square baking pan.
- Bake in 400 F (200 C) oven for about 25 minutes or until tester inserted in center comes out clean.
- Cut into rectangles to serve. *Makes 12 to 15 servings.*

APPLE MUFFINS

- In the Plain, Graham, Oat Bran or Cornmeal Muffins recipe, stir
$^3/_4$ cup (175 mL) finely chopped apple (peeled or unpeeled) and 1 tbsp
(15 mL) brown sugar into the egg mixture before pouring it into the
dry ingredients.

BERRY MUFFINS

- In the Plain, Graham, Oat Bran or Cornmeal Muffins recipe,
quickly fold $^3/_4$ cup (175 mL) fresh or frozen berries (whole blueberries, Saskatoons or raspberries or chopped strawberries) into the batter
immediately after it is mixed. (The muffins are best when dry, not
wet, berries are used. Roll fresh berries in paper towels to remove any
water clinging to them and use loose pack or drained frozen berries.)

CHEESE MUFFINS

- In the Plain, Graham, Oat Bran or Cornmeal Muffins recipe, fold
$1^1/_2$ cups (375 mL) shredded firm cheese (Cheddar, Edam, Gouda,
Swiss or Monterey Jack) into dry ingredients before adding the egg
mixture.

CINNAMON RAISIN MUFFINS

- In the Plain, Graham, Oat Bran or Cornmeal Muffins recipe, use
brown sugar instead of granulated, add 2 tsp (10 mL) cinnamon to
dry ingredients and fold $^3/_4$ cup (175 mL) well-drained plumped raisins
into the batter immediately after it is mixed.

CRANBERRY MUFFINS

- In the Plain, Graham, Oat Bran or Cornmeal Muffins recipe, fold
$^3/_4$ cup (175 mL) coarsely chopped cranberries mixed with 2 tbsp
(25 mL) granulated sugar into the batter immediately after it is mixed.
(I add this extra sugar with the cranberries because they are very tart.)

FRUIT MUFFINS

• In the Plain, Graham, Oat Bran or Cornmeal Muffins recipe, fold $^1/_2$ to $^3/_4$ cup (125 mL to 175 mL) chopped dried fruit (raisins, dates or apricots) into dry ingredients before adding the egg mixture.

NUTTY MUFFINS

• In the Plain, Graham, Oat Bran or Cornmeal Muffins recipe, fold $^1/_2$ to $^3/_4$ cup (125 mL to 175 mL) finely chopped nuts (walnuts, pecans, almonds or hazelnuts) into dry ingredients before adding the egg mixture.

MUFFIN TOPPINGS

• The above muffins, except for the Cheese Muffins, seem more glamorous if the batter in the muffin cups is sprinkled with a mixture of 2 tbsp (25 mL) granulated sugar and 1 tsp (5 mL) cinnamon before baking.

♦

HELPFUL HINT

To Plump Raisins
Place raisins in cup or bowl, cover with boiling water and let stand for about 5 minutes or until edges of raisins begin to look white.

BEST BRAN MUFFINS

These are the muffins I knew as a child and they are the ones my kids grew up on. I still like them better than any of the others.

◆

1 cup	natural bran or 100% bran cereal	250 mL
1 cup	milk	250 mL
1	egg	1
1/4 cup	melted butter or margarine	50 mL
1 tsp	vanilla	5 mL
1 cup	all-purpose flour	250 mL
1 tbsp	baking powder	15 mL
1/2 cup	firmly packed brown sugar	125 mL
1 tsp	cinnamon	5 mL
1/2 tsp	salt	2 mL

- In bowl, combine bran and milk; let stand for 10 minutes.
- Add egg, butter and vanilla, beat well.
- In mixing bowl, combine flour and baking powder. Stir in brown sugar, cinnamon and salt.
- Make a well in dry ingredients; add the liquid mixture all at once. Quickly stir only until combined.
- Spoon batter into buttered or paper-lined cups, filling each 2/3 full.
- Bake in 400 F (200 C) oven for 20 minutes or until browned.

Makes 12 muffins.

Variations

DATE BRAN MUFFINS

• Stir $^3/_4$ cup (175 mL) coarsely chopped dates into bran mixture.

FRUIT AND NUT BRAN MUFFINS

• Stir about $^1/_4$ cup (50 mL) each of chopped raisins and chopped nuts into bran mixture.

NUTTY BRAN MUFFINS

• Stir $^1/_2$ cup (125 mL) chopped walnuts into bran mixture.

RAISIN BRAN MUFFINS

• Stir 1 cup (250 mL) raisins into bran mixture.

◆

HELPFUL HINT

To Store Muffins
Place in covered container or sealed plastic bag to keep at room temperature for up to 2 days; in the freezer for up to 3 months. (It's best if muffins cool to room temperature before they are put in any container or bag.) Single muffins (split and buttered, if you wish) can be wrapped in plastic wrap, then frozen. A container full of individually wrapped muffins is handy when you are packing work or school lunches.

MARY'S COFFEE CAKE

For coffee klatsches in our neighborhood, we took turns having other young mothers over for coffee. Each one of us baked our own treats for the occasion. This coffee cake was one that I really liked, and I was delighted when Mary Wood wrote out the recipe for me.

◆

1 1/2 cups	all-purpose flour	375 mL
3/4 cup	granulated sugar	175 mL
1 tbsp	baking powder	15 mL
1/2 tsp	salt	2 mL
1/4 cup	butter	50 mL
1	egg	1
3/4 cup	milk	175 mL
1 tsp	vanilla	5 mL

Topping:

1 cup	firmly packed brown sugar	250 mL
1/2 cup	finely chopped nuts	125 mL
4 tbsp	all-purpose flour	60 mL
1 tsp	cinnamon	5 mL
1/4 cup	melted butter or margarine	50 mL

- In mixing bowl, combine flour, sugar, baking powder and salt.
- With pastry blender or 2 knives, cut in butter.
- In another bowl, beat together egg, milk and vanilla. Quickly stir into dry ingredients until just moistened.
- *Topping:* In bowl, combine brown sugar, nuts, flour and cinnamon. Stir in melted butter; mix well.
- Spread half of batter in buttered 8-inch (20 cm) square cake pan. Sprinkle half of brown sugar topping over top. Spoon on remaining batter, smoothing it with a knife. Sprinkle on remaining topping. Cut through layers with a knife (only once) making a zigzag motion to spread crumbs   through batter. Gently pat down to level mixture in pan.
- Bake in 375 F (190 C) oven for 30 to 35 minutes or until topping is golden brown. Serve warm.

Makes 12 servings.

CARROT NUT BREAD

When tea breads took on a healthier image, health food aficionados of the late '60s started baking carrot breads and cakes.

―――――――――――――――――   ◆   ―――――――――――――――――

3 cups	all-purpose flour	750 mL
1 tbsp	baking powder	15 mL
2 tsp	grated orange rind	10 mL
1^1/$_2$ tsp	ground cinnamon	7 mL
1 tsp	salt	5 mL
^{1}/$_2$ tsp	baking soda	2 mL
3	eggs	3
1^1/$_2$ cups	firmly packed brown sugar	375 mL
1 cup	vegetable oil	250 mL
1 tbsp	vanilla	15 mL
2 cups	coarsely grated carrots	500 mL
^{1}/$_2$ cup	finely chopped walnuts	125 mL
^{1}/$_2$ cup	coarsely chopped raisins	125 mL

• In large bowl, combine flour, baking powder, orange rind, cinnamon, salt and baking soda.
• In another bowl, beat eggs for about 2 minutes or until light yellow. Beat in sugar, oil and vanilla.
• Add egg mixture to dry ingredients; quickly stir until combined. Stir in carrots, walnuts and raisins until just mixed.
• Pour batter into 2 well-buttered 8^1/$_2$ x 4^1/$_2$ inch (22 x 11 cm/1.5 L) loaf pans.
• Bake in 375 F (190 C) oven for 60 to 70 minutes or until tester inserted in center comes out clean.
• Cool for 15 minutes in pan; then turn out onto wire racks to cool completely.
• Wrap tightly in foil or plastic wrap and allow to sit at room temperature overnight to mellow before slicing.

Makes 2 loaves, 32 to 40 slices.

Date Walnut Bread

Put your kitchen shears to use snipping the dates into small pieces. Chopping them with a knife may turn them into a sticky mess.

◆

1 cup	boiling water	250 mL
1 cup	finely chopped dates	250 mL
2 cups	all-purpose flour	500 mL
$^3/_4$ cup	packed brown sugar	175 mL
1 tsp	baking powder	5 mL
1 tsp	baking soda	5 mL
$^1/_2$ tsp	salt	2 mL
1	egg	1
2 tbsp	butter or margarine, melted	25 mL
1 cup	chopped walnuts	250 mL

• In small bowl, pour boiling water over dates; set aside.
• In mixing bowl, combine flour, brown sugar, baking powder, baking soda and salt; mix well.
• Beat egg, butter and nuts into date mixture. Add all at once to dry ingredients. Stir until all ingredients are just moistened.
• Spread in buttered 9 x 5-inch (23 x 13 cm/2L) loaf pan.
• Bake in 350 F (180 C) oven for 60 to 70 minutes or until tester inserted in center comes out clean. Cool for 10 minutes in pan. Turn out onto wire rack to cool completely.

Makes 1 loaf, 16 to 20 slices.

Variation

Orange Date Bread

• In place of $^1/_2$ cup (125 mL) of the boiling water, use $^1/_2$ cup (125 mL) orange juice; add 1 tbsp (15 mL) grated orange rind to the date mixture.

STEAMED BROWN BREAD

Although it's slower and the crust doesn't brown, steaming a quick bread is actually ovenless baking.

1¹/₂ cups	whole wheat flour	375 mL
1¹/₂ cups	all-purpose flour	375 mL
¹/₂ cup	100% bran cereal	125 mL
1 tsp	cinnamon	5 mL
1 tsp	baking powder	5 mL
1 tsp	baking soda	5 mL
¹/₂ tsp	ground nutmeg	2 mL
2 cups	sour milk or buttermilk	500 mL
¹/₂ cup	molasses	125 mL
¹/₂ cup	corn syrup	125 mL
1 tsp	vanilla	5 mL
1 cup	raisins	250 mL

• Wash, dry and butter two (369 g) coffee cans or three 19 oz (540 mL) juice or fruit cans. Dust inside with flour.
• In mixing bowl, combine flours, bran cereal, cinnamon, baking powder, baking soda and nutmeg.
• Combine sour milk, molasses, corn syrup and vanilla; mix well. Add to dry ingredients all at once with raisins. Stir just enough to moisten ingredients.
• Divide batter between prepared cans. Cover each can with foil; tie in place.
• Place cans on rack in Dutch oven or large soup kettle. Add boiling water to come halfway up cans. Cover tightly.
• Steam, over medium heat, for 2 hours or until tester inserted in center comes out clean, or tops spring back when touched.
• Cool for about 5 minutes in cans; then turn out onto wire rack to cool completely.

Makes 2 large or 3 small round loaves.

BANANA PECAN LOAF

For the richest banana taste, always use very ripe bananas. Their moistness and flavor result in a loaf that doesn't require the embellishment of butter or any other spread.

◆

$^{1}/_{3}$ cup	butter or margarine	75 mL
$^{3}/_{4}$ cup	granulated sugar	175 mL
2	eggs	2
1 tsp	vanilla	5 mL
1 cup	mashed ripe bananas (2 to 3)	250 mL
$^{1}/_{2}$ cup	commercial sour cream	125 mL
$1^{3}/_{4}$ cups	all-purpose flour	425 mL
$^{1}/_{3}$ cup	finely chopped pecans	75 mL
$1^{1}/_{2}$ tsp	baking powder	7 mL
$^{1}/_{2}$ tsp	baking soda	2 mL
$^{1}/_{2}$ tsp	salt	2 mL

• In mixing bowl, cream butter until soft. Add sugar and beat until light and fluffy. Beat in eggs, one at a time, and vanilla. Stir in bananas and sour cream until well blended.
• In another bowl, combine flour, pecans, baking powder, baking soda and salt. Add to banana mixture; stir until just combined.
• Pour into buttered 9 x 5-inch (23 x 13 cm/2 L) loaf pan.
• Or, alternatively, divide batter evenly among six 10-oz (284 mL) soup cans. To prepare empty cans, wash and dry well. Brush inside of cans with oil or butter. Cut waxed paper to line inside of cans (do not bother to put waxed paper on can bottoms). To make handling easier, place cans on cake pan or baking sheet.
• Bake in 350 C (180 C) oven for 60 to 70 minutes for loaf or 40 to 45 minutes for soup cans or until tester inserted in center comes out clean. Cool for 10 minutes in pan, then turn out onto wire rack to cool completely.

Makes 1 loaf (16 to 20 slices) or 6 small round loaves.

Variation

CHOCOLATE BANANA LOAF

• Reduce butter from $^1/_3$ cup (75 mL) to $^1/_4$ cup (50 mL). Melt $^1/_2$ cup (125 mL) chocolate chips and cool. Beat into butter mixture before adding eggs.

POPOVERS

The window of my first gas oven acted as a TV screen for the kids when they were preschoolers. I'd turn the oven light on and they'd watch as batters changed form and color. Young Bob found popovers provided the best show.

◆

1$^1/_2$ cups	all-purpose flour	375 mL
$^1/_2$ tsp	salt	2 mL
3	eggs	3
1$^1/_2$ cups	milk	375 mL

• Butter and lightly flour 12 large muffin cups or six $^1/_2$ cup (125 mL) custard cups. (Place these on a baking sheet to make handling easier.) Set aside.

• In mixer bowl or food processor, combine flour, salt, eggs and milk. Beat or process just until batter is smooth and light, the consistency of whipping cream. Do not overbeat.

• Fill prepared cups no more than $^2/_3$ full.

• Bake in preheated 450 F (230 C) oven for 20 minutes. Reduce heat to 350 F (180 C); bake for 15 minutes longer or until golden brown and sides and tops are firm to the touch. Take one out to test. Sides will collapse if they haven't been baked long enough.

• As soon as popovers are out of oven, with a sharp knife, make a small slit in side of each one to let steam escape. (This will prevent buildup of moisture which might cause them to collapse.)

• Serve immediately.

Makes 12 popovers.

Variations

CHEESY POPOVERS

- Instead of dusting muffin cups with flour, coat them with grated Parmesan cheese. Beat 2 tbsp (25 mL) grated Parmesan cheese into the batter of Popovers before baking.

LEMON OR ORANGE POPOVERS

- Beat 4 tsp (20 mL) granulated sugar and 2 tsp (10 mL) finely grated lemon or orange rind into the batter of Popovers before baking.

HELPFUL HINTS

Quick Breads or Tea Loaves
Mom kept one or two tea breads on hand for unexpected company, her sewing circle, after-school treats and Dad's bedtime snack. Now when I bake quick breads, I usually cut them in two after they've cooled. We eat one half and freeze the other for later use. That way the last half of a loaf doesn't dry out and we don't have a chance to tire of it. It also means that there are always several kinds on hand.

To Develop Flavor in Quick Breads
Quick bread loaves need time for their flavor to develop. You may be disappointed if you sample them when they are fresh out of the oven. Wrap cooled quick breads in waxed paper, foil or plastic wrap. Allow to stand for overnight or 24 hours to help the flavors mingle and mellow.

BARS & SQUARES

◆

At every church tea or pot luck supper I've attended there has always been a plateful of squares. There must be enough recipes for bars and squares to fill a book like this one.

I don't make them regularly except for a few favorites — Brownies and Matrimonial Cake. Mom had a pan of one or the other on hand most of the time for dessert (with a dish of home-canned fruit) or Dad's bedtime snack. In addition, she often made a pan of the fussier, more expensive squares (full of nuts and dried fruit) for bridge club or the choir socials.

Out of the hundreds I've tasted and the few dozen I've baked here is a small collection of recipes for the ones I liked best.

MATRIMONIAL CAKE

Somewhere between the late '40s and the '80s the name of this old-fashioned oatmeal cake changed to Date Squares. Pity! Doesn't Matrimonial Cake sound more exciting?

———————————— ◆ ————————————

Filling:

1 cup	chopped dates ($^1/_2$ lb/250 g)	250 mL
$^3/_4$ cup	boiling water	175 mL
1 tsp	vanilla	5 mL

Cake:

$^1/_2$ cup	butter	125 mL
$^3/_4$ cup	firmly packed brown sugar	175 mL
$1^1/_2$ cups	quick-cooking rolled oats (not instant)	375 mL
1 cup	all-purpose flour	250 mL
1 tsp	cinnamon	5 mL
1 tsp	baking powder	5 mL
$^1/_2$ tsp	baking soda	2 mL
$^1/_2$ tsp	salt	2 mL

• *Filling:* In small saucepan, combine dates and boiling water. Cook, stirring occasionally, for about 8 minutes or until mixture is a smooth paste. Stir in vanilla. Set aside to cool.

• *Cake:* In mixing bowl, cream butter and brown sugar until fluffy.

• In another bowl, combine rolled oats, flour, cinnamon, baking powder, baking soda and salt. Stir into creamed mixture until fine and crumbly.

• Press half of crumbly mixture onto bottom of buttered 8-inch (20 cm) square baking pan. Cover evenly with date filling. Sprinkle remaining crumbly mixture over top. Gently press in place.

• Bake in 350 F (180 C) oven for 30 minutes or until lightly browned. Cool.

• Cut into 2-inch (5 cm) squares to serve.

Makes 16 squares.

BEST QUICK BROWNIES

It's time to share the recipe for the best brownies in the world. These squares are so good, they don't need a frosting. Actually, they disappear so fast I seldom have a chance to make one anyway. The recipe comes from my Mom, who never depended on mixes. She made dozens of quick-to-fix treats from scratch.

◆

¹/₂ cup	butter	125 mL
2	squares unsweetened chocolate	2
1 cup	granulated sugar	250 mL
2	eggs, well beaten	2
1 tsp	vanilla	5 mL
³/₄ cup	all-purpose flour	175 mL
¹/₄ tsp	salt	1 mL
¹/₂ cup	chopped walnuts	125 mL

• Butter and lightly flour 8-inch (20 cm) square baking pan.
• In heavy saucepan, combine butter and chocolate. Melt over low heat, stirring constantly.
• Remove from heat. Stir in sugar, eggs, vanilla, flour and salt until smooth. Fold in nuts.
• Spread batter in prepared pan.
• Bake in 350 F (180 C) oven for 25 to 30 minutes or until firm and brownie begins to pull away from pan. Remove to wire rack to cool.
• Cut into 2-inch (5 cm) squares.

Makes 16 brownies.

CHOCOLATE PECAN BROWNIES

Turn these into decadent little diamonds by icing the panful with Chocolate Butter Cream frosting (see page 262).

—————————— ◆ ——————————

³/₄ cup	all-purpose flour	175 mL
¹/₂ cup	cocoa	125 mL
1 tsp	baking powder	5 mL
³/₄ cup	butter	175 mL
1¹/₄ cups	firmly packed brown sugar	300 mL
3	eggs	3
1 tsp	vanilla	5 mL
1 cup	chopped pecans	250 mL

• In bowl, sift or stir several times with a fork, flour, cocoa and baking powder.
• In another bowl, beat butter until soft. Gradually add sugar; cream until light and fluffy. Beat in eggs, one at a time. Stir in dry ingredients until smooth. Stir in vanilla. Fold in ¹/₂ cup (125 mL) chopped pecans.
• Pour into buttered 9-inch (23 cm) square baking pan. Sprinkle remaining pecans evenly on top.
• Bake in 350 F (180 C) oven for 30 minutes or until tester inserted in center comes out clean. Cool; cut into squares.

Makes 36 squares.

Variations

————————————

CHOCOLATE WALNUT OR ALMOND BROWNIES

• In place of pecans, use 1 cup (250 mL) chopped walnuts or unblanched almonds.

Chocolate Walnut and Raisin Brownies

• In place of pecans, use ¹/₂ cup (125 mL) chopped walnuts and ¹/₂ cup (125 mL) raisins.

Turtle Bars

Deciding what to call these bars was easy because they taste like the chocolates called Turtles.

——————————————— ◆ ———————————————

Base:

1 cup	all-purpose flour	250 mL
¹/₂ cup	whole wheat flour	125 mL
¹/₂ cup	granulated sugar	125 mL
³/₄ cup	butter	175 mL

Topping:

1 cup	firmly packed brown sugar	250 mL
¹/₂ cup	butter	125 mL
1¹/₂ cups	coarsely chopped pecans	375 mL
1 cup	semi-sweet chocolate chips	250 mL

• *Base:* In bowl, combine flours and granulated sugar. With pastry blender or 2 knives, cut in butter until mixture resembles coarse crumbs. Press onto bottom of unbuttered 13 x 9-inch (33 x 23 cm) baking pan.

• Bake in 350 F (180 C) oven for 15 minutes.

• *Topping:* In saucepan, combine brown sugar and butter. Bring to a boil and, stirring constantly, boil for 1 minute. Pour and spread evenly over baked layer. Sprinkle evenly with pecans.

• Return to 350 F (180 C) oven to bake for 15 minutes longer or until nuts begin to look toasted.

• Remove from oven and immediately sprinkle chocolate chips evenly over top. Let stand for about 5 minutes or until chocolate chips are soft. With knife, swirl through melted chocolate chips to haphazardly coat pecans with melted chocolate.

• Cut into bars or squares or break into pieces.

Makes 24 to 36 bars.

STRAWBERRY
CHEESECAKE SQUARES

All the ingredients of cheesecake are in this recipe but in different proportions, making it easy to pick up individual squares.

♦

$^1/_2$ cup	butter	125 mL
$1^1/_4$ cups	granulated sugar	300 mL
3	eggs	3
2 cups	all-purpose flour	500 mL
$^1/_2$ tsp	baking powder	2 mL
$^1/_2$ tsp	nutmeg	2 mL
1	package (250g) cream cheese	1
$^1/_2$ cup	strawberry jam or jelly	125 mL

• In bowl, beat butter until soft. Add 1 cup (250 mL) sugar and cream until light and fluffy. Beat in 2 eggs, one at a time.

• In another bowl, combine flour, baking powder and nutmeg. Stir into creamed mixture until well mixed. Spread evenly in a buttered 9-inch (23 cm) square baking pan.

• In the same bowl, beat together cream cheese, remaining sugar and remaining egg. Spread carefully over batter in pan. With a spoon, drop small dollops of jam (about 12) equal distance apart on the cheese mixture. With a knife or spatula, cut through the jam and cheese to create a swirl pattern.

• Bake in 350 F (180 C) oven for 35 minutes or until tester inserted in center comes out clean. Serve warm or cool. Cut into $1^1/_2$-inch (4 cm) squares.

• To store: Keep in covered container in refrigerator for up to 7 days; in freezer for 4 weeks.

Makes 36 squares.

MACAROON JAM BARS

Any one as fond of macaroons as I am will like these bars.

———————————— ♦ ————————————

Base:

$^{1}/_{2}$ cup	butter	125 mL
$^{1}/_{4}$ cup	granulated sugar	50 mL
1	egg	1
1 cup	all-purpose flour	250 mL
1 tsp	baking powder	5 mL
$^{1}/_{4}$ tsp	salt	1 mL
$^{3}/_{4}$ cup	raspberry, strawberry or apricot jam	175 mL

Topping:

$^{1}/_{2}$ cup	granulated sugar	125 mL
2 tbsp	soft butter	25 mL
1	egg	1
1 tsp	vanilla	5 mL
$1^{1}/_{2}$ cups	desiccated coconut	375 mL

• *Base:* In mixing bowl, cream together butter and sugar until light and fluffy. Beat in egg.
• In another bowl, combine flour, baking powder and salt. Stir into creamed mixture; mix well.
• Pat onto bottom of lightly buttered 8-inch (20 cm) square baking pan. Spread with jam.
• *Topping:* In same bowl, cream together sugar and butter until light and fluffy. Beat in egg and vanilla. Stir in coconut. Spread evenly over jam.
• Bake in 350 F (180 C) oven for 35 to 40 minutes or until top is golden brown.
• Set on wire rack to cool. Cut into 2-inch (5 cm) squares.

Makes 16 squares.

CRISP OATMEAL BUTTERSCOTCH BARS

I think of this crunchy sweet as the grandaddy of the granola bar. It's a winner in school lunches.

♦

$^1/_2$ cup	butter	125 mL
$^3/_4$ cup	packed brown sugar	175 mL
$^1/_4$ cup	corn syrup	50 mL
Pinch	salt	Pinch
1 tsp	vanilla	5 mL
1 tsp	vinegar	5 mL
2$^1/_2$ cups	quick-cooking rolled oats (not instant)	625 mL

• In saucepan, melt butter. Stir in brown sugar, corn syrup and salt. Heat until sugar melts. Stir in vanilla and vinegar. Add rolled oats; stir until well mixed.
• Spread in 15$^1/_2$ x 10$^1/_2$-inch (39 x 26 cm) jelly-roll pan. With moistened fingers, press firmly in place.
• Bake in 350 F (180 C) oven for 15 minutes or until lightly browned. Let cool for 5 minutes.
• Cut lengthwise into 6 strips and crosswise into 8 strips.

Makes 48 bars.

Variations

OATMEAL AND SUNFLOWER BUTTERSCOTCH BARS

• Add $^1/_4$ cup (50 mL) sunflower seeds with the rolled oats.

Banana Pecan Loaf, Chocolate Banana Nut Loaf,
Carrot Nut Bread, Baking Powder Biscuits

◆

Cherry Mallow Squares, Lemon Shortbread Bars, Turtle Bars

Peanut Butter Crisscrosses, Gingerbread Men,
Chocolate Chip Cookies, Sugar Cookies

◆

Maple Chiffon Bundt Cake, Cupcakes with Maple Glaze

CHERRY COCONUT WALNUT SQUARES

In several cookbooks, especially in Mom's older ones, baked combinations such as this one were referred to as Mystery Cake or Dream Cake.

◆

Base:

¹/₂ cup	soft butter	125 mL
¹/₃ cup	firmly packed brown sugar	75 mL
¹/₂ tsp	vanilla	2 mL
1 cup	all-purpose flour	250 mL

Topping:

2	eggs	2
¹/₂ cup	firmly packed brown sugar	125 mL
¹/₂ cup	corn syrup	125 mL
1 tsp	vanilla	5 mL
¹/₄ cup	all-purpose flour	50 mL
¹/₂ tsp	baking powder	2 mL
¹/₄ tsp	salt	1 mL
1 cup	coarsely chopped walnuts	250 mL
¹/₂ cup	desiccated coconut	125 mL
¹/₂ cup	quartered candied cherries	125 mL

- *Base:* In bowl, cream butter and sugar until light and fluffy. Add vanilla. Stir in flour until mixture is crumbly. Pat onto bottom of lightly buttered 8-inch (20 cm) square baking pan.
- Bake in 350 F (180 C) oven for 10 minutes.
- *Topping:* In bowl, beat together eggs, sugar, corn syrup and vanilla.
- In another bowl, combine flour, baking powder and salt. Stir into egg mixture until well mixed. Stir in walnuts, coconut and cherries. Spread over baked base.
- Bake in 350 F (180 C) oven for 35 to 40 minutes longer or until tester inserted in center comes out clean. Set pan on wire rack to cool.

Makes 16 to 20 squares or bars.

CHERRY MALLOW SQUARES

The marshmallow topping of these squares is delightful and contrasts beautifully with their cookie-like base.

◆

Base:

³/₄ cup	butter	175 mL
¹/₃ cup	brown sugar	75 mL
1¹/₂ cups	all-purpose flour	375 mL

Topping:

2	envelopes unflavored gelatin	2
¹/₂ cup	cold water	125 mL
1¹/₂ cups	granulated sugar	375 mL
¹/₃ cup	water	75 mL
1 tsp	vanilla	5 mL
¹/₂ tsp	almond flavoring	2 mL
¹/₂ cup	chopped candied cherries	125 mL
¹/₂ cup	chopped blanched almonds	125 mL
¹/₄ cup	desiccated coconut	50 mL

• *Base:* In mixing bowl, cream butter and sugar until light and fluffy. Stir in flour until mixture resembles fine crumbs. Press into lightly buttered 9-inch (23 cm) square pan. Prick with fork.

• Bake in 325 F (160 C) oven for 30 minutes or until golden. Cool.

• *Topping:* Sprinkle gelatin over cold water; set aside to soften.

• In saucepan, combine sugar and water. Place over high heat; boil for 2 minutes. Stir in gelatin until dissolved.

• Pour into electric mixer bowl. Beat until very stiff. Beat in vanilla and almond flavoring. Fold in cherries and almonds. Spread on cool crust; smooth top and sprinkle evenly with coconut.

• Set aside for 2 hours or until topping is set. Cut into squares.

Makes 16 or 25 squares.

LEMON SHORTBREAD BARS

The lemon custard topping melts into the rich buttery base.

♦

Base:

1 cup	all-purpose flour	250 mL
$^1/_2$ cup	granulated sugar	125 mL
$^1/_2$ cup	butter	125 mL

Topping:

1 cup	granulated sugar	250 mL
2 tbsp	all-purpose flour	25 mL
$^1/_2$ tsp	baking powder	2 mL
$^1/_2$ tsp	baking soda	2 mL
$^1/_4$ tsp	salt	1 mL
	Grated rind of 1 lemon	
	Juice of 1 lemon	
3	eggs	3
	Icing sugar	

• *Base:* In bowl, combine flour and sugar. Cut in butter until mixture resembles fine crumbs. Press evenly over bottom of lightly buttered 8-inch (20 cm) square baking pan.

• Bake in 350 F (180 C) oven for 15 minutes or until edges begin to brown. Remove from oven and cool for about 10 minutes.

• *Topping:* While crust is baking, in bowl, combine sugar, flour, baking powder, baking soda, salt and lemon rind.

• In another bowl, beat together lemon juice and eggs. Stir into sugar mixture until smooth. Pour over warm crust.

• Return to 350 F (180 C) oven for 15 minutes or until topping is set. Dust with icing sugar. Cool in pan.

• Cut into bars or squares.

Makes 16 or 18 bars.

GRANDMA'S PUFFED WHEAT CAKE

Sometimes Mom hid her Puffed Wheat Cake because Sis and I would pig out on it whenever we had a chance. My children did when she introduced it to them but, being a grandmother, she thought that was okay.

◆

8 cups	puffed wheat	2 L
1 cup	firmly packed brown sugar	250 mL
$1/_2$ cup	corn syrup	125 mL
$1/_2$ cup	butter or margarine	125 mL
Pinch	salt	Pinch

• Butter 8-inch (20 cm) square baking pan or dish.
• Place puffed wheat in deep pan or roasting pan. Crisp in 200 F (100 C) oven for 5 to 10 minutes.
• Meanwhile, in saucepan, combine brown sugar, corn syrup, butter and salt. Stir well. Bring to a boil, stirring, over medium heat. Boil rapidly for 1 minute.
• Immediately pour over warm, crisped puffed wheat. Stir quickly until all puffed wheat is covered with brown sugar syrup.
• Spread in prepared pan. With buttered fingers or metal spoon, press in place. Set aside to cool.
• Cut into 2-inch (5 cm) squares.

Makes 16 squares.

Variations

PEANUTTY PUFFED WHEAT CAKE

• In place of 1 cup (250 mL) of the puffed wheat, use 1 cup (250 mL) peanuts.

COOKIES

◆

There's nothing homier than a cookie jar filled to the brim with edible gems waiting for raiders. Hardly anyone, except a skinny dieter I know, can resist freshly-baked, homemade cookies.

My children loved cookies and milk for after school snacks. So much so that I nearly rationed the treats. The thought crossed my mind once when son Bob and two of his pals finished off most of a three quart jug of milk and nearly a whole batch of Chocolate Chip cookies.

Since making cookies takes less time and less skill than baking cakes, they are one of the first things children can bake on their own. They love the results and lap up the compliments.

This collection includes recipes for all the different types of cookies along with a few tips on storing them.

OATMEAL COCONUT CRISPS

When Susan, Patti and Bob were children they called these Our Dad's Cookies because they taste like the commercial ones.

◆

1 cup	butter or margarine	250 mL
1/2 cup	granulated sugar	125 mL
1/2 cup	packed brown sugar	125 mL
1	egg	1
2 cups	quick-cooking rolled oats (not instant)	500 mL
1 cup	all-purpose flour	250 mL
1/2 cup	whole wheat flour	125 mL
2 tsp	baking powder	10 mL
1/2 tsp	salt	2 mL
1 cup	unsweetened desiccated coconut	250 mL

• In mixing bowl, cream butter and sugars until light and fluffy. Beat in egg.
• In another bowl, combine rolled oats, flours, baking powder and salt. Stir into creamed mixture until well mixed. Add coconut; mix until well distributed.
• Drop by heaping teaspoonfuls (5 mL) onto lightly buttered baking sheet. Flatten with fingers.
• Bake in 375 F (190 C) oven for about 15 minutes or until golden brown.

Makes about 6 dozen cookies.

OLD-FASHIONED HERMITS

I have to admit that I was never enthusiastic about Hermits or Rock cookies when I was a kid. Mom said they were good for us, but I thought other foods — stews, meat loaf, macaroni and cheese, bread puddings — were the good-for-you stuff, not cookies. Now, it's clear Mom was right. The nuts, dates and raisins do make these Hermits far more nourishing than Shortbread or Sugar Cookies.

◆

1¹/₂ cups	packed brown sugar	375 mL
³/₄ cup	butter	175 mL
2	eggs	2
1 tsp	vanilla	5 mL
2 cups	all-purpose flour	500 mL
1¹/₂ tsp	cinnamon	7 mL
1 tsp	baking powder	5 mL
¹/₂ tsp	baking soda	2 mL
¹/₂ tsp	nutmeg	2 mL
Pinch	cloves	Pinch
Pinch	salt	Pinch
2 tbsp	water	25 mL
1 cup	raisins	250 mL
1 cup	finely chopped dates	250 mL
1 cup	coarsely chopped walnuts	250 mL

• In mixing bowl, cream together sugar and butter until light and fluffy. Beat in eggs and vanilla.
• In another bowl, combine flour, cinnamon, baking powder, baking soda, nutmeg, cloves and salt. Stir into creamed mixture alternately with water. Stir in raisins, dates and walnuts.
• Drop by heaping teaspoonfuls (5 mL) on buttered baking sheet.
• Bake in 350 F (180 C) oven for 15 to 18 minutes or until lightly browned. Remove to wire racks to cool.

Makes 4 to 5 dozen.

Variations

CHOCOLATE PEANUT HERMITS

• In place of dates and walnuts, use chocolate chips and peanuts.

FRUITCAKE NUGGETS

• In place of dates and walnuts, use 1 cup (250 mL) candied mixed fruit and 1 cup (250 mL) coarsely chopped unblanched almonds.
• Sprinkle raisins, candied fruit and almonds with 2 tbsp (25 mL) brandy or liqueur or orange juice; allow to marinate for about 10 minutes. Once cookie dough is ready, form spoonfuls of dough into balls before placing them on baking sheets. Bake as directed.

♦

HELPFUL HINTS

To Store Cookies
• Store crisp cookies in container with loose-fitting lid.
• To restore crispness (if cookies happen to soften): Place cookies on baking sheet. Heat in 300 F (150 C) oven for 2 to 5 minutes.
• Soft cookies keep best in airtight cookie cans, jars or plastic containers.
• If soft cookies or cookies containing fruit become too dry, add cut apple or orange, or piece of bread to their airtight container to soften them. Change often; it may start to mold.
• To refresh soft cookies, place them in a covered casserole and heat in 300 F (150 C) oven for about 8 minutes.
• The most important tip about storing cookies is to store crisp ones separately from soft ones. Do not mix the two.

Chocolate Pecan Drop Cookies

In these cookies the chocolate is right in the cookie dough, making it a wonderful base for the nuts.

◆

2	squares unsweetened chocolate	2
¹/₂ cup	butter or margarine	125 mL
1 cup	packed brown sugar	250 mL
1	egg	1
2¹/₂ cups	all-purpose flour	625 mL
1 tsp	baking powder	5 mL
¹/₂ tsp	baking soda	2 mL
¹/₄ tsp	salt	1 mL
¹/₂ cup	commercial sour cream	125 mL
1 tsp	vanilla	5 mL
1 cup	chopped pecans	250 mL

• In small pan over boiling water, melt chocolate. (Or melt it in microwave oven following manufacturer's directions.) Cool to room temperature.
• In mixing bowl, cream together butter and sugar until light and fluffy. Blend in melted chocolate. Beat in egg.
• In another bowl, combine flour, baking powder, baking soda and salt.
• Stir into chocolate mixture alternately with sour cream; mix well. Stir in vanilla. Add pecans; mix well.
• Drop by heaping teaspoonfuls (5 mL) about 2 inches (5 cm) apart on buttered baking sheets.
• Bake in 350 F (180 C) oven for 10 to 12 minutes or until centers feel firm to the touch.

Makes 5 to 6 dozen.

Variations

CHOCOLATE RAISIN DROP COOKIES

• In place of 1 cup (250 mL) chopped pecans, use 1 cup (250 mL) raisins.

CHOCOLATE RAISIN NUT DROP COOKIES

• In place of 1 cup (250 mL) chopped pecans, use $^1/_2$ cup (125 mL) raisins and $^1/_2$ cup (125 mL) chopped nuts (walnuts, hazelnuts, almonds, peanuts).

♦

HELPFUL HINTS

Cookie Tips
• Baking sheets are best buttered with unsalted butter or shortening.
• Oven rack should be in the center of the oven for baking cookies. If two racks are used, arrange racks to divide oven into three. At least 2 inches (5 cm) of oven rack should show all around baking sheet for most even circulation of heat. Try not to set one sheet directly under the other.
• Cookies are best cooled on a wire rack with air circulating around them.

CHOCOLATE CHIP COOKIES

The home economist who made the first chocolate chip cookies, the Toll House Cookies, stirred bits of chocolate into a cookie batter when she discovered she was out of raisins. They were such a hit that by the early '40s some food manufacturers developed chocolate chips for home baking.

◆

1 cup	butter or shortening	250 mL
1/2 cup	granulated sugar	125 mL
1/2 cup	firmly packed brown sugar	125 mL
2	eggs	2
1 tsp	vanilla	5 mL
2 cups	all-purpose flour	500 mL
1 tsp	baking soda	5 mL
1/2 tsp	salt	2 mL
1 cup	semi-sweet chocolate chips	250 mL
3/4 cup	chopped walnuts or pecans	175 mL

• In mixing bowl, cream together butter and sugars until light and fluffy. Beat in eggs and vanilla.
• In another bowl, combine flour, soda and salt. Add to creamed mixture; mix well. Stir in chocolate chips and walnuts until well mixed.
• Drop by teaspoonfuls (5 mL) onto buttered baking sheets.
• Bake in 375 F (190 C) oven for 10 to 12 minutes or until lightly browned. Remove to wire racks to cool.

Makes 6 dozen, or 3 dozen big ones.

SHORTBREAD

Sometimes Mom turned these into what she called Melting Moments. As a child that name made this common Christmas cookie far more exciting and romantic. Now, just like Mom, I make them for bridal and spring and summer tea parties.

◆

1 cup	butter	250 mL
³/₄ cup	icing sugar or fruit powdered berry sugar	175 mL
2 cups	all-purpose flour	500 mL
1 tbsp	cornstarch	15 mL
Pinch	each of baking powder and salt	Pinch
	Small pieces candied cherry (optional)	

• In mixing bowl, cream butter and icing sugar until light and fluffy. Stir in flour, cornstarch, baking powder and salt until very smooth.
• Form into a firm ball. Place on lightly floured surface. Lightly knead 5 to 6 times.
• Form level teaspoonfuls (5 mL) into small balls. Place 2 inches (5 cm) apart on unbuttered baking sheet. With fingertips or fork, gently press each ball to slightly flatten it. If desired, place a cherry piece in center of each.
• Bake in 325 F (170 C) oven for about 15 minutes or until edges are slightly golden and firm to the touch. Cool.

Makes 5 to 6 dozen.

Variation

MELTING MOMENTS

• Lightly flatten the little balls of dough on the baking sheet and forget the tidbit in the center. Sandwich baked and cooled cookies together with tinted (if desired) Fluffy or Chocolate Butter Cream Frosting (see page 262).

CRINKLY
GINGERSNAPS

These look like Dad and my husband, Jim's, favorite old-fashioned store-bought cookie. Jim tells me he prefers mine, a sure way to encourage me to make them often.

♦

¹/₃ cup	butter	75 mL
1 cup	firmly packed brown sugar	250 mL
1	egg	1
¹/₄ cup	molasses	50 mL
1 tsp	white vinegar	5 mL
1³/₄ cups	all-purpose flour	425 mL
2 tsp	ground ginger	10 mL
1 tsp	baking soda	5 mL
¹/₂ tsp	cinnamon	2 mL
¹/₄ tsp	salt	1 mL
Pinch	cloves	Pinch
¹/₄ cup	granulated sugar	50 mL

• In electric mixer bowl, cream butter and brown sugar. Add egg, molasses and vinegar; beat until light and fluffy.
• In separate bowl, combine flour, ginger, baking soda, cinnamon, salt and cloves; mix well. Gradually beat into butter mixture until well blended. Gather and press dough into big ball.
• Pinch off enough at a time to roll by hand into small balls, 1 inch (2.5 cm) in diameter. Dip each ball into granulated sugar. Place sugar side up and 2 inches (5 cm) apart on lightly buttered baking sheet.
• Bake in 350 F (180 C) oven for about 12 minutes or until edges are lightly browned and tops have many cracks in them.
• Remove to wire racks to cool.

Makes 5 to 6 dozen.

Peanut Butter Crisscrosses

No cookie recipe collection would be complete if these weren't included. Everyone seems to like them. I've even been known to ration them just to make sure a batch would last more than 2 days.

◆

¹/₂ cup	butter or shortening	125 mL
¹/₂ cup	peanut butter	125 mL
¹/₂ cup	firmly packed brown sugar	125 mL
¹/₂ cup	granulated sugar	125 mL
1	egg	1
2 tbsp	orange juice	25 mL
1¹/₂ cups	all-purpose flour	375 mL
1 tsp	baking soda	5 mL
¹/₂ tsp	baking powder	2 mL
¹/₄ tsp	salt	1 mL

• In electric mixer bowl, cream butter. Beat in peanut butter and sugars until light and fluffy. Beat in egg and orange juice.
• In another bowl, combine flour, baking soda, baking powder and salt. Stir into peanut butter mixture, mixing well to form a stiff dough.
• Wrap dough in waxed paper and chill for 30 to 40 minutes until firm enough to handle. Take 1 heaping tablespoonful (15 mL) of dough at a time and roll into a ball.
• Place balls 3 inches (8 cm) apart on unbuttered baking sheets. With floured fork, flatten crisscross fashion.
• Bake in 375 F (190 C) oven for 12 minutes or until golden brown. Remove to wire racks to cool.

Makes 5 dozen.

PECAN CRESCENTS

I associate these buttery-nut cookies with the festive Christmas season because Mom never made them at any other time of the year.

———————————— ♦ ————————————

¹/₂ cup	butter	125 mL
¹/₃ cup	firmly packed brown sugar	75 mL
1 tsp	vanilla	5 mL
1 cup	cake and pastry flour	250 mL
¹/₄ tsp	baking powder	1 mL
Pinch	salt	Pinch
1 cup	ground pecans	250 mL
	Icing sugar	

• In bowl, cream together butter and sugar until light and fluffy. Blend in vanilla.
• In another bowl, combine flour, baking powder and salt. Blend into creamed mixture until smooth. Add pecans; mix well.
• Form dough, about a tablespoonful (15 mL) at a time, into small crescents. Place on unbuttered baking sheet.
• Bake in 350 F (180 C) oven for about 15 minutes or until lightly browned. Dust with icing sugar while warm.
• Store in covered container between sheets of waxed paper.

Makes about 48.

Variations

ALMOND CRESCENTS

• In place of brown sugar and ground pecans, use granulated sugar and ground almonds; add ¹/₂ tsp (2 mL) almond flavoring.

WALNUT-HAZELNUT LOGS

• In place of pecans, use finely chopped walnuts and hazelnuts. Roll into small log shapes.

GINGERBREAD MEN

My Christmas baking always includes Gingerbread Men or Ladies, Dolls, Teddy Bears, Santas, Christmas Trees or Wreaths. They are delightful little gifts for friends and family, youngsters and adults alike. Because the dough doesn't spread as it bakes, the shapes are firm and crisp with sharp edges. That quality also makes this an excellent dough for making gingerbread houses.

$\blacklozenge$

$^1/_2$ cup	butter	125 mL
$^1/_2$ cup	granulated sugar	125 mL
1	egg	1
$^1/_2$ cup	fancy molasses	125 mL
1 tbsp	vinegar	15 mL
2 cups	all-purpose flour	500 mL
1 tsp	baking soda	5 mL
1 tsp	ground ginger	5 mL
1 tsp	cinnamon	5 mL
$^1/_2$ tsp	cloves	2 mL
$^1/_2$ tsp	salt	2 mL

• Lightly butter and flour baking sheets.
• In mixing bowl, cream butter and sugar until light and fluffy. Beat in egg, molasses and vinegar.
• In another bowl, combine flour, baking soda, ginger, cinnamon, cloves and salt. Stir into molasses mixture until well mixed.
• Transfer to lightly floured surface. Form into a ball and knead 6 to 8 times. Chill in refrigerator for about 20 minutes.
• Divide dough into 2 or 3 pieces. On lightly floured surface, roll each piece to about $^1/_8$ inch (3 mm) thickness. With floured cookie cutters, cut into assorted shapes. Lift onto prepared baking sheets.
• Bake in 350 F (180 C) oven for 10 minutes or until beginning to brown around edges. Cool for 2 to 3 minutes. Remove to wire rack to cool.
• Decorate, as desired, with Royal Frosting (see page 261).

Makes 3 to 4 dozen, depending on size of cookie cutter.

CRISP OATMEAL COOKIES

The scribbled recipe in Mom's collection says, as so many do, "add enough flour to make a stiff dough." Once I made them far too stiff and the cookies became hard rather than crunchy. What I suggest here is just about right.

◆

1 cup	butter or margarine	250 mL
$^1/_2$ cup	packed brown sugar	125 mL
$^1/_2$ cup	granulated sugar	125 mL
1	egg	1
1 tsp	vanilla	5 mL
$1^1/_2$ cups	all-purpose flour	375 mL
2 tsp	baking powder	10 mL
1 tsp	cinnamon	5 mL
$^1/_2$ tsp	salt	2 mL
$2^1/_2$ cups	quick-cooking rolled oats (not instant)	625 mL

• In mixing bowl, cream butter and sugars until light and fluffy. Beat in egg and vanilla.
• In another bowl, combine flour, baking powder, cinnamon and salt. Stir into creamed mixture. Mix in rolled oats to form a soft but not sticky dough. Chill for about 20 minutes to firm dough.
• On floured surface, roll out dough to $^1/_8$ inch (3 mm) thickness. With $2^1/_2$-inch (6 cm) round cookie cutter, cut out cookies. Place about 2 inches (5 cm) apart on lightly buttered or nonstick baking sheet.
• Bake in 350 F (180 C) oven for 10 to 12 minutes or until golden brown. Remove to wire racks to cool.

Makes 7 dozen.

OATMEAL DATE COOKIES

The texture of these cookies changes depending on how long they've been filled. At first they are crunchy with fruity paste oozing from the center, then they become more chewy as the moistness of the filling softens the cookies. Either way, they rate in the top ten of our best cookie list.

◆

1	batch Crisp Oatmeal Cookies (see page 235)	1

Filling:

1 cup	chopped dates	250 mL
1 tsp	grated orange rind	5 mL
1/2 cup	orange juice	125 mL

- Make Crisp Oatmeal Cookies.
- *Filling:* In saucepan, combine dates, orange rind and juice. Bring to a boil, reduce heat and cook for about 3 minutes, stirring occasionally until smooth. Remove from heat; set aside to cool.
- Sandwich cookies together with cooled date filling.

Makes 3 1/2 dozen.

Variations

OATMEAL TEA COOKIES

- Form Crisp Oatmeal Cookie dough into small balls the circumference of a dime. Place on buttered baking sheet. With floured fork, flatten each one. Bake as directed. *Makes about 10 dozen.*

OATMEAL DATE TEA COOKIES

- Sandwich Oatmeal Tea Cookies together with Date Filling (see above). *Makes 5 dozen.*

SUGAR COOKIES

For decorating the Christmas tree, I sometimes make sugar cookie angels and birds. They look delightful dancing among the boughs with gingerbread men. Both are smart presents for little people.

◆

1 cup	butter or shortening	250 mL
1¼ cups	granulated sugar	300 mL
1	egg	2
2 tsp	vanilla	10 mL
3 cups	all-purpose flour	750 mL
1 tsp	salt	5 mL
1 tsp	baking powder	5 mL

- In mixing bowl, cream together butter and sugar until light and fluffy. Beat in eggs and vanilla.
- In another bowl, combine flour, salt and baking powder. Stir into creamed mixture until well blended.
- Press into a ball. Chill for about 20 minutes until firmer.
- On lightly floured surface, roll out dough to ⅛ inch (3 mm) thickness. With floured cookie cutters, cut into assorted shapes. Lift onto lightly buttered baking sheets.
- Bake in 350 F (180 C) oven for 8 to 10 minutes or until lightly browned. Remove to wire racks to cool.

Makes 6 to 7 dozen, depending on size of cookie cutter.

BUTTERSCOTCH NUT SLICE

Icebox cookies like these are crunchy. You'll find thin ones the crispest.

◆

¹/₂ cup	butter or shortening	125 mL
³/₄ cup	packed brown sugar	175 mL
1	egg	1
1 tsp	vanilla	5 mL
1¹/₂ cups	all-purpose flour	375 mL
¹/₂ cup	finely chopped pecans	125 mL
1 tsp	baking powder	5 mL
¹/₂ tsp	baking soda	2 mL
¹/₂ tsp	salt	2 mL

• In mixing bowl, cream together butter and sugar until light and fluffy. Beat in egg and vanilla.
• In another bowl, combine flour, pecans, baking powder, baking soda and salt. Stir into creamed mixture to make a soft dough.
• Shape into 2 long rolls, 2 inches (5 cm) in diameter; wrap in waxed paper. Chill overnight or for 8 hours.
• When ready to bake, cut dough into slices ¹/₄ inch (5 mm) thick. Place on buttered baking sheets.
• Bake in 375 F (190 C) oven for 8 minutes or until golden around the edges. Remove to wire racks to cool.

Makes 4 dozen.

Variation

FRUIT AND NUT SLICE
• Add ¹/₂ cup (125 mL) raisins or candied mixed fruit.

PINWHEELS

These crisp chocolate and cream pinwheels look smashing on their own or in an assortment of cookies.

— ♦ —

1	batch Butterscotch Nut Slice dough (see page 238)	1
1	square unsweetened chocolate, melted	1

• Prepare Butterscotch Nut Slice dough, omitting nuts, if you wish. Divide the dough into 2 equal portions.
• Stir melted chocolate into half of the dough until thoroughly blended. (Leave other half plain.)
• Chill both halves for about 30 minutes or until firm enough to roll.
• Roll out plain dough on floured plastic wrap to form 16 x 6-inch (40.5 x 15 cm) rectangle. Roll chocolate dough to same size on another piece of plastic wrap. Place chocolate dough on top of plain dough, pressing gently to hold doughs together.
• Starting from one wide end, roll up like a jelly roll, making sure center is tight. Wrap in plastic wrap; chill overnight.
• Cut into $\frac{1}{8}$ inch (3 mm) thick slices. Place $1\frac{1}{2}$ inches (4 cm) apart on buttered baking sheets.
• Bake in 375 F (190 C) oven for 8 to 10 minutes or until firm.

Makes 4 dozen.

— ♦ —

HELPFUL HINT

Juice Can Molds
Small juice cans make handy molds for refrigerator cookies. Pack dough into can and chill. At baking time, remove bottom of can with can opener, then press against it to push out dough — just enough for one cookie at a time. Cut against the can to help cookies keep their round shape.

COCONUT
MACAROONS

These macaroons have a curious crunchy, melt-in-your-mouth texture. When the atmosphere is humid, they soften a bit and I recrisp them by popping them into a warm oven for a few minutes.

◆

2	egg whites	2
Pinch	salt	Pinch
$^3/_4$ cup	granulated sugar	175 mL
$^1/_2$ tsp	cornstarch	2 mL
1 tsp	vanilla	5 mL
$^1/_2$ tsp	vinegar	2 mL
$1^1/_2$ cups	unsweetened desiccated coconut	375 mL

• Line baking sheets with brown paper (from paper bag) or baking paper.
• In electric mixer bowl, beat egg whites and salt until soft peaks form. Gradually beat in sugar and continue beating until stiff and sugar has dissolved. (A bit of mixture rubbed between finger and thumb feels smooth when sugar is completely dissolved.) Beat in cornstarch. Stir in vanilla and vinegar. Fold in coconut.
• Drop by teaspoonful (5 mL) on prepared baking sheets.
• Bake in preheated 350 F (180 C) oven for 3 minutes. Without opening door, turn off heat and leave in oven overnight or at least 8 hours until dry. With thin metal spatula carefully lift from paper.
• To store: Keep in a loosely covered container for up to 4 weeks.

Makes about 4 dozen.

BRANDY BALLS

A dozen or two of these sitting in tiny paper cups make a grand "something from my kitchen" gift. For Christmas I put together a batch or two just for that purpose.

◆

1 cup	semi-sweet chocolate chips	250 mL
1/2 cup	granulated sugar	125 mL
1/3 cup	brandy or rum	75 mL
1/4 cup	corn syrup	50 mL
2 tbsp	seedless jam or jelly	25 mL
1	package (8 oz/250 g) vanilla wafers, finely crushed (2 1/2 cups/625 mL)	1
1 cup	finely chopped walnuts	250 mL
	Granulated sugar	

• In top of double boiler, melt chocolate chips over hot (not boiling) water, or in microwave oven following manufacturer's directions.
• Stir in sugar, brandy, corn syrup and jam. Blend in wafer crumbs and nuts; mix thoroughly. (Or the melted chocolate and remaining ingredients can be combined in food processor, scraping down container once or twice, for 1 to 2 minutes. This will make a finer mixture.) Chill for about 20 minutes or until firm.
• Shape 1 heaping teaspoonful (5 mL) at a time into small balls. Roll in granulated sugar.
• Set aside in cool place (not refrigerator) to ripen for 2 days.
• Store in covered container in cool place for up to 6 weeks.

Makes about 5 dozen.

Variation

ANISETTE BALLS

• In place of brandy, use anisette.

PEANUT BUTTER WINKS

My son Bob called these "balls of fudge" and always asked for "s'more please."

◆

2 cups	icing sugar	500 mL
1 cup	crunchy peanut butter	250 mL
¼ cup	soft butter	50 mL
3	squares semi-sweet chocolate	3
1 cup	chopped peanuts or desiccated coconut	250 mL

• In mixing bowl, cream together icing sugar, peanut butter and butter until light and fluffy. Cover and refrigerate overnight to chill well.

• Shape 1 heaping teaspoonful (5 mL) at a time into small balls; set on waxed paper-lined tray.

• In small saucepan, melt chocolate over low heat, or in microwave oven following manufacturer's directions. Cool until chocolate thickly coats metal spoon and barely drips. Dip half of each ball in chocolate and then into chopped nuts.

• Place, nutty end down, on waxed paper. Allow to set at room temperature for 2 hours or until firm.

• To store: Place in covered container with waxed paper between layers. Keep container in cool, dry place.

Makes about 3 dozen.

Variation

PEANUT BUTTER FUDGE

• Spread peanut butter mixture in waxed paper-lined 8-inch (20 cm) square cake pan.

CAKES

♦

When I was young, prairie kitchens bubbled over with the scent of cakes, cookies and squares baking, just as, I'm sure, maritime kitchens did. It's in that era that most of my recipes have their roots.

Traditionally, Mom always had a prettily decorated, light, moist cake for every special family event — birthday, christening, anniversary, graduation — and so have I.

Mom turned out so many different ones, it's hard for me to remember all the varieties. But, I can hear her say, "Use fresh eggs, take care measuring, beat in a little extra air and bake your cake in a reliable oven."

All cakes fit one of these classifications: Angel cakes (use only egg whites); sponge cakes (use whole eggs, separated); butter cakes (use butter and whole eggs); genoise or chiffon (use liquid fats and whole eggs, separated). You'll find several examples of each in my recipes. And, while you're baking think about what Dad used to say to me. "There's always praise for the cook who bakes a good cake."

HELPFUL HINT

To Mix Cake Batters

The mixing method used in the Basic Plain Cake and its variations is the conventional one. I would stick with it if the mixing equipment you have is no stronger than a hand mixer. However, if you have an electric mixer on a stand and with its own bowl, the one-bowl method is easier and speedier.

• First, place all of the ingredients in the mixer bowl, making sure the butter is soft and at room temperature. Then, beat them together at medium-low for about 30 seconds to incorporate the dry and wet ingredients.

• Beat at medium for 3 minutes, scraping down the bowl once or twice, or until mixture is light and fluffy.

• Spread evenly in prepared pans or paper-lined muffin cups.

• Bake as directed.

HELPFUL HINT

How To Fill and Frost Layer Cakes

To make and decorate a layer cake, place one cake layer on cake plate. Spread its top evenly with frosting. Arrange second layer on frosted layer pressing gently to hold it in place. Spread frosting evenly around side of stacked layers, then spread top with frosting. Finish with spoon swirls or zigzag knife design or decorate as desired.

BASIC PLAIN CAKE

Cake batters like this one were always beaten by hand with a spoon or an egg beater until the late '40s when Mom acquired an electric hand mixer. I still keep an egg beater in the drawer, for nostalgia's sake I guess. I never use it.

◆

²/₃ cup	butter or margarine	150 mL
1 cup	granulated sugar	250 mL
2	eggs	2
2 cups	sifted cake and pastry flour	500 mL
2¹/₂ tsp	baking powder	12 mL
¹/₂ tsp	salt	2 mL
1 cup	milk	250 mL
1 tsp	vanilla	5 mL
	Fluffy Butter Cream Frosting (see page 262)	

• Lightly butter 8 or 9-inch (20 or 23 cm) square or two 8-inch (20 cm) round layer cake pans. Dust lightly with flour or line bottoms with waxed paper cut to fit.
• In electric mixer bowl, cream butter. Add sugar and cream together until light and fluffy. Beat in eggs, one at a time.
• Sift, or with fork lightly stir together, flour, baking powder and salt. Beat flour mixture alternately with milk into creamed mixture, starting and ending with flour. Add vanilla. Beat for 1 minute longer.
• Spread batter in prepared cake pan or pans.
• Bake in 350 F (180 C) oven for 45 to 50 minutes for square cake, 30 to 35 minutes for layer cakes, or until tester inserted in center comes out clean. Cool for 5 minutes in pan.
• Turn out onto cake rack to cool completely.
• Spread cake (and fill between layers) with frosting.

Makes 1 square cake or 1 layer cake, 12 to 16 pieces.

Variations

EASY BANANA CAKE

• Beat 1 cup (250 mL) mashed ripe bananas (about 3) into creamed mixture; use only $^1/_2$ cup (125 mL) milk and fold $^1/_2$ cup (125 mL) finely chopped (not ground) pecans or walnuts into batter, if desired. Frost with Fluffy Butter Cream Frosting (see page 262) or 7-Minute Fluffy Frosting (see page 266).

EASY POPPY SEED CAKE

• Soak $^1/_2$ cup (125 mL) poppy seeds in 1 cup (250 mL) boiling water while preparing cake. Drain very well then fold poppy seeds into batter before spreading it in pans. Frost with Orange Butter Cream Frosting (see page 263).

EASY SPICE CAKE

• In place of granulated sugar, use firmly packed brown sugar; add 1 tsp (5 mL) cinnamon, $^1/_2$ tsp (2 mL) ground ginger, $^1/_2$ tsp (5 mL) nutmeg and $^1/_4$ tsp (1 mL) ground nutmeg or allspice to dry ingredients. Top with Lazy Day Broiled Frosting (see page 264).

EASY WHITE CAKE

• In place of 1 egg, use 2 egg whites. Frost with tinted 7-Minute Fluffy Frosting (see page 266).

CUPCAKES

• Line 18 medium muffin cups with a double layer of paper baking cups. (For some reason when two are used for each cupcake, the baked cupcake is easier to remove from the one baking cup it bakes in.)
• Spoon any of the cake batters into the paper-lined muffin cups.
• Bake in 375 F (190 C) oven for 20 to 30 minutes or until tops spring back when lightly touched.

ELVIS PRESLEY CAKE

Almost every time I visited Mom in the '50s, she had just baked or was going to bake this cake. Perhaps she was inspired by the star's popularity on the "Ed Sullivan Show" or maybe she thought we'd think she was really "with it."

◆

1¹/₂ cups	packed brown sugar	375 mL
1 cup	quick-cooking rolled oats (not instant)	250 mL
³/₄ cup	butter	175 mL
¹/₂ cup	finely chopped dates	125 mL
1 cup	boiling water	250 mL
1 cup	all-purpose flour	250 mL
1 tsp	baking soda	5 mL
1 tsp	cinnamon	5 mL
1 tsp	ground allspice	5 mL
2	eggs, well beaten	2
¹/₂ cup	finely chopped walnuts	125 mL
	Brown Sugar Fudge Frosting (see page 265)	

• In small bowl, combine brown sugar, rolled oats, butter, dates and water.
• In mixing bowl, combine flour, soda, cinnamon and allspice. Stir in date mixture and beaten eggs, mix well. Fold in walnuts.
• Pour into lightly buttered and floured 8- or 9-inch (20 or 23 cm) square cake pan.
• Bake in 350 F (180 C) oven for about 55 minutes or until lightly browned and tester inserted in center comes out clean.
• Cool in the pan before frosting. Cover top with Brown Sugar Fudge Frosting. Cut into squares to serve.

Makes 1 square cake, 12 to 16 pieces.

RAISIN CRUMB CAKE

Raisin Crumb Cake appeared regularly for Dad's bedtime snack, which was as much of a ritual at our house as breakfast, dinner and supper. Sometimes Mom made it in minutes while my sister and I did the dishes. The crumbly topping replaces frosting.

♦

$^{3}/_{4}$ cup	butter	175 mL
$1^{1}/_{2}$ cups	firmly packed brown sugar	375 mL
2 cups	all-purpose flour	500 mL
1 tsp	cinnamon	5 mL
$^{1}/_{2}$ tsp	salt	2 mL
$^{1}/_{2}$ tsp	ground cardamom or nutmeg	2 mL
$^{1}/_{4}$ tsp	mace	1 mL
1 tsp	baking soda	5 mL
$^{1}/_{2}$ tsp	baking powder	2 mL
2	eggs	2
$^{3}/_{4}$ cup	sour milk or buttermilk	175 mL
1 tsp	vanilla	5 mL
$^{1}/_{2}$ cup	raisins	125 mL

- Lightly butter and flour 9-inch (23 cm) square cake pan.
- In mixing bowl, cream butter and sugar until light and fluffy.
- Add flour, cinnamon, salt, cardamom and mace. Mix and blend until mixture resembles fine crumbs. Remove $^{3}/_{4}$ cup (175 mL) for crumb topping.
- Blend baking soda and baking powder into remaining crumbly mixture. Add eggs and sour milk. Beat for about 2 minutes or until smooth and creamy. Stir in vanilla and raisins.
- Spread batter in prepared cake pan. Sprinkle reserved crumb mixture over top; lightly press in place.
- Bake in 350 F (180 C) oven for 40 to 45 minutes or until tester inserted in center comes out clean.

Makes 1 square cake, 12 to 16 pieces.

Devil's Food Cake

For dedicated chocoholics you can double the dose of chocolate by frosting this rich concoction with more chocolate.

◆

3	squares semi-sweet chocolate	3
1¼ cup	milk	300 mL
¾ cup	packed brown sugar	175 mL
2	eggs, separated	2
2 cups	sifted cake and pastry flour	500 mL
2 tsp	baking powder	10 mL
½ tsp	baking soda	2 mL
½ tsp	salt	2 mL
½ cup	butter	125 mL
¾ cup	granulated sugar, divided	175 mL
	7-Minute Fluffy Frosting (see page 266)	

- Butter and lightly flour one 8 or 9-inch (20 to 23 cm) square pan or two 8 or 9-inch (20 to 23 cm) round layer cake pans.
- In top of double boiler, over (not in) hot water, heat chocolate, milk and brown sugar, stirring until chocolate melts. In small bowl, beat egg yolks. Beat in small amount of hot mixture then beat this yolk mixture back into chocolate mixture. Continue to cook, stirring, for 1½ minutes or until mixture thickens. Set aside to cool.
- In bowl, combine flour, baking powder, baking soda and salt.
- In electric mixer bowl, cream butter with ½ cup (125 mL) granulated sugar until light and fluffy. Beat in dry ingredients alternately with chocolate mixture, beginning and ending with flour mixture.
- In clean mixer bowl and with clean beaters, beat 2 egg whites until frothy. Gradually add remaining sugar; beat until stiff satiny peaks form. Fold in chocolate batter. Pour into prepared cake pan or pans.
- Bake in 350 F (180 C) oven for about 30 to 35 minutes or until tester inserted in center comes out clean. Cool in pans.
- Frost or fill and frost with 7-Minute Fluffy Frosting.

Makes 1 square cake or 1 layer cake, 12 to 16 pieces.

CARROT CAKE

During the health food craze of the late '70s there were many variations of this cake. True, the carrots are nutritious but don't be fooled. This is a rich, moist cake that becomes loaded with calories when it's frosted with cream cheese or butter cream frosting.

♦

1 cup	granulated sugar	250 mL
1/2 cup	firmly packed brown sugar	125 mL
1 cup	vegetable oil	250 mL
4	eggs	4
1 tbsp	frozen orange juice concentrate	15 mL
2 cups	all-purpose flour	500 mL
2 tsp	cinnamon	10 mL
1 1/2 tsp	baking soda	7 mL
1 tsp	baking powder	5 mL
1/2 tsp	salt	2 mL
1/2 tsp	ground cloves	2 mL
2 tsp	vanilla	10 mL
2 1/2 cups	finely shredded carrots	625 mL
1/2 cup	finely chopped nuts	125 mL
	Cream Cheese Frosting (see page 263) or Orange Butter Cream Frosting (see page 263)	

• Butter and lightly flour one 13 x 9-inch (33 x 23 cm) baking pan, two 8 or 9-inch (20 or 23 cm) round layer cake pans or one 10-inch (25 cm) tube pan.
• In mixing bowl, beat together sugars and oil. Beat in eggs, one at a time, and orange juice concentrate.

- In another bowl, combine flour, cinnamon, baking soda, baking powder, salt and cloves. Gradually stir into creamed mixture. Blend in vanilla. Fold in carrots and nuts. Spoon into prepared cake pan or pans.
- Bake in 325 F (160 C) oven for about 50 minutes for baking pan and tube pan; for about 35 minutes for layer cakes; or until tester inserted in center comes out clean. Remove to wire racks to cool for 5 minutes.
- Leave cake in baking pan, cool and frost. Remove layers or tube cake from pans, cool on wire racks then fill or frost as required.

Makes 1 sheet cake or tube cake or 2 layer cakes, 12 to 16 pieces.

Variations

DELUXE CARROT CAKE

- Fold $^3/_4$ cup (175 mL) chopped raisins into batter with carrots; mix well.

CHOCOLATE CARROT CAKE

- Fold $^1/_2$ cup (125 mL) chocolate chips into batter with the carrots in the Carrot Cake or with carrots and raisins in Deluxe Carrot Cake.

ZUCCHINI CAKE

- In place of shredded carrot, use shredded zucchini.

DELUXE ZUCCHINI CAKE

- In place of shredded carrot, use finely shredded zucchini in Deluxe Carrot Cake recipe.

CHOCOLATE ZUCCHINI CAKE

- Fold $^1/_2$ cup (125 mL) chocolate chips into batter with zucchini in Zucchini Cake or with zucchini and raisins in Deluxe Zucchini Cake.

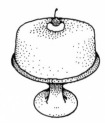

LIGHT CHIFFON CAKE

Ever since developing this lighter version of chiffon cake for my cookbook *Light & Easy Choice Desserts* (Grosvenor House Press, 1986), it's become my comfort cake. I make it more often than any other cake because it's both light in texture and taste and has fewer calories per slice than most other cakes.

———————————— ♦ ————————————

²/₃ cup	granulated sugar, divided	175 mL
2 tsp	baking powder	10 mL
¹/₂ cup	water	125 mL
¹/₄ cup	canola or safflower oil	50 mL
2	egg yolks	2
¹/₂ tsp	vanilla or almond flavoring	2 mL
4	egg whites	4
¹/₂ tsp	salt	2 mL
¹/₄ tsp	cream of tartar	1 mL

- In bowl, combine flour, ¹/₃ cup (75 mL) sugar and baking powder. Stir to combine.
- Make a well in dry ingredients; pour in water, oil, egg yolks and vanilla. Beat for 1 minute or until very smooth.
- In large mixing bowl, with clean beaters, beat egg whites, salt and cream of tartar until soft peaks form. Gradually add remaining sugar and beat for 1 or 2 minutes longer or until very stiff and shiny.
- With wire whisk, gently fold egg yolk mixture into stiffly beaten egg whites until blended and mixture is even-colored.

- Pour into unbuttered 10-inch (23 cm) tube pan. With knife, cut through batter to remove air bubbles. Smooth top.
- Bake in 325 F (160 C) oven for 50 minutes or until golden and top springs back when lightly touched in the center.
- Invert pan allowing cake to hang upside down on its own stand or a funnel to cool for at least 1 hour. With sharp knife loosen edge. Remove to cake plate.

Makes one 10-inch (25 cm) tube cake, 12 to 16 servings.

Variations

LIGHT CHOCOLATE CHIFFON CAKE

- In place of $^{1}/_{4}$ cup (50 mL) cake and pastry flour, use $^{1}/_{4}$ cup (50 mL) cocoa. Sift with flour mixture.

LIGHT ORANGE CHIFFON CAKE

- In place of water, use $^{1}/_{2}$ cup (125 mL) orange juice; fold 2 tsp (10 mL) grated orange rind into batter just before it is poured into tube pan. Drizzle Orange Glaze (recipe follows) over top of cooled inverted cake.

ORANGE GLAZE

- In bowl, combine $^{1}/_{4}$ cup (50 mL) orange juice, 2 tsp (10 mL) lemon juice and 1 cup (250 mL) icing sugar; stir until well blended. Add about 1 tsp (5 mL) grated orange rind, if desired. Drizzle over inverted cake.

MAPLE CHIFFON BUNDT CAKE

At least once a year, when new maple syrup is available, this is my choice for a stunning, sophisticated dessert.

———————————————— ◆ ————————————————

2 cups	sifted cake and pastry flour	500 mL
1 cup	firmly packed brown sugar	250 mL
1 tsp	baking soda	5 mL
1 tsp	salt	5 mL
³/₄ cup	maple syrup	175 mL
¹/₂ cup	vegetable oil	125 mL
¹/₄ cup	water	50 mL
5	eggs	5
1 tsp	vanilla	5 mL
¹/₂ tsp	maple flavouring	2 mL
¹/₂ tsp	cream of tartar	2 mL
	Maple Glaze (recipe page 256)	
¹/₂ cup	coarsely chopped walnuts (optional)	125 mL

• In electric mixer bowl, combine flour, ¹/₂ cup (125 mL) brown sugar, baking powder and salt. Add syrup, oil, water, egg yolks, vanilla and maple flavouring. Beat, scraping down the sides of the bowl occasionally, for about 1 minute until smooth.

• In clean bowl, with clean beaters, beat egg whites and cream of tartar until soft peaks form. Gradually beat in remaining brown sugar, until stiff, shiny peaks form and sugar is dissolved. With wire whisk, fold in flour mixture until evenly blended.

• Pour into lightly buttered 10-inch (25 cm) Bundt or tube pan.

• Bake in 350 F (180 C) oven for 50 to 55 minutes or until top springs back when lightly touched in center.

• Invert pan, allowing cake to hang upside down on its own stand or a funnel to cool. With knife loosen edges. Place on cake plate, top side down.

• Glaze with Maple Glaze and sprinkle with nuts, if desired.

Makes 1 Bundt or tube cake, 12 to 16 pieces.

SPONGE CAKE

Feathery-light sponge cake depends on stiffly beaten egg whites for its lightness and on the fat from egg yolks for some richness. It has no baking powder or additional added fat. This is the best cake for trifle or baked Alaska.

◆

1 cup	sifted cake and pastry flour	250 mL
1/4 tsp	salt	1 mL
4	eggs, separated	4
2/3 cup	granulated sugar	150 mL
1/4 cup	hot water	50 mL
1 tsp	vanilla	5 mL

- In bowl, combine flour and salt.
- In another bowl, beat egg yolks and 1/3 cup (75 mL) sugar until creamy and doubled in bulk. Beat in hot water then vanilla.
- Sift flour mixture over top of yolk mixture in 2 batches. With wire whisk, fold in until blended.
- In electric mixer bowl, beat egg whites with remaining sugar until stiff, shiny peaks form and sugar is dissolved. With wire whisk, fold in egg yolk and flour batter.
- Spread in waxed paper-lined 9-inch (23 cm) square or tube pan.
- Bake in 350 F (180 C) oven for 40 to 45 minutes or until golden and center springs back when lightly touched.
- Invert pan on wire rack to cool. With thin-bladed knife loosen cake; remove from pan.

Makes 1 square or tube cake, 12 to 16 pieces.

Variations

CHOCOLATE SPONGE CAKE

• In place of 1 cup (250 mL) sifted cake and pastry flour, use $^2/_3$ cup (150 mL) sifted cake and pastry flour plus $^1/_3$ cup (75 mL) cocoa.

GENOISE (BUTTERY SPONGE CAKE)

• Before spooning Sponge Cake batter into pan, carefully and thoroughly fold $^1/_4$ cup (50 mL) melted butter into the batter.

CHOCOLATE GENOISE (BUTTERY CHOCOLATE SPONGE CAKE)

• Before spooning Chocolate Sponge Cake batter into pan, carefully and thoroughly fold $^1/_4$ cup (50 mL) melted butter into the batter.

JELLY ROLL

• Either the Genoise or Chocolate Genoise (see above) may also be baked in a jelly-roll pan and used in recipes calling for a jelly roll.

MAPLE GLAZE

◆

$^1/_4$ cup	maple syrup	50 mL
1 tsp	vanilla	5 mL
1 cup	icing sugar	250 mL

• In bowl, combine maple syrup, vanilla and icing sugar. Stir until smooth and the consistency of thick sauce. Drizzle over inverted cake.

Makes $^1/_2$ cup (125 mL) glaze.

ANGEL FOOD CAKE

Mom's angel food cake whipped up from farm fresh eggs was heavenly. For several years running, it was the only kind I wanted for my birthday cake.

◆

1¹/₂ cups	egg whites (approximately 12)	375 mL
1 tsp	cream of tartar	5 mL
¹/₂ tsp	salt	2 mL
1¹/₃ cups	fine granulated sugar, divided	325 mL
1 cup	sifted cake and pastry flour	250 mL
1 tsp	vanilla	5 mL
	7-Minute Fluffy Frosting (see page 266) (optional)	

• In mixer bowl, beat egg whites, cream of tartar and salt until frothy. Gradually add ³/₄ cup (175 mL) sugar and continue beating until stiff, shiny peaks form and sugar is dissolved. (A bit of the mixture feels smooth when squashed between finger and thumb.)
• In another bowl, lightly combine flour and remaining sugar. Sift over egg white mixture in 3 batches and with wire whisk, fold in until there are no little lumps of flour.
• Spoon into ungreased 10-inch (25 cm) tube pan. With knife, cut through batter to remove bubbles. Smooth top.
• Bake in 350 F (180 C) oven for about 40 minutes or until top is golden and springs back when lightly touched.
• Invert pan allowing cake to hang upside down on its own stand or a funnel for at least 1 hour. With sharp knife loosen around edge; remove from pan to cake plate.
• Frost with 7-Minute Fluffy Frosting, if desired.

Makes 1 angel food cake, 12 to 16 servings.

Variations

CHOCOLATE ANGEL FOOD CAKE

• In place of $^1/_4$ cup (50 mL) cake and pastry flour, use $^1/_4$ cup (50 mL) cocoa. Combine and sift with flour.

LEMON ANGEL FOOD CAKE

• Add 2 tbsp (25 mL) lemon juice to egg whites before beating. Fold 2 tsp (10 mL) grated lemon rind into batter before pouring it into tube pan.

MARBLE ANGEL FOOD CAKE

• Make Angel Food Cake batter; divide into 2 portions. To one fold in a mixture of 2 tbsp (25 mL) cake and pastry flour and 2 tbsp (25 mL) granulated sugar; to the other fold in 3 tbsp (45 mL) cocoa and 2 tbsp (25 mL) granulated sugar. In heaping spoonfuls place one and then the other in tube pan.

GOLDEN JELLY ROLL

After making an Angel Food Cake there are always twelve leftover egg yolks. Mom used them to made this jelly roll and Lemon Butter (see page 311).

◆

8	egg yolks	8
$^3/_4$ cup	granulated sugar	175 mL
$^1/_2$ cup	hot water	125 mL
1 tsp	vanilla	5 mL
1 cup	sifted cake and pastry flour	250 mL
1 tsp	baking powder	5 mL
$^1/_2$ tsp	salt	2 mL
$^3/_4$ cup	jam or jelly	175 mL

- Lightly butter and, with waxed paper, line bottom of 15$^1/_2$ x 10$^1/_2$-inch (39 x 27 cm/2 L) jelly-roll pan.
- In electric mixer bowl, beat egg yolks and sugar until pale yellow and mixture ribbons from beaters. Beat in hot water and vanilla.
- In another bowl, combine flour, baking powder and salt. Sift over egg yolk mixture in 2 portions, gently folding after each. Spread in prepared jelly-roll pan.
- Bake in 375 F (190 C) oven for about 12 minutes or until golden and top springs back when lightly touched in center. Cut around edges with sharp knife. Invert pan with cake onto clean dishtowel.
- Remove pan. Carefully peel off waxed paper. With sharp knife, cut off about $^1/_4$-inch (5 mm) strip from each edge. (These are crusty and may cause cracking if left on.)
- Beginning at narrow end, roll up warm cake with towel, into a cylinder. Overwrap with waxed paper or plastic wrap. Set aside, seam side down, for about 45 minutes or until cool.
- Carefully unroll and remove towel. Spread to the edges with jam. Reroll, gently pressing into shape. Place seam side down on cake plate or serving tray.

Makes 12 to 16 slices.

Variation

MOCHA JELLY ROLL

- In place of hot water, use hot strong coffee. In place of 1 cup (250 mL) cake and pastry flour, use $^2/_3$ cup (150 mL) cake and pastry flour plus $^1/_2$ cup (125 mL) cocoa. Fill with Flavored Whipped Cream (page 267) or Chocolate Whipped Cream (see page 268).

WEDDING CAKE

This light fruitcake, which is my favorite Christmas cake, was a big hit at stepson Steve's wedding. It does not require ripening so I made it just three weeks before the big day. It gave me time to splash the layers with brandy a couple of times before I decorated them with a cover of rolled fondant, garlands of Royal Frosting (see page 261) and tiny nosegays of pink straw flowers.

◆

2 lbs	golden raisins	1 kg
1 lb	red candied cherries	500 g
1 lb	candied yellow and green pineapple, diced	500 g
1 lb	blanched almonds	500 g
5 cups	all-purpose flour, divided	1.25 L
2 cups	butter	500 mL
2 cups	granulated sugar, divided	500 mL
¹/₂ tsp	salt	2 mL
6	eggs, separated	6
1 tbsp	almond flavoring	15 mL
¹/₂ cup	milk	125 mL
³/₄ cup	brandy	175 mL
1 tsp	cream of tartar	5 mL

• Thoroughly butter one set of tier pans: one 9-inch (23 cm), one 7-inch (17.5 cm) and one 5-inch (12.5 cm). Or three 9 x 5-inch (23 x 13 cm) loaf pans. Line each with heavy brown paper cut to fit. Lightly butter inside of paper lining.

• In large bowl, combine raisins, cherries, candied pineapple, almonds and 1 cup (250 mL) flour.

• In electric mixer bowl, cream butter, 1¹/₂ cups (375 mL) sugar and salt until well blended. Beat in egg yolks and almond flavoring until very light and fluffy.

• Stir together milk and brandy. Add remaining flour alternately with liquid, making the last addition the flour mixture. Mix thoroughly but lightly after each.

• In another bowl, with clean beaters, beat egg whites and cream of tartar. Gradually add remaining sugar. Continue to beat until stiff but moist peaks form. Fold into batter. Then fold in floured fruit mixture.

- Spoon into prepared pans, filling pans about $^2/_3$ full. Smooth tops.
- Bake in 300 F (150 C) oven for $2^1/_2$ to $3^1/_2$ hours, depending on size of pan, until tester inserted in center comes out clean.
- Cool for 10 minutes. Remove from pans, take off paper and set on wire racks to cool.
- To store: Lightly sprinkle cakes with sherry or brandy, if you wish. Wrap them individually in plastic wrap to mellow for 24 hours before cutting. Or keep in cool place for up to 4 weeks; freeze for up to 3 months.

Makes layers for three-tier wedding cake or 3 loaves fruitcake.

ROYAL FROSTING

Once this ornamental or decorator icing is exposed to air, even for a short time, it becomes as firm as rock-hard candy. That makes it ideal for decorating sugar cookies, gingerbread houses and especially wedding cakes. It is also known as ornamental or decorator frosting.

———————————— ♦ ————————————

1	egg white	1
2 cups	icing sugar	500 mL
3	drops glycerin or vegetable oil	3

- In small bowl, beat egg white until foamy. Sift in icing sugar in 3 batches; beat until smooth after each addition. Blend in glycerin. If too thick, blend in a bit of water, 1 drop at a time, until desired consistency is reached. If too thin add a bit more icing sugar, 1 tsp (5 mL) at a time.
- If several different colors are desired, divide among small bowls and tint each portion with food coloring, a drop at a time, to make desired colors. Cover bowls with damp cloths or paper towels to prevent the formation of a hard crust on the surface and eventual drying out.
- To use, place in decorator bag fitted with the desired tip. Twist top of bag to hold frosting in. Holding bag like you would a large pencil, press designs or writing on cookies or cake.

Makes about $1^1/_4$ cups (300 mL).

FLUFFY BUTTER CREAM FROSTING

For icing Mom creamed together butter and icing sugar. Then she thinned it slightly with a few drops of milk or cream and stirred in more icing sugar until she had the texture she wanted. This version with the egg white is fluffier but, like her icing, it spreads easily and stays creamy and soft. It makes an excellent covering for cakes and filling for both cakes and cookies.

◆

1	egg white	1
2 cups	icing sugar	500 mL
$^1/_2$ cup	soft butter	125 mL
1 tsp	vanilla or almond flavoring	5 mL

• In electric mixer bowl, beat egg white until frothy. Add $^1/_2$ cup (125 mL) icing sugar. Beat until soft peaks form. Beat in butter and remaining icing sugar until smooth. Beat in vanilla.

Makes about $1^1/_2$ cups (375 mL).

Variations

TINTED BUTTER CREAM FROSTING

• Blend food coloring, a drop at a time, into portions of Fluffy Butter Cream Frosting to make tinted frosting.

CHOCOLATE BUTTER CREAM FROSTING

• Melt 1 square semi-sweet chocolate, cool to room temperature and beat into Fluffy Butter Cream Frosting.

OTHER FLAVORS

If you prefer other flavors, in place of vanilla in either Fluffy Butter Cream Frosting or Chocolate Butter Cream Frosting, use any of the following: peppermint flavoring, any liqueur, brandy or rum, lemon or orange juice plus a bit of grated rind, or instant coffee powder.

CREAM CHEESE FROSTING

As a change from butter cream frosting, use this on any spicy or fruit-flavored cake.

♦

1	package (250 g) cream cheese ($^1/_2$ lb)	1
$^1/_4$ cup	butter	50 mL
$1^1/_2$ cups	sifted icing sugar	375 mL
2 tsp	vanilla or orange flavored-liqueur	10 mL

• In bowl, beat cream cheese and butter until well creamed. Stir in icing sugar and vanilla until well blended and smooth.

Makes about 2 cups (500 mL).

Variation

ORANGE CREAM CHEESE FROSTING

• In place of vanilla use 2 tsp (10 mL) frozen orange juice concentrate; blend 1 tsp (5 mL) grated orange rind into creamed mixture.

LAZY DAY BROILED FROSTING

As the butter and sugar melt under the broiler, a caramalized topping flows over the cake.

———————————————— ◆ ————————————————

¹/₄ cup	soft butter	50 mL
1 cup	packed brown sugar	250 mL
2 tbsp	milk	25 mL
1 cup	flaked or desiccated coconut	250 mL

• In bowl, cream butter. Stir in brown sugar and milk until smooth. Add coconut and mix well. Spread on cake in pan.
• Place under broiler about 6 inches (15 cm) from heat for about 3 minutes or until golden and bubbly.

Makes enough for 8- or 9-inch (20 or 23 cm) square or round cake.

CRUMB TOPPING

This is a quick and easy finishing touch for any of the Basic Plain Cake variations (see page 245).

———————————————— ◆ ————————————————

¹/₂ cup	all-purpose flour	125 mL
¹/₃ cup	packed brown sugar	75 mL
¹/₃ cup	soft butter	75 mL
¹/₃ cup	finely chopped nuts	75 mL
¹/₂ to 1 tsp	cinnamon	2 to 5 mL

• In bowl, combine flour and brown sugar. Rub in butter until crumbly. Stir in nuts and cinnamon. Sprinkle over cake batter before baking it.

Makes enough for one 8- or 9-inch (20 or 23 cm) square or round cake.

BROWN SUGAR FUDGE FROSTING

In some old-fashioned cookbooks, this is called Penuche.

———————————— ◆ ————————————

²/₃ cup	packed brown sugar	150 mL
¹/₄ cup	milk or cream	50 mL
¹/₄ cup	butter	50 mL
¹/₂ cup	sifted icing sugar	125 mL

• In saucepan, combine brown sugar, milk and butter. Heat to boiling and boil for 3 minutes. Remove from heat. Allow to cool for about 4 minutes.
• Beat in icing sugar and continue beating for about 3 minutes until light and creamy. Pour evenly over cooled cake.

Makes enough for one 8- or 9-inch (20 to 23 cm) square cake.

Variations

—————————

BUTTERSCOTCH SAUCE

• Add ¹/₄ to ¹/₂ cup (50 to 125 mL) water. Stir ¹/₂ tsp (2 mL) vinegar into sauce after beating in the icing sugar.

BRANDY, RUM OR WHISKEY SAUCE

• In place of vinegar, add 1 tbsp (15 mL) brandy, rum or rye whiskey to Butterscotch Sauce.

7-Minute Fluffy Frosting

Because this boiled frosting is soft and marshmallowy when it's freshly made, it is easy to spread into lovely professional-looking swirls.

♦

1 cup	granulated sugar	250 mL
1/4 cup	corn syrup	50 mL
1/4 cup	water	50 mL
1/2 tsp	salt	2 mL
Pinch	cream of tartar	Pinch
2	egg whites	2
1 tsp	vanilla	5 mL

• In top of double boiler, combine sugar, corn syrup, water, salt, cream of tartar and egg whites.
• Place over rapidly boiling water. With rotary beater or electric mixer, immediately start beating and continue beating for 6 to 7 minutes or until stiff, shiny peaks form.
• Remove from heat. Beat in vanilla and continue beating for about 30 seconds longer to cool slightly.

Makes enough for one 8- to 9-inch (20 to 23 cm) layer cake (filling and frosting).

Variations

Seafoam Frosting

• In place of granulated sugar, use firmly packed brown sugar.

Peppermint Frosting

• In place of vanilla, stir in 1/4 tsp (1 mL) peppermint frosting. Tint pink or pale green, if desired. (Good on chocolate cake.)

FLAVORED WHIPPED CREAM

Whipped cream can be made ahead if icing sugar rather than granulated sugar is added. The little bit of cornstarch in icing sugar helps prevent the whipped cream from weeping.

◆

1 cup	cold whipping cream	250 mL
$^1/_3$ cup	icing sugar	75 mL
2 tsp	vanilla	10 mL

• With rotary beaters or wire whisk, whip cream in cold bowl until soft peaks form. Beat in icing sugar and vanilla for about 40 seconds until well blended and slightly firmer soft peaks form. Be cautious because, in an instant, overbeating can turn whipped cream into butter.

Makes 2 cups (500 mL), enough for one jelly roll or pumpkin pie or 12 cream puffs.

Variation

OTHER FLAVORS

• In place of vanilla, use any liqueur or orange juice, or 1 tsp (5 mL) almond flavoring or lemon juice.

CHOCOLATE WHIPPED CREAM

Some gourmets and chefs have a far more elegant name for this concoction — ganache. It is used for fillings and toppings for sponge cakes and tortes.

————————————————— ◆ —————————————————

1 cup	whipping cream	250 mL
2	squares semi-sweet chocolate	2
2 tbsp	icing sugar	25 mL
1 tsp	vanilla, brandy or liqueur	5 mL

• In small saucepan, combine whipping cream and chocolate squares. Place over medium heat. Stir until chocolate melts. It will look speckled but whisk or beat with a spoon until a smooth creamy chocolate color.

• Pour into bowl. Refrigerate, stirring once or twice, for about 2 hours or until it is firm.

• With electric or rotary beater, beat until soft peaks form that hold their shape. Beat in icing sugar and vanilla.

Makes 2 cups (500 mL), enough for one jelly roll or 12 cream puffs.

PIES

◆

Men like pies. Have you ever seen them at church suppers or picnics? They're never satisfied with one piece, they have to eat several.

According to the *Laura Secord Canadian Cookbook*, pie was the most popular dessert at that time. It was certainly Mom's favorite one for Sunday night family dinners for as long as I can remember.

Her pastry was wonderful but she didn't spare the lard or shortening. I'm a little more frugal with the fat, however.

Pies are winners in the sweets category as far as my husband Jim is concerned. Before I even ask him what he'd like for dessert, I know he'll say pie. He prefers fruit ones but has never turned away a piece with cream filling.

Pies are heartier than many other desserts, so it's a good idea to plan to serve them as the finishing touch to light meals.

TO MAKE PIE SHELLS AND TARTS

For double-crust pie:
- Cut dough in half; form into 2 round balls.
- On lightly floured surface, with floured rolling pin (or one fitted with a stocking), roll each ball from the center to the outside edge to form a round shape about $^1/_4$ inch (5 mm) thick. It is best not to turn the flattened pieces over to roll on the other side.
- Fit one round into 9-inch (23 cm) pie plate without stretching it. Trim to the edge of the pie plate. Fill this shell with filling as directed in recipe being used.
- Roll second round of pastry loosely around rolling pin. Lift and center it over filling. Unroll it from rolling pin.
- With scissors, trim around pastry allowing a $^1/_2$-inch (1 cm) over-hang. Gently lift the edge of the bottom crust and tuck and fold this overhang over it. Press together firmly to form a raised rim. Flute or crimp rim to form an attractive edge around pie.
- With sharp knife, cut several slashes in top crust for steam vents.

For unbaked single crust:
- Cut dough in half; form into 2 round balls.
- Roll dough allowing for a $^1/_2$-inch (1 cm) overhang to fit a 9-inch (23 cm) pie plate. Without stretching rolled dough, gently press onto bottom and sides of pie plate. With scissors, trim overhang to $^1/_2$ inch (1 cm) all around.
- Fold and tuck overhang under to make a double layer of pastry. Press together to form a rim around edge of pie plate. Flute or crimp rim to make an attractive edge. Use in pie recipe calling for an unbaked pie shell.

For baked single crust or shell:
- Line pie plate with one pastry round following the above directions.
- With tines of fork, prick bottom in about 2 dozen places. Then gently press a piece of foil onto bottom and up sides of pastry. Prick or slash foil in several places for steam to escape. This will help prevent pastry from shrinking while it bakes. Some cooks sprinkle small steel pastry weights or dried beans over bottom, but I find this really isn't necessary, the foil does the job as long as it has the pricks or slashes to allow steam to escape.
- Bake in 425 F (220 C) oven for 12 minutes; carefully remove foil; continue to bake for 5 to 7 minutes longer or until light golden brown.
- Cool. Use as baked shell to be filled later.

For tart shells:
- Working quickly, roll out $^1/_3$ or $^1/_2$ prepared pastry dough to $^1/_4$-inch (5 mm) thickness.
- With floured round cookie cutter or rim of glass, cut out rounds large enough to fit onto bottom and up sides of tart pans.
- For recipes calling for unbaked tart shells, follow recipe directions for baking.
- For recipes calling for baked tart shells, handle as directed for baked pastry shell or blind in above recipe.

FLAKY PASTRY

Lard makes the crisp, flaky pastry I like. When it's really cold, it's easy to cut it into the flour mixture, leaving some of the chunks larger than others. It's the larger pieces that melt between the layers of dough and make the baked pastry flaky.

——————————————— ◆ ———————————————

$1^3/_4$ cups	all-purpose flour	425 mL
$^1/_2$ tsp	salt	2 mL
$^2/_3$ cup	cold lard	150 mL
$^1/_3$ cup	ice water	75 mL

- In mixing bowl, combine flour and salt. With pastry blender or 2 knives, cut half the lard into flour until mixture resembles fine crumbs, then cut in the remainder until it is the size of peas.
- With fork stir in water, a little at a time, until dough clings together and easily comes away from sides of bowl. Form into a firm ball.
- Work quickly to make pie or tart crusts (see page 272). The best pastry comes from dough that is not handled too much.

Makes pastry for two 9-inch (23 cm) single pie shells, one 9-inch (1 L/ 23 cm) double-crust pie or 12 to 14 medium tart shells.

NO-FAIL PASTRY

At first I wondered about the amount of pastry I'd have from making up a whole pound of lard at one time, now I'm sold on it. I've experimented with a mixture of flours and prefer this one. For savory pies (quiches and tourtières), I replace the cake and pastry flour with whole wheat flour. The dough stores so well, I like to keep it on hand.

◆

4 cups	all-purpose flour	1 L
2 cups	cake and pastry flour	500 mL
1 tbsp	granulated sugar	15 mL
2 tsp	salt	10 mL
2 tsp	baking powder	10 mL
1 lb	lard	454 g
1	egg, beaten	1
1 tbsp	lemon juice or vinegar	15 mL
	Cold water	

• In large bowl, combine flours, sugar, salt and baking powder.
• With pastry blender or 2 knives, cut lard into dry ingredients until mixture is the texture of coarse crumbs. (This can be done in the food processor, but you must be careful not to over process the mixture. Just in case that happens, keep out about $1/4$ lb (125 g) lard and cut it into the processed crumbly mixture by hand.)
• In measuring cup, combine egg and lemon juice. Add enough water to make 1 cup (250 mL); stir well. Gradually add to crumbly mixture and quickly stir with fork until mixture holds together. Form into a ball.
• Cut into 6 even pieces. Form each into small round pattie. Use immediately for pie crusts or tart shells or keep for later use.
• To store: Wrap each pattie with plastic wrap. (I like to make the patties, which defrost more readily than balls, to fit into plastic tubs that once held sour cream, cottage cheese or yogurt. A 2-cup (500 mL) tub holds 3 wrapped patties.) Refrigerate for up to 2 weeks or freeze for up to 3 months. Defrost and allow to sit at room temperature for 10 to 15 minutes for easier rolling.

Makes enough for 3 double-crust pies or 6 pie shells.

CRUMB CRUST

Before the days of the food processor, a rolling pin was used to crush graham wafers for crumb crusts. Mom's instructions say "roll fine."

— ◆ —

1¼ cups	wafer crumbs	300 mL
2 tbsp	granulated sugar or packed brown sugar	25 mL
⅓ cup	melted butter	75 mL
1 tbsp	warm water	15 mL

• In bowl, combine crumbs and sugar. With fork, work in butter and water until evenly distributed. Firmly press mixture on bottom and up sides of 9-inch (23 cm) pie plate.
• Bake in 350 F (180 C) oven for 8 to 10 minutes or until just beginning to lightly brown.

Makes one 9-inch (23 cm) crumb crust.

STREUSEL TOPPING

If you wish, you can use this crumbly mixture in place of the top crust in most fruit pies.

— ◆ —

¼ cup	all-purpose flour	50 mL
¼ cup	brown sugar	50 mL
¼ cup	butter	50 mL
1 tbsp	oat bran or wheat germ (optional)	15 mL
½ tsp	cinnamon	2 mL

• In bowl, combine flour and brown sugar. With pastry blender or fingers, cut or rub in butter. Blend in oat bran, if desired, and cinnamon.

Makes ¾ cup (175 mL).

WATERLOO MARKET
APPLE PIE

After a full morning at the Waterloo, Ontario market picking and choosing wonderful stuff — pork loins, prime rib of beef, chicken sausages, round rye bread, pickled baby corn, knitted toques and mittens — we were ready for lunch. We selected potato and bacon soup from one stall, Oktoberfest sausage in a bun from another and from still another, a superb open-face apple pie. Topped off with good hearty coffee, it's a lunch that makes my list of unforgettable meals. Here's my interpretation of the pie.

◆

1	9-inch (23 cm) unbaked Flaky Pastry (see page 271) pie shell	
²/₃ cup	packed brown sugar	150 mL
¹/₄ cup	all-purpose flour	50 mL
¹/₂ tsp	cinnamon	2 mL
¹/₄ tsp	salt	1 mL
2 tbsp	butter	25 mL
5 to 6	apples (about 4 cups/1 L slices)	5 to 6
1 cup	commercial sour cream	250 mL

• Prepare pie shell.
• In bowl, combine brown sugar, flour, cinnamon and salt. With pastry blender or fingers, cut or rub in butter until mixture resembles fine crumbs. Sprinkle about 2 tbsp (25 mL) over bottom of pie crust.
• Peel and core apples. Cut into wedges about 1 inch (2.5 cm) thick at the widest part. Arrange slices, with thickest part down, in a circle around outside of pastry shell. Repeat with another circle of slices in center.
• Sprinkle half the remaining crumbs over apples. Pour sour cream over top. Sprinkle with remaining crumbs.
• Bake in 400 F (200 C) oven for 10 minutes then reduce heat to 350 F (180 C). Continue to bake for 30 minutes longer or until apples are tender and top turns golden.

Makes one 9-inch (23 cm) pie, 6 servings.

OLD-FASHIONED APPLE PIE

In first year home economics classes we learned that pie-making requires a special touch. My friend, Eileen Gray, has it. Even the pies she made then were amazing. Her apple pies are always wonderful. She says, "Work fast and use enough water in the pie dough."

◆

	Flaky Pastry for 9-inch (23 cm) pie (see page 271)	
1 cup	lightly packed brown sugar	250 mL
2 tbsp	quick-cooking minute tapioca or 3 tbsp (45 mL) all-purpose flour	25 mL
$^1/_2$ tsp	cinnamon	2 mL
$^1/_4$ tsp	nutmeg	1 mL
7 or 8	large tart apples	7 or 8
2 tsp	butter (optional)	10 mL
2 tbsp	milk	25 mL
2 tsp	granulated sugar	10 mL

• Line pie plate with pastry; roll out pastry top following flaky pastry recipe.
• In bowl, combine brown sugar, minute tapioca, cinnamon and nutmeg.
• Peel, core and slice apples. Sprinkle with sugar mixture; toss to coat apple slices. Arrange in layers in pastry shell. Dot with butter, if desired.
• Place top pastry round over apples. Trim pastry, leaving about 1-inch (2.5 cm) overhang. Tuck overhang under trimmed bottom pastry. Pinch edge to form rim around pie, then flute or crimp rim. Cut slashes in crust or prick with fork to create steam vents.
• Brush milk over crust. Sprinkle with sugar.
• Bake in 400 F (200 C) oven for 10 minutes; reduce heat to 350 F (180 C); continue baking for 35 to 40 minutes longer or until pastry is golden and fruit is tender.

Makes one 9-inch (23 cm) pie, 6 to 8 servings.

STREUSEL APPLE PIE

• Sprinkle Streusel Topping (see page 273) evenly over top of apples instead of adding top crust. Bake as directed.

PECAN PIE

A few of my extra pounds are probably due to sampling too many pecan pies. Some were so syrupy sweet, they made my teeth scream. But this version rates among the best I've tasted since my introduction to this pie in 1956 in the United States.

♦

1	9-inch (23 cm) unbaked pie shell	1
3	eggs	3
1/2 cup	granulated sugar	125 mL
Pinch	salt	Pinch
1 cup	corn syrup	250 mL
1/3 cup	melted butter	75 mL
1 cup	pecan halves or pieces	250 mL

• Prepare pie shell
• In mixing bowl, beat together eggs, sugar and salt. Stir in corn syrup and butter until thoroughly mixed. Add pecans; mix well.
• Pour into unbaked pie shell.
• Bake in 375 F (190 C) oven for 10 minutes; reduce heat to 350 F (180 C); continue to bake for 35 to 40 minutes longer or until tester inserted between edge and center comes out clean.
• Cool before serving.

Makes one 9-inch (23 cm) pie, 8 servings.

MOM'S SPICY PUMPKIN PIE

Dad was always exuberant over Mom's pumpkin pie. In his opinion, no one else's ever matched hers. As best as I can remember, this is what she used for it.

♦

1	9-inch (23 cm) unbaked pie shell	1
³/₄ cup	packed brown sugar	175 mL
1 tbsp	all-purpose flour	15 mL
1¹/₂ tsp	cinnamon	7 mL
¹/₂ tsp	ground ginger	2 mL
¹/₄ tsp	each grated nutmeg, ground allspice and cloves	1 mL
¹/₄ tsp	salt	1 mL
2	eggs	2
1³/₄ cups	mashed cooked pumpkin or 1 14 oz/398 mL can	425 mL
¹/₂ cup	evaporated milk or milk	125 mL
¹/₂ cup	whipping cream	125 mL
1 tsp	vanilla	5 mL
	Flavored Whipped Cream (see page 267)	

• Prepare pie shell.
• In bowl, combine brown sugar, flour, cinnamon, ginger, nutmeg, allspice, cloves and salt.
• In mixing bowl, lightly beat eggs; whisk in pumpkin, flour mixture, evaporated milk, whipping cream and vanilla.
• Pour into prepared pastry shell.
• Bake in 425 F (210 C) oven for 15 minutes; reduce oven temperature to 325 F (160 C) and bake pie for 35 to 40 minutes longer or until tester inserted halfway between center and edge comes out clean.
• Cool. Serve garnished with Flavored Whipped Cream.

Makes one 9-inch (23 cm) pie, 6 to 8 servings.

FRESH BERRY PIE

When I close my eyes and think of fresh berry pie, I smell and see one plump with Saskatoon berries. Some of its sweet purple juice bubbles through the vents in the flaky golden crust. That's the berry pie I knew when I was a child. Mom always made several after berry-picking jaunts to prairie bluffs or the banks of the South Saskatchewan River near Langham.

♦

	Flaky Pastry for 9-inch (23 cm) double-crust pie (see page 271)	
³/₄ cup	granulated sugar	175 mL
4 tbsp	all-purpose flour or 3 tbsp (45 mL) quick-cooking tapioca	60 mL
¹/₂ tsp	cinnamon	2 mL
4 cups	berries (Saskatoons, blueberries, elderberries, raspberries or strawberries or combination of 2 or 3)	1 L
2 tsp	butter (optional)	10 mL
Glaze:		
2 tbsp	milk	25 mL
1 tbsp	granulated sugar	15 mL

• Roll out half of pastry to fit 9-inch (23 cm) pie plate.
• In small bowl, combine sugar, flour and cinnamon. Sprinkle over berries; lightly mix. Pour into prepared crust. Dot with butter, if desired.
• Roll remaining pastry to fit over top and allow for ¹/₂-inch (1 cm) overhang. Place on top of filling. Tuck overhang under edge of bottom crust. Pinch together to form rim. Crimp rim, as desired. Cut slashes in top crust for steam vents.

- *Glaze:* Brush milk on top and edge of pie crust. Sprinkle with granulated sugar.
- Bake in a 425 F (210 C) oven for 10 minutes. Reduce heat to 350 F (180 C); bake for 25 to 30 minutes longer or until crust is golden brown.

Makes one 9-inch (23 cm) pie, 6 to 8 servings.

Variations

APRICOT OR PEACH PIE

- In place of berries, use 4 cups (1 L) sliced fresh apricots or peaches for the berries.

RHUBARB PIE

- In place of berries, use (1 L) cut-up rhubarb; increase sugar to $1^1/_3$ cups (325 mL); increase flour to 6 tbsp (90 mL), or minute tapioca to $^1/_3$ cup (75 mL).

STRAWBERRY OR SASKATOON RHUBARB PIE

- In place of 2 cups (500 mL) berries, use 2 cups (500 mL) cut-up rhubarb; increase sugar by 2 tbsp (25 mL) and flour by 1 tbsp (15 mL).

SOUR CHERRY PIE

- In place of berries, use 4 cups (1 L) pitted sour red cherries; increase sugar to $1^1/_4$ cups (300 mL); add $^1/_2$ tsp (2 mL) almond extract.

MINCEMEAT SUNDAE PIE

The ice cream mellows the richness of the mincemeat and extends its exotic flavor in this make ahead pie.

◆

Crumb Crust:

	Crumb Crust mixture, using vanilla wafers (see page 273)	
¹/₂ cup	finely chopped pecans	125 mL
¹/₂ tsp	cinnamon	2 mL

Filling:

6 cups	vanilla ice cream	1.5 L
1 cup	mincemeat	250 mL

Warm Caramel Sauce:

1 cup	firmly packed brown sugar	250 mL
1 cup	whipping cream	250 mL
1 tsp	vanilla	5 mL

• *Crust*: Prepare vanilla Crumb Crust mixture; stir in pecans and cinnamon.
• Press onto bottom and 1¹/₂ inches (3.5 cm) up sides of 10-inch (25 cm/3L) buttered springform pan. Freeze for 30 minutes.
• *Filling*: In cold bowl, stir ice cream to soften slightly; fold in mincemeat until evenly distributed. Pack into crumb crust.
• Cover and freeze for at least 6 hours or overnight.
• To store: Keep wrapped pie in freezer for up to 4 weeks.
• *Warm Caramel Sauce*: In small saucepan, combine sugar and whipping cream. Bring to a boil; cook, stirring occasionally, for 3 to 4 minutes or until thick enough to coat spoon. Do not overcook. Stir in vanilla.
• At serving time, cut pie into wedges. Drizzle Warm Caramel Sauce over each. Serve immediately.

Makes 8 to 10 servings.

CREAM PIE

Plain home cooked puddings turn into special desserts when they're poured into a crunchy crust and topped with feathery meringue or whipped cream.

--- ◆ ---

1	9-inch (23 cm) baked pie shell or crumb crust	1
1	batch Vanilla Cream Pudding and Pie Filling (see page 291) Meringue Topping (see page 288) or Flavored Whipped Cream (see page 267)	1

- Prepare pie shell. Cool.
- Pour warm filling into pie shell.
- Top with Meringue Topping and bake as directed or once filling has cooled, top with Flavored Whipped Cream.

Makes one 9-inch (23 cm) pie, 6 servings.

Variations

BANANA CREAM PIE

• In place of Vanilla Cream Pudding and Pie Filling, use Banana Cream Pudding and Pie Filling (see page 292), making sure all the banana slices are coated with pudding.

CHOCOLATE CREAM PIE

• In place of Vanilla Pudding and Pie Filling, use Chocolate Pudding and Pie Filling (see page 292).

COCONUT CREAM PIE

• Stir 1 cup (250 mL) shredded or desiccated coconut into warm Vanilla Pudding and Pie Filling before pouring it into its pie shell. If using Meringue Topping, sprinkle $^1/_4$ cup (50 mL) coconut over top before baking. If using Flavored Whipped Cream topping, garnish top with $^1/_4$ cup (50 mL) toasted coconut.

FLAPPER PIE

• In place of Vanilla Pudding and Pie Filling, use Butterscotch Pudding and Pie Filling (see page 292). If using Meringue Topping, sprinkle it with about $^1/_3$ cup (75 mL) finely chopped nuts before baking. Or, if using Flavored Whipped Cream, garnish it with the nuts.

Jelly Roll, Flavored Whipped Cream and Berry Sauce

◆

Streusel Apple Pie, Cherry Pie, Peach Pie

◆

Strawberry Shortcake

Ambrosia Fruit Bowl

♦

LEMON MERINGUE PIE

Sometimes Mom made lemon meringue pie from a packaged mix. Even though she usually did a fine job of camouflaging it, we'd find out. We preferred her from-scratch pie and no substitute could match it.

◆

1	9-inch (23 cm) baked pie shell	1
1¼ cups	granulated sugar	300 mL
¼ cup	all-purpose flour	50 mL
¼ cup	cornstarch	50 mL
½ tsp	salt	2 mL
2¼ cups	boiling water	550 mL
3	egg yolks	3
⅔ cup	lemon juice	150 mL
2 tbsp	grated lemon rind, optional	25 mL
1 tbsp	cold butter	15 mL
	Meringue Topping (see page 288)	

• Prepare pie shell.
• In heavy saucepan, combine 1 cup (250 mL) sugar, flour, cornstarch and salt. Stir in boiling water. Cook over medium heat, stirring constantly, for about 5 minutes or until thickened. (Or, cook mixture in top of double boiler over boiling water.)
• Remove from heat. Stir in lemon juice, lemon rind, if desired and butter until it melts. Pour into pie shell.
• Spread Meringue Topping over top right to and touching the crust.
• Bake in 325 F (160 C) oven for about 18 minutes or until delicately browned. Cool to room temperature before serving.

Makes one 9-inch (23 cm) pie, 6 to 8 servings.

IRISH COFFEE PIE

A dessert that tastes like an after-dinner drink or liqueur is a delightful finishing touch to a special dinner.

◆

Crust:

1	batch graham cracker Crumb Crust (see page 273)	1
¹/₂ cup	finely chopped pecans	125 mL

Filling:

1	envelope unflavored gelatin	1
¹/₄ cup	cold water	50 mL
²/₃ cup	milk	150 mL
¹/₂ cup	granulated sugar, divided	125 mL
2 tbsp	instant coffee granules	25 mL
Pinch	salt	Pinch
2	eggs, separated	2
¹/₃ cup	Irish whiskey	75 mL
¹/₂ cup	whipping cream	125 mL
¹/₂ cup	toasted finely chopped pecans	125 mL

• Mix chopped pecans into the crumb crust mixture. Press into 9-inch (23 cm) pie plate.
• Bake in 375 F (190 C) oven for 10 minutes until lightly browned. Set aside to cool.
• Sprinkle gelatin over cold water. Let stand for 5 minutes to soften.
• In small heavy saucepan, heat together milk, ¹/₄ cup (50 mL) sugar, coffee granules and salt, stirring until coffee is completely dissolved.
• Beat together egg yolks and whiskey. Stir a little of the hot milk mixture into egg yolk mixture then stir this back into milk mixture. Cook over medium heat, stirring constantly, for about 2 minutes or until mixture thickens slightly. Do not allow to boil. Remove from heat.

- Immediately stir in softened gelatin until it dissolves. Pour into bowl; chill for 25 minutes or until consistency of egg white.
- In electric mixer bowl, beat egg whites until frothy. Add remaining sugar; beat until stiff, satiny peaks form. Fold into gelatin mixture.
- Whip cream and fold into egg white and gelatin mixture. Chill in refrigerator for about 20 minutes or until partially set.
- Spoon into cooled pie shell, mounding filling. Chill for 3 to 4 hours or until set.
- Garnish with toasted pecans.

Makes 8 servings.

Variations

KAHLUA CHIFFON PIE

- In place of Irish whiskey, use coffee-flavored liqueur, such as Kahlua.

GRAND MARNIER PIE

- Omit coffee granules. In place of Irish whiskey, use orange-flavored liqueur, such as Grand Marnier.

IRISH COFFEE, KAHLUA OR GRAND MARNIER MOUSSE

- Make the filling only, omitting the pie crust. Serve in stemmed glasses.

BUTTER TARTS

The crackled yellow edges of this page in Mom's carbon-copied recipe book tell me she made these tarts often when she was a young bride. I like them best with currants, but usually when I'm in the mood to make them, I have only raisins on hand.

◆

	Flaky Pastry (see page 271)	
¹/₂ cup	packed brown sugar	125 mL
¹/₃ cup	soft butter	75 mL
1 cup	corn syrup	250 mL
2	eggs, lightly beaten	2
1 tsp	vinegar	5 mL
1 tsp	vanilla	5 mL
Pinch	salt	Pinch
Pinch	cinnamon	Pinch
³/₄ cup	currants or plumped raisins	175 mL

• Prepare pastry. Roll out and with cookie cutters cut into circles to line 24 medium muffin cups. Set aside.
• In bowl, stir together brown sugar and butter until blended. Stir in corn syrup, eggs, vinegar, vanilla, salt and cinnamon.
• Distribute currants among pastry-lined muffin cups. Carefully pour butter mixture into muffin cups, filling them ²/₃ full.
• Bake in 375 F (190 C) oven for 5 minutes. Reduce heat to 325 F (160 C) and continue to bake for 15 to 20 minutes longer or until pastry is golden. Try to prevent filling from bubbling.

Makes 24.

Variation

RAISIN NUT BUTTER TARTS

• In place of currants, use ¹/₃ cup (75 mL) plumped raisins and ¹/₃ cup (75 mL) coarsely chopped nuts.

LEMON DELIGHT
TARTS

Seeing these sensational lemon gems in the kitchen told us it was Mom's turn to entertain the Ladies' Aid or sewing circle. Whenever I serve them I receive the same compliments as my mother did.

◆

1	batch Flaky Pastry (see page 271)	1
1	batch Lemon Butter (see page 311)	1

- Prepare pastry and bake as 24 small tart shells.
- Spoon Lemon Butter into tart shells no longer than 8 hours before serving.
- Refrigerate until serving time.

Makes 24 tarts.

Variation

CREAMY LEMON DELIGHT TARTS

- Fold $^1/_2$ cup (125 mL) Lemon Butter into 1 cup (250 mL) firm whipped cream. Spoon mixture into baked tart shells. Garnish each tart with small strawberries (or slices), raspberries or blueberries and a tiny mint leaf, if desired. Fill tart shells no longer than 3 hours ahead and refrigerate until serving time.

MERINGUE TOPPING

Very early in my cooking experiences I learned that meringue for a pie topping is best when all the sugar in it is completely dissolved.

———————————————— ♦ ————————————————

3	egg whites	3
¹/₄ tsp	cream of tartar	1 mL
Pinch	salt	Pinch
¹/₄ cup	granulated sugar	50 mL

• In electric mixer bowl, beat egg whites, cream of tartar and salt until frothy. Gradually beat in sugar. Continue to beat until sugar is completely dissolved and stiff glossy peaks form that do not curl over when beaters are lifted.

• Spoon on top of pie filling, spreading meringue right to and touching edge of crust to prevent shrinking. With spreader or spoon, swirl in an attractive design.

• Bake in 325 F (160 C) oven for about 18 minutes or until delicately browned.

• Cool at room temperature for about an hour before serving. Do not refrigerate.

Makes enough for one 9-inch (23 cm) pie.

DESSERTS

◆

At Mom's table every dinner and supper included dessert. It pleased Dad because as far as he was concerned a meal without a sweet treat for a finale was incomplete. During the week it was usually creamy milk pudding or home-canned peaches, pears or plums with cookies, satisfying bread or rice pudding, fruit crumble or crisp or a single layer cake with ice cream.

My family desserts have been a bit different. They've included far more fresh fruit simply because it's been more available than it ever was in Mom's day.

For celebrations and Sunday family dinners she turned out perfect cream puffs, fat jelly rolls, frosted cakes and scrumptious pies. They made such an impression on me I still think of them as special desserts. In addition, during my fifty years of cooking I've added others — creamy cheesecakes, airy mousses and fruit-filled tortes.

AMBROSIA FRUIT BOWL

In Greek and Roman mythology, ambrosia is the food of the gods.

———————————————— ♦ ————————————————

2	seedless navel oranges	2
2	bananas	2
1 cup	fresh or canned pineapple chunks	250 mL
1 cup	green or red seedless grapes	250 mL
2 tbsp	icing sugar	25 mL
$^1/_4$ cup	sweetened flaked coconut	50 mL

• Peel oranges including white membrane. With a sharp knife slip each section away from the inside white membrane into a bowl.
• Peel cut bananas in $^1/_4$-inch (5 mm) slices. Add banana slices, pineapple and grapes to orange sections.
• Fold in icing sugar and coconut.
• Refrigerate for at least 2 hours to chill thoroughly.

Makes 5 to 6 servings.

Variation

————————————

APRICOT OR PEACH AMBROSIA

• In place of oranges, use 4 to 6 apricots or 2 firm, ripe peaches (or nectarines).

VANILLA CREAM PUDDING AND PIE FILLING

This cream pudding serves two purposes. First, I think of it as a comforting dessert and then, once it is contained in a pie shell it becomes a yummy cream pie. You will need the full batch to fill a pie shell, but if six servings of pudding are too many, these recipes can be halved (using 1 egg). If you prefer a thinner pudding, stir in a little more milk.

◆

³/₄ cup	granulated sugar	175 mL
¹/₄ cup	all-purpose flour	50 mL
¹/₄ cup	cornstarch	50 mL
3 cups	milk	750 mL
3	egg yolks, slightly beaten	3
	or 2 eggs	
1 tbsp	vanilla	25 mL

• In heavy saucepan, combine sugar, flour and cornstarch. Gradually stir in milk. Bring to a boil, stirring occasionally, over medium heat. Cook, stirring constantly, for 3 minutes.
• Remove from heat. Slowly stir about 1 cup (250 mL) of hot mixture into egg yolks. Return egg mixture back to hot mixture in saucepan. Return to heat; cook, stirring constantly, for 1 to 2 minutes or until thickened. Remove from heat.
• Stir in vanilla. Cover top closely with plastic wrap to prevent skin from forming. Cool to room temperature.

Makes 6 servings or filling for one 9-inch (23 cm) pie shell.

Variations

BANANA CREAM PUDDING AND PIE FILLING

• Reduce vanilla to 1 tsp (5 mL). Prepare pudding and cool. Cut 3 bananas into $1/2$-inch (1 cm) slices. Fold into pudding.

BUTTERSCOTCH PUDDING AND PIE FILLING

• In place of granulated sugar, use 1 cup (250 mL) firmly packed brown sugar. Add it to saucepan with 2 tbsp (25 mL) butter; cook until sugar melts. Beat together flour, cornstarch and milk. Stir into brown sugar mixture, bring to boil and cook, stirring constantly, for 3 minutes. Then add egg yolks and finish as directed.

CHOCOLATE CREAM PUDDING AND PIE FILLING

• Add $1/2$ cup (125 mL) more sugar. Coarsely chop 3 squares unsweetened chocolate and add to saucepan with milk. Then cook as directed.

HELPFUL HINT

Pudding and Pie Filling Tip
For pudding or pies topped with Flavored Whipped Cream, in place of 3 egg yolks, use 2 whole eggs. For pies topped with Meringue Topping, use 3 egg yolks because the remaining whites can be used for the meringue.

OLD-FASHIONED BREAD PUDDING

If there's anything that's comfort food, this is it. My children, husband and friends usually ask me to make it again and again.

When Mom created her glorious version out of her own homemade loaves, Dad gilded it with the thick pouring cream we always had on hand. I prefer using a variation of Butterscotch Sauce (see page 265), especially with whiskey added, but always feel like it truly is gilding the lily.

◆

3	eggs	3
$^{1}/_{2}$ cup	granulated sugar	125 mL
2 cups	milk	500 mL
1 tsp	cinnamon	5 mL
$^{1}/_{4}$ tsp	nutmeg	1 mL
1 tsp	vanilla	5 mL
3 cups	cubed stale bread (about 4 slices)	750 mL
$^{3}/_{4}$ cup	raisins or dried currants	175 mL
2 tsp	butter	10 mL

• In mixing bowl, beat eggs and sugar until foamy. Stir in milk, cinnamon, nutmeg and vanilla.
• Add bread cubes and raisins; mix well. Allow bread to soak up egg-milk mixture for about 5 minutes.
• Use half the butter to butter shallow 6 cup (1.5 L) baking dish. Pour in bread mixture. Top with bits of remaining butter.
• Bake in 350 F (180 C) oven for about 50 minutes or until thin knife blade inserted in center comes out clean. This method gives a golden brown crust and crunchy toasted top.
• For a more custard-like pudding, place baking dish in pan of hot water. Bake in 375 F (190 C) oven for 50 to 60 minutes or until tester inserted in center comes out clean.

Makes 4 to 6 servings.

Variations

BUTTERSCOTCH BREAD PUDDING

• In place of granulated sugar, use $^3/_4$ cup (175 mL) firmly packed brown sugar.

CHOCOLATE BREAD PUDDING

• Beat $^1/_3$ cup (75 mL) cocoa into egg and sugar mixture.

COCONUT BREAD PUDDING

• Stir $^1/_4$ cup (50 mL) shredded or flaked coconut into bread mixture and sprinkle top of pudding in baking dish with another $^1/_4$ cup (50 mL) coconut.

DATE OR FIG BREAD PUDDING

• In place of raisins, use $^3/_4$ cup (175 mL) chopped dates or figs.

NUTTY BREAD PUDDING

• Add $^1/_2$ cup (125 mL) chopped nuts, preferably pecans or walnuts, to any of the above bread pudding recipes.

MERINGUE-CROWNED BREAD PUDDING

• In any of the above bread pudding recipes, use 2 egg yolks in place of 1 of the eggs. Bake pudding as directed. Make a meringue by beating 2 egg whites with a pinch of salt and 2 tbsp (25 mL) icing sugar until stiff peaks form. Spread over hot pudding. Return to 300 F (150 C) oven for 8 to 10 minutes or until meringue is golden brown. (This pudding, sometimes called the Queen of Puddings, can be embellished even more by spreading the baked pudding with jam or jelly before covering it with meringue.)

Old-Fashioned Baked Rice Pudding

My pudding never seems to reach the same level of excellence as Mom's. It must have been the oven of that old wood stove that made the difference. As soon as we were off to the four room school across the road from us, she'd put this mixture in the oven. By noon its cinnamon-scented sweet aroma surrounded us.

$\blacklozenge$

2¼ cups	milk	550 mL
½ cup	uncooked long-grain rice	125 mL
⅓ cup	granulated sugar	75 mL
¼ tsp	salt	1 mL
Pinch	ground cinnamon or nutmeg	Pinch
2 tbsp	raisins	25 mL
1 tsp	vanilla	15 mL

• In lightly buttered 4-cup (1 L) casserole or baking dish, combine milk, rice, sugar, salt and cinnamon.
• Bake, uncovered, in 250 F (120 C) oven for 30 minutes. Stir well. Continue baking for 30 minutes longer.
• Stir in raisins. Bake, stirring occasionally, for 1½ hours longer or until rice is tender, milk is absorbed and top is golden. Stir in vanilla.

Makes 4 servings.

Variations

Quick Rice Pudding

• In place of baking rice pudding, in 6-cup (1.5 L) saucepan, combine milk, rice and salt. Bring to a boil, reduce heat and simmer, uncovered, stirring occasionally, for 15 minutes. Stir in sugar, raisins and cinnamon. Cover and continue simmering for 20 minutes or until rice is tender. Stir in vanilla.

JIM'S EASY CHERRY PUDDING

The first time I tasted this tasty concoction at Jim's house, I realized it was what I call "crumble." For him, it was just as the title says. His daughter, Laura, gave him the recipe when he was a widower on his own. It became the one baked fruit dessert he could master.

◆

$\frac{1}{2}$ cup	soft butter or margarine	125 mL
$1\frac{1}{3}$ cups	granulated sugar, divided	325 mL
1 cup	all-purpose flour	250 mL
2 tsp	baking powder	10 mL
$\frac{1}{2}$ tsp	salt	2 mL
$\frac{1}{2}$ cup	milk	125 mL
1	egg	1
2 cups	pitted red sour cherries, fresh, frozen, or canned	500 mL

- In 9-inch (23 cm) baking dish, melt butter.
- In bowl, combine 1 cup (250 mL) sugar, flour, baking powder and salt. Lightly beat together milk and egg. Stir into dry ingredients until mixed. Spoon over melted butter. Do not mix.
- Pour undrained cherries over batter. Do not mix.
- Sprinkle remaining sugar over cherries.
- Bake in 350 F (180 C) oven for about 1 hour or until golden and tester inserted in center comes out clean.

Makes 6 to 8 servings.

Variation

APPLE, PEACH, PLUM, STRAWBERRY OR RASPBERRY CRUMBLE

- In place of cherries, use 2 cups (500 mL) sliced fruit or berries or any combination of fruits and berries.

SASKATOON BERRY COBBLER

I had been living in the East for about 15 years when a friend from Saskatoon, Saskatchewan, brought me a quart of canned Saskatoons. We made a cobbler and ate it together. What a treat! It was like eating a memory and brought back visions of the prairies.

♦

1	batch Flaky Pastry (see page 271)	1
4 cups	Saskatoon berries or blueberries	1 L
$^3/_4$ cup	granulated sugar, divided	175 mL
Pinch	cinnamon	Pinch
2 tbsp	cold butter	25 mL
	Table cream or ice cream	

• On lightly floured surface, with floured rolling pin, roll out pastry into a large circle about 14 inches (35 cm) in diameter. Roll around rolling pin; unroll pastry over 9-inch (23 cm) round and 2-inch (5 cm) deep baking dish or casserole. Press pastry onto bottom and up sides. Allow extra pastry to hang over edge.

• Spoon berries into pastry shell. Sprinkle with $^1/_2$ cup (125 mL) sugar and cinnamon. Dot with little pieces of butter.

• Bring pastry, hanging over the edge, up and over berries. It will not meet in the middle. Use any pastry pieces that might have fallen off to cover more of the fruit. Sprinkle crust with remaining sugar.

• Bake in 425 C (220 C) oven for 40 minutes or until berries are bubbling and crust is golden brown.

• Serve warm with ice cold table cream.

Makes 6 servings.

Variations

APPLE OR PEACH COBBLER

• In place of berries, use sliced apples or peaches.

PEACH MELBA CRISP

The combination of peaches and ice cream with raspberry sauce is known as Peach Melba. I call this crisp "melba" because it has the same tastes and you can always serve it with ice cream, pouring cream or plain yogurt.

◆

3 cups	sliced peaches (6 medium)	1.5 L
1 cup	raspberries or blueberries	250 mL
1 cup	all-purpose flour, divided	250 mL
2 tbsp	granulated sugar	25 mL
$^1/_2$ cup	packed brown sugar	125 mL
$^1/_4$ cup	oat bran or wheat germ	50 mL
1 tsp	cinnamon	5 mL
$^1/_3$ cup	butter or margarine	75 mL

• In 8 or 9-inch (20 or 23 cm) baking dish, combine peaches and raspberries. Add 1 tbsp (15 mL) flour and granulated sugar; stir into fruit.
• In small bowl, combine remaining flour, brown sugar, oat bran, and cinnamon. With pastry blender or 2 knives, cut in butter until crumbly but evenly mixed. Sprinkle over fruit.
• Bake in 375 F (190 C) oven for 30 to 35 minutes or until peaches are tender and topping browned and crisp.
• Serve topped with ice cream, if desired.

Makes 6 servings.

Variations

PEACH, PEAR, APPLE OR PLUM CRISP

• In place of peaches and raspberries, use 4 cups (1 L) sliced peaches, pears, apples or plums.

LEMON PUDDING CAKE

A pudding cake is another example of the astonishing things that can happen to a wet, runny batter when it goes into a hot oven. In half an hour, this type of batter turns into tender cake sitting on top of its own smooth sauce.

◆

1 tbsp	soft butter	15 mL
$^2/_3$ cup	granulated sugar, divided	150 mL
2 tsp	grated lemon rind	10 mL
3	eggs, separated	3
$^1/_4$ cup	all-purpose flour	50 mL
1 cup	milk	250 mL
$^1/_3$ cup	lemon juice	75 mL

• In large bowl, cream butter and $^1/_3$ cup (75 mL) sugar until fluffy. Add lemon rind and egg yolks; beat well. Stir in flour alternately with milk. Stir in lemon juice.
• In another bowl, beat egg whites with remaining sugar until stiff, satiny peaks form. Fold into egg yolk mixture.
• Pour into 8-inch (20 cm) round or square baking dish. Set in pan filled with $1^1/_2$ inches (3.5 cm) hot water.
• Bake in 350 F (180 C) oven for 25 to 30 minutes or until golden brown and top springs back when touched in center.
• Serve warm or cool. Top each spoonful of the cake with sauce from the bottom of the baking dish.

Makes 6 to 8 servings.

Variation

RASPBERRY PUDDING CAKE

• Spread 1 cup (250 mL) raspberries on bottom of baking dish. Pour Lemon Pudding Cake batter over berries.

STRAWBERRY
SHORTCAKE

The best strawberry shortcakes were the ones Mom made from the wild strawberries Sis and I picked when we were young kids in Radisson, Saskatchewan. Whenever we managed to cart home a jam pail full of berries, a big round sandwich of feathery biscuit, overflowing with tiny succulent strawberries and slathered with whipped farm cream would appear as a teatime specialty or suppertime dessert. The shortcake was always warm because it was fresh from the oven (that's when it's best). This version is close to the one I remember and the one my children love.

◆

2 cups	all-purpose flour	500 mL
2 tbsp	granulated sugar	25 mL
1 tbsp	baking powder	15 mL
¹/₂ tsp	salt	2 mL
¹/₂ cup	cold butter	125 mL
¹/₂ cup	milk or light cream	125 mL
Glaze:		
1 tsp	milk	5 mL
1 tsp	granulated sugar	5 mL
Filling:		
2 cups	sliced strawberies	500 mL
2 tbsp	(approx.) granulated sugar	25 mL
1 tbsp	sherry	15 mL
1 cup	whipping cream	250 mL
6 to 8	whole strawberries	6 to 8

- In large bowl, combine flour, 2 tbsp (25 mL) sugar, baking powder and salt; mix well.
- With pastry blender or 2 knives, cut in butter until mixture resembles coarse crumbs.
- Add milk and stir quickly with fork. Form into ball and turn dough out onto lightly floured surface.
- Knead quickly, about 10 to 12 times, then shape into 8-inch (20 cm) round about $^1/_2$ inch (1 cm) thick. Place on nonstick baking sheet.
- *Glaze:* Lightly brush top with milk and sprinkle with 1 tsp (5 mL) sugar.
- Bake in 425 F (220 C) oven for 15 to 18 minutes or until golden brown.
- *Filling:* In small bowl, combine sliced strawberries, 2 tbsp (25 mL) sugar and sherry; stir gently. Let stand at room temperature.
- To assemble: Split warm biscuit round in half. Place bottom half on serving plate. Spoon sliced berries over biscuit bottom, reserving any juice; top with biscuit top.
- Whip cream and sweeten if desired. Dot biscuit top with dollops of whipped cream. Drizzle reserved strawberry juice over whipped cream and garnish with whole strawberries.

Makes 6 to 8 servings.

Variations

PEACH SHORTCAKE

- In place of strawberries, use 2 cups (500 mL) sliced peaches; in place of sherry, use orange-flavored liqueur or peach schnappes.

ORANGE SHORTCAKE

- In place of strawberries, use 2 cups (500 mL) sliced navel oranges; in place of sherry, use orange-flavored liqueur.

PEACH SHORTCAKE MERINGUE TORTE

When I think of all the delectable desserts I've eaten or concocted in the past 50 years, this is the one that stands out as my favorite. It has everything — buttery almond-scented cake, pillowy-light meringue, crunchy toasted almonds and tangy fruit covered with cool whipped cream.

◆

¹/₂ cup	butter	125 mL
1¹/₂ cups	granulated sugar, divided	375 mL
4	eggs, separated	4
¹/₂ cup	milk	125 mL
1 tsp	almond flavoring	5 mL
1 cup	sifted cake and pastry flour	250 mL
1¹/₂ tsp	baking powder	7 mL
¹/₂ tsp	salt, divided	2 mL
1 cup	sliced blanched almonds	250 mL
Topping:		
2 cups	sliced fresh peaches (2 to 3)	500 mL
1 cup	whipping cream	250 mL
¹/₄ cup	icing sugar	50 mL
¹/₂ tsp	almond flavoring	2 mL

• Lightly butter bottoms of two 9-inch (23 cm) round cake pans. Line bottoms only with waxed paper cut to fit.
• In electric mixer bowl, cream butter and ¹/₂ cup (125 mL) sugar; beat until light and fluffy. Beat in egg yolks, milk and almond flavoring until light and fluffy.
• Combine flour, baking powder and ¹/₄ tsp (1 mL) salt. Gradually beat into butter mixture until well mixed. (Batter will be thick.)

- Divide batter evenly between prepared pans. Smooth tops.
- In clean electric mixer bowl, with clean beaters, beat egg whites with remaining salt until foamy. Gradually beat in remaining sugar, about 2 tbsp (25 mL) at a time, until stiff, satiny peaks form and sugar granules are dissolved.
- Divide and spread evenly over each pan of batter. Sprinkle each top with almonds.
- Bake in 350 F (180 C) oven for 35 minutes or until nuts are toasted and tester inserted in center comes out clean. (Meringue topping will look puffed and irregular.)
- With knife, loosen around edges to release meringue from pan edge. Cool on cake racks.
- Carefully remove from pans. Place one cake on cake plate meringue side down. Place the other one on another plate, board or rack with meringue side up.
- *Topping*: Prepare peaches. Drain and reserve 8 pieces for garnish.
- In small bowl, whip cream. Fold in icing sugar and almond flavoring. Remove $^1/_2$ cup (125 mL) for garnish; set aside.
- Fold remaining fruit into remaining whipped cream. Spread on cake on cake plate. Place second cake, meringue side up on top.
- Garnish with reserved whipped cream and fruit.
- Serve immediately or chill in refrigerator for up to 6 hours before serving.

Makes 8 servings.

HELPFUL HINT

To Remove Cake From Pan
Invert pan with cake in it onto cloth or paper towel-covered rack. Remove pan. Place a wire rack, board or plate on cake bottom and holding both racks turn cake over. Remove rack and towel. Replace any loose almonds or crumbs.

CREAMY CHEESECAKE

In the late '50s Lindy's of New York made cheesecake famous in North America. Sis introduced it to our family. This is an adaptation of her recipe.

— ◆ —

Crust:

1 cup	vanilla wafer crumbs (24 wafers)	250 mL
1/4 cup	butter, melted	50 mL

Filling:

1 1/2 lb	cream cheese	750 g
1 cup	granulated sugar	250 mL
2 tbsp	all-purpose flour	25 mL
1/4 tsp	salt	1 mL
4	eggs	4
1/4 cup	milk	50 mL
1 tsp	vanilla	5 mL
1 cup	commercial sour cream	250 mL

Topping:

Berry or Fruit Sauce (see page 305)

• *Crust:* Thoroughly combine vanilla crumbs and melted butter. Press onto bottom of 10-inch (25 cm) springform pan.
• *Filling:* In electric mixer bowl or food processor, beat cream cheese until smooth. Beat in sugar, flour, salt, milk, eggs and vanilla for 2 minutes or until very smooth. Pour over crust.
• Bake in 400 F (200 C) oven for 10 minutes. Reduce heat to 250 F (120 C). Bake for 55 minutes longer or until center is barely firm.
• Spread sour cream evenly over cheesecake. Turn off oven and leave cheesecake in oven for 30 minutes or until nearly cooled.
• With knife blade, loosen cake from rim of pan. Cool completely.
• Loosen from pan and slide onto flat-bottomed cake plate.
• *Topping:* Spread Berry or Fruit Sauce over top.

Makes 8 to 10 servings.

Variations

CHOCOLATE CHEESECAKE

• To cream cheese mixture, add 6 melted squares semi-sweet chocolate. Top with Flavored Whipped Cream just before serving.

LIQUEUR-FLAVORED CHEESECAKE

• In place of milk in cream cheese mixture, use amaretto, coffee- or orange-flavored liqueur, rum or brandy. Omit sour cream.

BERRY OR FRUIT SAUCE

◆

For a sundae topping, it is hard to beat lightly sweetened pure berry or fruit purée. The flavor variations are endless.

2 cups	fresh, frozen or canned raspberries, strawberries, blueberries, blackberries, or Saskatoons, or sliced peaches, apricots, pears, bananas, or any combination	500 mL
$^1/_2$ cup	granulated sugar	125 mL
$^1/_2$ tsp	vanilla, almond flavoring or rose water	2 mL

• In food processor blender, process fruit until puréed. Let stand at room temperature for about 1 hour. Stir occasionally to make sure sugar dissolves. If purée contains seeds from the berries used, press through a sieve to remove seeds.
• To store: Pour into covered container and refrigerate for up to 7 days; or freeze for up to 6 months.

Makes 1 cup (250 mL).

GINGERBREAD

Warm gingerbread is wonderful! It's one of my favorite desserts after a light supper. And my son, Bob, loves it. We both think it's best with lightly sweetened whipped cream. It's also good with cold Spiced Apple Sauce (see page 321).

--- ♦ ---

$^1/_2$ cup	soft butter	125 mL
$^1/_3$ cup	firmly packed brown sugar	75 mL
1	egg	1
2 cups	all-purpose flour	500 mL
$1^1/_2$ tsp	baking soda	7 mL
1 tsp	baking powder	5 mL
1 tsp	ground ginger	5 mL
1 tsp	cinnamon	5 mL
$^1/_2$ tsp	salt	2 mL
$^1/_2$ cup	fancy molasses	125 mL
$^2/_3$ cup	boiling water	150 mL
	Flavored Whipped Cream (see page 267)	

• In mixing bowl, cream butter and sugar until light and fluffy. Beat in eggs.
• In another bowl, combine flour, baking soda, baking powder, ginger, cinnamon and salt.
• In measuring cup, combine molasses and boiling water.
• Stir dry ingredients into creamed mixture alternately with molasses mixture, starting and ending with dry ingredients.
• Spoon into buttered and floured 9-inch (23 cm) square cake pan.
• Bake in 350 F (180 C) oven for 35 to 40 minutes.

Makes 9 servings.

Maple Flan

If you like Crème Caramel, you'll find this maple syrup coated custard sensational.

♦

1 cup	maple syrup, divided	250 mL
4	eggs	4
4	egg yolks	4
1 tsp	vanilla	5 mL
$^1/_4$ tsp	ground ginger	1 mL
$2^1/_4$ cups	milk	550 mL

• Pour $^3/_4$ cup (175 mL) maple syrup into heavy-bottomed saucepan.
• Heat to boiling, then boil for about 4 to 6 minutes or until up reaches the hard ball stage (250 F/125 C on candy thermometer), when ball will hold its shape but still be pliable when dropped into ice water. Watch carefully because seconds past this point syrup is apt to burn.
• Pour syrup into a hot clean, straight-sided 6-cup (1.5L) soufflé dish or casserole. Turn dish around and around until syrup coats bottom and halfway up sides. Allow to cool completely while making custard.
• In bowl, stir eggs, egg yolks, remaining maple syrup, vanilla and ginger together until creamy and smooth. Pour and stir milk slowly into egg mixture until smooth and thoroughly mixed.
• Pour through sieve into prepared dish. Cover dish with waxed paper or aluminum foil.
• Set in shallow pan partially filled with boiling water.
• Bake in 350 F (180 C) oven for about 1 hour or until custard is firm and set.
• Let custard cool until just warm or chill about 4 hours in refrigerator. Unmold onto serving dish with turned-up lip to hold syrup.

Makes 6 servings.

CREAM PUFFS

My daughter, Susan, was about five when she first noticed how a pan of small doughy mounds put into the oven came out an hour or so later as big, hollow golden puffs. She found the miraculous change amazing.

♦

1 cup	water	250 mL
¹/₂ cup	butter	125 mL
1 tsp	granulated sugar	5 mL
Pinch	salt	Pinch
1 cup	all-purpose flour	250 mL
1 tsp	baking powder	5 mL
3	eggs	3
2	egg whites	2
	Flavored Whipped Cream (see page 267) or Chocolate Whipped Cream (see page 268)	
	Chocolate Sauce (see page 322) or icing sugar	

• In saucepan, combine water, butter, sugar and salt. Bring to a rapid boil. As soon as butter melts, add flour and baking powder all at once. With wooden spoon stir quickly until mixture forms a cooked ball of dough and leaves the side of the pan. Immediately remove from heat. Cool for 5 minutes. Transfer to electric mixer bowl or food processor.

• Add eggs and egg whites one at a time; beat or process until mixture is smooth after each addition. Or beat by hand. (When each egg is first beaten into mixture the dough becomes slippery and breaks apart. This is normal. Keep right on beating. As each egg is incorporated, the dough will become smooth and shiny.)

• Spoon or pipe batter from piping bag fitted with large plain tip onto lightly buttered baking sheets in 12 large mounds, 18 medium or 24 small, about 2 inches (5 cm) apart to allow for expansion.

• Bake in 400 F (200 C) oven for 15 minutes. Reduce heat to 350 F (180 C). Bake for 20 minutes longer or until golden brown and firm to touch.

• Remove from oven but leave oven on. With spatula loosen each puff from pan. Cut a slash or small hole in the side of each puff to release steam and later use for filling.

- Leave puffs on pan and return to oven. Reduce heat to 200 F (100 C). Leave puffs in oven for 1 hour to dry and crisp.
- To store: Place puffs in airtight container. Keep at room temperature overnight, in refrigerator for up to 1 week or in freezer for up to 4 weeks. To recrisp, heat in 200 F (100 C) oven for about 10 minutes.
- To fill: Put Flavored Whipped Cream into pastry bag fitted with medium plain tube. Pipe into slash or hole made in side of puffs. Or split puffs and fill with whipped cream. Drizzle Chocolate Sauce over tops or dust with icing sugar.

Makes 12 large, 18 medium or 24 small puffs.

Variations

CREAM PUFF SWANS

Whenever Mom added a pan of little question mark shapes when she was making cream puffs, I knew something special was coming up. She never had a bride's or baby's shower or fancy afternoon tea without a tray of long-necked swans dusted with icing sugar for her guests to admire and then devour.

- To form swan heads and necks: Place raw cream puff paste in decorating bag fitted with large plain round writing tip. Press dough onto buttered baking sheets in the shape of 2-inch (5 cm) long question marks, making a thicker dollop at the beginning of each for head. Bake in 400 C (200 F) oven for about 12 minutes or until golden brown. For swan bodies, make remainder of dough into cream puffs.
- To assemble swans: When cream puffs are cool, cut top third off each. Set aside. Fill bottom (swan's body) with Flavored Whipped Cream (see page 267). Cut reserved cream puff top in half. Arrange in filling as wings. Place swan's neck in place using wings to keep it steady. Dust the whole swan with sifted icing sugar.
- For an elegant dessert, float the swans on a puddle of Chocolate Sauce (see page 322) or Berry or Fruit Sauce (see page 305).

ÉCLAIRS

• Spoon or pipe cream puff dough into 4- to 6-inch (10 to 15 cm) logs onto buttered baking sheets.

PROFITEROLES

French chefs cut small cream puffs horizontally in half and fill them with Flavored Whipped Cream (see page 267). Usually three at a time are put on individual dessert plates, then drizzled with Chocolate Sauce (see page 322) or Berry or Fruit Sauce (see page 305).

LEMON CREAM ROLL

Whenever I make an angel food cake, I make this jelly roll dessert to use up the leftover egg yolks. If there is any of the Lemon Cream Roll left over, I wrap and freeze it for another day. Or you can freeze the roll. Simply cut off slices when you need dessert.

◆

1	baked Golden Jelly Roll (see page 258)	1
1	batch Lemon Butter (see page 311), made with 4 egg yolks	1
1 cup	whipping cream	250 mL
	Icing sugar	

• Bake and cool Golden Jelly Roll.
• Prepare and chill Lemon Butter.
• Whip cream until firm peaks form. Fold in Lemon Butter.
• Unroll jelly roll. Remove towel.
• Spread cream mixture on jelly roll right out to the edges. Reroll jelly roll. Place seam side down on serving platter. Lightly dust with icing sugar.
• To store: Wrap tightly in plastic wrap. Keep in refrigerator for up to 3 days; in freezer for up to 6 weeks.

Makes 8 to 10 servings.

LEMON BUTTER

Other cookbooks, particularly English ones, call this lemon curd or cheese. At any given time, I usually have some perched on my refrigerator shelf beside the jams and jellies. It's delicious on warm toast or muffins and as a rich filling for tart shells (see page 271) and jelly roll (see page 256).

♦

2	eggs or 4 egg yolks	2
1/2 cup	granulated sugar	125 mL
	Juice of 1 lemon	
2 tbsp	butter	25 mL

• In heavy saucepan or top of double boiler, beat eggs until foamy. Beat in sugar and lemon juice.
• Cook over medium-low heat or boiling water, stirring, for 4 to 5 minutes or until custardlike and mixture thickly coats a metal spoon. Remove from heat.
• Beat butter into warm mixture.
• Pour into covered container. Store in refrigerator.
• To store: Keep in refrigerator for up to 4 weeks.

Makes about 1 cup (250 mL).

Variations

LEMON LIME BUTTER

• Use half lemon and half lime juice.

APRICOT BUTTER

• Use only 2 tbsp (25 mL) lemon juice. Add 1/4 cup (50 mL) puréed, cooked dried apricots to egg and sugar mixture.

ENGLISH TRIFLE

We lived in the East for at least five years before I copied the English Trifle we loved in the dining room at the old Lord Simcoe Hotel in Toronto. I had never made it before. It's one of the best make-ahead desserts and actually improves when it's been in the refrigerator overnight. I vary the taste by using different flavored jams or jellies — strawberry, raspberry, apple, even cranberry sauce — and canned frozen or fresh fruit — strawberries, peaches, apricots, pears or any combination.

◆

1	baked Sponge Cake (see page 255)	1
1	batch Cream Custard (see page 313)	1
1/2 cup	sherry	125 mL
1 cup	black or red currant jelly	250 mL
1 cup	fresh or defrosted frozen unsweetened raspberries	250 mL
1 cup	whipping cream	250 mL
2 tbsp	icing sugar	25 mL
	mint leaves (optional)	

• Bake Sponge Cake a day ahead.
• Make Cream Custard; cover top with plastic wrap. Chill.
• Trim any brown edges from cake; cut into 1-inch (2.5 cm) squares. Arrange in bottom of large glass serving bowl. Sprinkle sherry over cake cubes.
• In saucepan over low heat, melt jelly; brush evenly over cake. Cover with raspberries. (Reserve several for garnish if desired.)
• Spread half Cream Custard over berries.
• In small bowl, beat whiping cream and icing sugar until soft peaks form; fold into remaining Cream Custard. Spread over trifle. Smooth surface.
• Refrigerate, covered, for at least 4 hours.
• Garnish with whole raspberries and mint leaves, if desired.

Makes 8 servings.

CREAM CUSTARD

A real homemade custard like this one belongs in trifle. It's also good served warm or well chilled with unfrosted cake and/or sliced fruit and berries. My aunt called that combination cottage pudding.

♦

1 cup	milk	250 mL
1 cup	whipping cream	250 mL
4	egg yolks	4
1/4 cup	granulated sugar	50 mL
1/4 cup	cornstarch	50 mL
1 tbsp	vanilla	15 mL

• In saucepan, heat milk and cream to a boil; remove from heat.
• In electric mixer bowl or with wire whisk in large bowl, beat egg yolks for 2 minutes or until thickened. Gradually beat in sugar until mixture falls in ribbons when beaters are lifted from bowl. Beat in cornstarch until smooth. Whisking constantly, pour in cream mixture in a steady stream. Pour mixture back into saucepan.
• Heat over medium heat, stirring constantly, until mixture just comes to a simmer. Reduce heat and cook at simmer, stirring constantly for about 3 minutes, until thickened. Stir in vanilla.
• Set pan in cold water to stop the cooking and cool quickly.
• To store: Refrigerate, covered, for at least 1 hour or until cold or for up to 2 days.

Makes 2 1/2 cups (625 mL).

MERINGUES WITH ALMOND CREAM

Meringues make a glamorous finale for a meal and small ones add a special touch to a tray of cookies. The meringue from this recipe can also be made into small rosettes (about 24).

◆

2	egg whites	2
Pinch	cream of tartar	Pinch
Pinch	salt	Pinch
$^1/_2$ cup	granulated sugar (fine, if possible)	125 mL
$^1/_2$ tsp	vanilla	

Almond Cream:

1 cup	whipping cream	250 mL
2 tbsp	icing sugar	25 mL
2 tsp	amaretto	10 mL
2 tbsp	toasted finely chopped almonds	25 mL

• Line baking sheet with brown paper, baking paper or lightly buttered and floured foil.
• In electric mixer bowl, beat egg whites, cream of tartar and salt until foamy. Gradually beat in sugar until stiff and satiny.
• Spoon into decorating bag fitted with large star tip. Pipe meringue (or spoon it) into round circles 4 inch (10 cm) in diameter with a rim around outside of each circle.
• Bake in 200 F (100 C) oven for 35 minutes or until very delicately golden. Turn off oven and leave meringues inside overnight or for 8 hours to dry thoroughly.
• To store: Place meringues in airtight container or plastic bag to keep for up to 6 weeks.
• *Almond Cream:* Whip cream until fluffy. Add icing sugar and amaretto, beating just until stiff. Fold in half of almonds.
• Divide cream evenly among meringues. Garnish with remaining almonds. Serve immediately.

Makes 4 servings.

Variation

MERINGUES WITH BERRIES OR FRUIT

• In place of amaretto, use 1 tsp (5 mL) orange-flavored liqueur or orange juice; in place of almonds, fold $^1/_2$ cup (125 mL) blueberries, raspberries or quartered strawberries or chopped peaches or nectarines into whipped cream. Garnish with whole berry or fruit slice.

MAGIC CHOCOLATE MOUSSE

For a divine frozen chocolate dessert find a few minutes to make this mousse ahead then freeze it for at least 4 hours or overnight.

◆

1 cup	whipping cream, divided	250 mL
3	squares semi-sweet chocolate	3
$^1/_4$ cup	icing sugar	50 mL
2 tsp	brandy or orange-flavored liqueur	10 mL

• In saucepan, heat $^1/_4$ cup (50 mL) whipping cream and chocolate together over low heat until chocolate melts. Whisk until smooth. Chill for 15 minutes.
• Beat remaining whipping cream with icing sugar. When thick, add brandy and chilled chocolate mixture; beat until fluffy.
• Spoon into parfait glasses, cover and chill for at least 2 hours. (For frozen parfait, freeze for at least 4 hours.)
• To store: Wrap well; freeze for up to 2 weeks.

Makes 4 servings.

STRAWBERRY
CHARLOTTE RUSSE

From my experience, lady fingers don't seem to be as available as they once were. When I give up looking for them in the stores, I use strips of sponge, or unrolled jelly roll cake. Or the filling on its own makes a wonderful fruit mousse.

♦

20 to 24	small soft ladyfingers	20 to 24
2	envelopes unflavored gelatin	2
1/2 cup	orange juice, divided	125 mL
4	eggs, separated	4
1/2 cup	granulated sugar	125 mL
2 cups	crushed strawberries	500 mL
1/2 tsp	ground nutmeg	2 mL
1 cup	whipping cream	250 mL
1 tsp	vanilla	5 mL

• Wrap and tie 3 inch (8 cm) waxed paper or foil collar around an 8-inch (20 cm) springform pan.
• Cut tips from one end of ladyfingers so they will stand. Arrange, round side up, around inside edge of pan.
• Sprinkle gelatin over 1/4 cup (50 mL) orange juice, to soften.
• In top of double boiler, beat together remaining orange juice, egg yolks and sugar. Set over simmering water. Stir constantly until mixture thickens. Add gelatin mixture and stir until gelatin dissolves. Remove from heat and stir in strawberries and nutmeg. Chill for about 25 minutes or until partially set and the consistency of egg white.
• Whip cream; stir in vanilla. Fold into strawberry mixture.
• Beat egg whites until stiff but not dry. Fold into strawberry mixture until no streaks of white show. Spoon mixture into ladyfinger-lined pan.
• Chill for about 4 hours or overnight to set. Remove collar and springform ring. Garnish with sweetened whipped cream, if desired.

Makes 10 to 12 servings.

BERRIED PASSION

The peaches were luscious in a creation similar to this one that was served to me at the 1985 Penticton Peach Festival. I could hardly wait to try it with strawberries.

◆

Crust:

1 cup	vanilla wafer crumbs (24 wafers)	250 mL
1/4 cup	finely chopped almonds	50 mL
1/4 cup	butter, melted	50 mL

Filling:

1	batch Cream Custard (see page 313)	
1 cup	cream cheese (1/2 lb/250 g)	250 mL
3/4 cup	icing sugar	175 mL
1/2 cup	whipping cream	125 mL
4 cups	strawberries, raspberries or blueberries	1 L

Topping:

1/2 cup	whipping cream	125 mL
1/4 cup	icing sugar	50 mL
1 tsp	vanilla	5 mL
1/4 cup	finely chopped toasted almonds	50 mL

• *Crust:* In bowl, combine crumbs, almonds and butter; mix well. Press onto bottom of 11 x 7-inch (28 x 18 cm) baking dish.
• Bake in 350 F (180 C) oven for 15 minutes or until golden. Cool.
• *Filling:* Prepare Cream Custard; cool.
• In electric mixer bowl, beat cream cheese and 3/4 cup (175 mL) icing sugar for about 2 minutes or until smooth. Whip 1/2 cup (125 mL) whipping cream. Fold into cheese mixture. Spread evenly over crust.
• Reserve 6 to 8 strawberries for garnish. Arrange remaining straw-berries, stem-end down, in layer over cream cheese mixture.
• Spread Cream Custard evenly over berries. Cover with plastic wrap. Chill in refrigerator for 3 hours or overnight.
• *Topping:* At serving time, whip cream. Fold in icing sugar and vanilla. Spread evenly over custard.
• Garnish with slices of reserved berries and toasted almonds.

Makes 8 to 10 servings.

Frozen Lemonade Loaf

This freezer cake is known for its tongue-tingling tartness and refreshing coolness. Stored like bricks of ice cream, it's great to have on hand when surprise company pops in. Loaves keep for 6 weeks.

◆

1	envelope unflavored gelatin	1
1/4 cup	cold water	50 mL
6	eggs, separated	6
3/4 cup	granulated sugar	175 mL
1	can (6 oz/175 mL) frozen lemonade concentrate	1
1/2 cup	corn syrup	125 mL
1 cup	whipping cream	250 mL
1	10-inch (25 cm) angel food cake	

- With strips of waxed paper cut to allow for an overhang at ends and sides, line two 9 x 5-inch (23 x 13 cm) loaf pans.
- Sprinkle gelatin over cold water to soften for 5 minutes.
- In top of double boiler, whisk together egg yolks, sugar and undiluted lemonade. Place over boiling water. Cook, stirring, for about 7 minutes or until mixture thickens and coats a metal spoon.
- Remove from heat. Stir in softened gelatin until it melts. Cool.
- In electric mixer bowl, beat egg whites until soft peaks form. Gradually add corn syrup and continue beating until stiff, satiny peaks form. Fold into cooled custard.
- Whip cream until soft peaks form. Fold into custard mixture.
- Break angel food into small pieces, about 2-inches (5 cm) square. Gently fold into custard mixture.
- Spoon into prepared pans. Smooth top with spatula. Fold overlapping waxed paper over top. Cover with plastic wrap. Freeze overnight.

Makes 2 loaves to keep frozen and cut as needed.

ICE CREAM

I have fond childhood memories of Sunday afternoon ice cream-making sessions. My cousin, Earl, and his brothers took turns turning the big handle on the wooden ice cream maker until it would barely move. After it set for a bit, we'd line up for bowls full. Now I make ice cream an easier way, in my electric ice cream machine. It still tastes as good as it did when I was a child and better than most store-bought varieties.

◆

1 cup	milk	250 mL
¹/₂ cup	granulated sugar	75 mL
1 tbsp	all-purpose flour	15 mL
2	egg yolks	2
1 cup	table cream	250 mL
1 tsp	vanilla	5 mL

- In saucepan, bring ³/₄ cup (175 mL) milk to a boil.
- In small dish, combine remaining milk, sugar and flour; mix well. Stir into hot milk. Cook, stirring constantly, for about 5 minutes.
- In bowl, beat egg yolks; stir in a little thickened milk, return to saucepan; cook for 1 minute longer. Cool.
- Stir in cream and vanilla. Strain, if not perfectly smooth.
- Pour into an ice cream maker. Follow manufacturer's instructions and freeze until soft-textured ice cream forms. Serve immediately. Or, spoon into bowl or container. Cover and freeze for at least 2 hours.
- To store: Keep in covered container in freezer for up to 4 weeks.

Makes 4 servings.

Variations

CHOCOLATE ICE CREAM

• Add 1$\frac{1}{2}$ squares semi-sweet chocolate, coarsely chopped, to cold milk in saucepan. Bring to a boil and as chocolate melts, beat until smooth before adding remaining ingredients.

PEACH ICE CREAM

• Add 1 cup (250 mL) finely chopped peaches to mixture just before freezing. Makes 6 servings.

STRAWBERRY ICE CREAM

• Combine 1 cup (250 mL) crushed strawberries and 2 tbsp (25 mL) granulated sugar. Let stand for about 20 minutes, stirring occasionally until sugar dissolves. Add just before pouring mixture into freezer.

FRUIT SHERBET

• Omit flour and do not cook mixture. Dissolve sugar in milk. In place of egg yolks, add 1 beaten egg white; in place of table cream, use 1 cup (250 mL) orange, cranberry or raspberry juice or puréed berries, peaches or pineapple and 1 tsp (5 mL) lemon juice.

FRUIT ICE OR SORBET

• Omit egg white in Fruit Sherbet. In place of milk, use 1 cup (250 mL) fruit juice or puréed fruit.

SPICED APPLE SAUCE

If cinnamon hearts are unavailable, a cinnamon stick plus a bit of red food coloring dropped into the simmering sugar solution will add spiciness and color to apples. You might want to stock up on the candies around Valentine's day when they are available. They keep from one year to the next.

◆

4	large apples (1^1/$_3$ lb/575 g)	4
1 cup	water	250 mL
^{1}/$_2$ cup	granulated sugar	125 mL
^{1}/$_4$ cup	red cinnamon hearts	50 mL
Pinch	salt	Pinch

• Cut each apple into 8 even wedges. Peel each wedge and remove core.
• In saucepan, combine water, sugar, cinnamon heart candies and salt. Bring to a boil, stirring until candies dissolve.
• Add apple wedges. Bring to a boil, reduce heat and simmer for 5 minutes or until apples are tender and translucent.
• Serve warm, at room temperature or chilled.

Makes 3 to 4 servings.

Variation

SPICED PEACH SAUCE

• In place of apples, use 8 peeled peaches, cut in sixths. Omit red cinnamon hearts. Add cinnamon stick to sugar solution. Remove after 5 minutes.

Best Chocolate Sauce

This is as good on ice cream as any of the chocolate sauces I have tasted on sundaes in ice cream parlors.

❖

2	squares semi-sweet chocolate	2
1 tbsp	butter	15 mL
2/3 cup	granulated sugar	150 mL
2/3 cup	evaporated milk or table cream	150 mL
2 tbsp	corn syrup	25 mL
1 tsp	vanilla or liqueur	5 mL

• In small, heavy saucepan, combine chocolate, butter, sugar, evaporated milk and corn syrup. Over medium heat, bring to a gentle boil, stirring constantly. Continue to stir and cook for 5 minutes until smooth and thickened. Stir in vanilla.
• Cool for 5 minutes. Pour into container with tight-fitting lid.
• To store: Keep at room temperature for up to 4 weeks.

Makes about 1 1/4 cups (300 mL).

Variation

Hot Fudge Sauce

• Add an additional 1 tbsp (15 mL) butter to Chocolate Sauce. Cook for 1 to 2 minutes longer. Serve hot.

COOKTIONARY

There's a special jargon associated with cooking. Knowing even some of it makes it much easier to follow a recipe, and, more importantly, to end up with a successful dish.

◆

COOKING METHODS

(What the recipe is talking about.)

Bake: Cook by dry heat in an oven or oven-type appliance, such as a toaster oven.

Barbecue: Grill or roast by dry heat on a rack or spit over the hot coals of a barbecue.

Blanch: Submerge food in boiling water for a very short time to slightly precook it, soften it and/or loosen the peel. This is usually followed by plunging the food into cold water to stop the precooking.

Boil: Heat or cook in a liquid (at 212 F/100 C) that bubbles constantly; the bubbles break on the surface.

Braise: Cook food at a low temperature in a small amount of water in a tightly covered pan.

Broil: Cook under the direct dry heat of the broiler unit of a gas or electric range.

Brown: Cook in hot fat on the top of the stove, in a hot oven or under a hot broiler until outside of food browns.

Caramelize: Cook sugar in a pan with a little water until it melts and turns into an amber brown syrup.

Coddle: Cook in a hot liquid that is just below the boiling point.

Deep Fry: Cook in enough very hot oil or fat to cover food.

Fry: Cook in a shallow layer about 1/8 inch (3 mm) of hot oil or fat in a skillet or saucepan.

Melt: Heat a firm fat or dissolvable solid food to change it to its liquid state.

Microwave: Cook food in a microwave oven. Microwaves cook quickly but do not brown food.

Parboil: Partially cook food in boiling water.

Poach: Cook immersed in gently simmering liquid.

Preheat: Turn on oven or broiler to heat to the desired cooking temperature 10 to 15 minutes before using.

Reduce: Boil liquid quickly to evaporate moisture and decrease and concentrate the amount of liquid.

Refresh: Put hot food in cold water or under cold running water to stop the cooking. It helps retain the color in vegetables and prevents overcooking.

Roast: Cook by dry heat, uncovered, in an enclosed oven or oven-like appliance.

Sauté: Cook, partly cook or brown in a small amount of hot fat.

Simmer: Cook in liquid in pan over just enough heat so that the surface of the liquid barely ripples and does not bubble.

Steam: Cook in a covered container over or in boiling water so that the food cooks by the vapor rising through it and the steam trapped in the container.

Stew: Cook in liquid at a low temperature for a long time.

Stir-braise: Mix food with an up-and-down motion as it cooks in a small amount of liquid in a hot skillet or saucepan.

Stir-fry: Lift and stir food as it cooks in a small amount of hot oil or fat in a skillet or wok over moderately high to high heat.

Toast: Brown food by dry heat in an oven, toaster or pan.

HANDLING INGREDIENTS

(How to do what the recipe directs.)

Baste: Brush or spoon liquid — juice, vegetable oil, pan drippings, natural juice or sauce — over food as it cooks to add flavor and keep it moist. Bulb basters are perfect for this job.

Beat: Mix ingredients together by stirring briskly in an over-and-over action with a spoon, fork or whisk, or in an around-and-around action with a beater, to make a mixture smooth and incorporate air.

Blend: Stir or mix two or more ingredients together until mixture is smooth. (Not as vigorous as beating.)

Bone: Remove meat from bones of fish, poultry or meat by cutting meat away from bones with a very sharp thin-bladed (boning) knife.

Bread: Coat food which is moist or moistened with milk or egg with cracker or bread crumbs.

Brush On: Spread liquid on food with a small brush. (Natural bristles are best.)

Chill: Cool foods in refrigerator or over cracked ice or briefly in the freezer.

Chop: Cut into pieces using a knife, cleaver, food chopper or processor.

Coat: Cover all sides of food with another liquid or dry ingredient such as egg, milk, flour or crumbs.

Combine: Mix two or more foods together.

Core: Remove inedible seed, pit or center part of vegetables or fruit.

Crisp: Make food crunchy and firm by allowing vegetables to stand in ice water or bread to dry in oven.

Crumb: Change food to very small pieces such as rolling dry bread into crumbs or pulverizing them in a food processor.

Cube: Cut food into small squares about $1/2$ to $3/4$ inch (1 to 2 cm) square.

Cut In: Work fat into flour mixture with pastry blender or cutting action of two forks or knives until mixture is evenly textured.

Defat or Degrease: Remove fat from pan or surface liquid that food is cooking in by skimming it from the surface with a spoon and blotting excess off with paper; by lifting it from a well-chilled mixture once it has congealed; or by removing visible fat before food is cooked.

Deglaze: Gather flavor from pan after roasting or sautéeing food (and after degreasing pan) by adding liquid to pan and scraping up any brown bits stuck to pan and dissolving them. This makes a natural jus (juice) or sauce.

Dice: Cut food into very small cubes about ⅛ inch (3 mm) square.

Disjoint: Divide poultry into pieces by cutting it apart at its joints.

Drain: Place food in strainer to allow liquid to run off food or pour off liquid from food using something to hold food from falling out of bowl or pan.

Dredge: Coat food with flour by rolling it in flour or shaking it in a bag containing flour.

Dust: Shake or sprinkle a dry powder over food or pan, as in dusting top of cake with icing sugar.

Flake: Pull food apart gently with the tines of a fork until it separates into pieces, as in flaking cooked fish.

Fold: Blend one delicate ingredient or mixture into another using a spoon, rubber scraper or whisk, moving it down and across bottom of bowl and up and over mixture until it is well blended.

Garnish: Add pieces of food or mixtures in contrasting colors and textures to cooked or prepared food to decorate it.

Glaze: Brush or spoon a thin layer of pan juices, syrup or jelly onto the surface of food to coat it, as in brushing melted jelly over fruit slices to finish a fruit dessert.

Grate: Rub hard food across the rough part of a grater to make very fine bits of food such as grated lemon rind.

Grease: (Synonymous with *butter* in this book.) Brush or spread a thin coat of butter, shortening, oil or margarine on baking sheets or pans to keep food from sticking.

Grind: Cut food, such as nuts or meat, into tiny particles by putting it through a grinder or processing it to a ground state.

Julienne: Cut food, such as vegetables, into thin matchstick like pieces.

Knead: Work food by hand by folding it over and pushing it with the heel of the hand or in the mixer or food processor until it feels smooth and elastic.

Macerate: Soak in a flavored (often liqueur- or liquor-based) liquid to enhance flavor and, as in the case of dried fruits, to soften them.

Marinate: Allow food to stand or soak in a flavored liquid (usually acidic in the case of meat) to add flavor and make meat more tender.

Mince: Chop very finely.

Mix: Stir or combine ingredients until evenly blended.

Peel: Remove outer coating (peel) and stem from vegetable or fruit with knife or appropriate tool. (Same as *pare*, the term used in some cookbooks.)

Pit: Remove pit or seeds from vegetables or fruits. (Sometimes the term *seed* is used as in the case of tomatoes.)

Purée: Press cooked or soft food through a sieve or food mill, or mash to a smooth consistency, or process in blender or food processor until blended and smooth.

Score: Cut shallow incisions in the surface of food, usually in a diamond pattern, as decoration and to allow seasonings to be absorbed as in baked ham.

Season: Add salt, seasonings, flavorings and/or herbs and spices to food to flavor it.

Separate: Divide food into its components such as the yolk from the white in an egg.

Shred: Cut food, such as cabbage, into fine slivers or thin strips with a knife, shredder or food processor.

Sift: Pass granular or powdery foods, such as flour or sugar, through a screen or sieve to separate the grains, make them somewhat finer, lighten the consistency and sometimes separate fine-grained from coarser food particles.

Skewer: Close or fasten an opening in food, as in a stuffed chicken, with metal or wooden pins to hold it in place while cooking. Or thread food on a long wooden or metal stick or pin for barbecuing, broiling or grilling.

Skim: Remove top layer from the surface of food using a spoon or skimmer, as in removing fat from a soup or stew.

Slice: Cut food horizontally or vertically into thick or thin pieces.

Stir: Mix two or more foods together, usually with a spoon, using a circular motion until ingredients are evenly distributed.

Thicken: Change consistency of a thin mixture to a denser one by stirring in a thickener, such as flour, cornstarch, egg yolks or potatoes, and cooking it.

Toss: Mix foods by lifting and turning them with two forks or salad servers.

Unmold: Remove food, such as a set gelatin mixture, from a mold.

Whip: Beat rapidly and steadily with a whisk, rotary beater or electric mixer until mixture expands in volume, seems lighter and in most cases is thicker, as in whipped cream.

Whisk: Beat food with a wire whisk made for the purpose.

TESTS FOR DONENESS

◆

(How to tell when food is cooked.)

FOOD	IT IS DONE WHEN
Baking powder biscuits *Yeast rolls*	One fresh from the oven is broken open and the soft center springs back after being pressed lightly with a finger.
Muffins *Buttercakes* *Quick breads* *Steamed breads*	Wire cake tester, toothpick or broom straw inserted in the center has no food particles clinging to it after it is pulled out.
Yeast bread	Loaf sounds hollow when top crust is tapped with knuckles and loaf shrinks from sides of pan.

Angel cakes *Sponge cakes* *Jelly rolls* *Soufflés*	Spot close to center springs back into shape after being pressed lightly with a finger.
Pastry shell *Tart shells*	Crust appears crisp as it is touched with a fork and is golden brown.
Two-crust *pies*	Cake tester inserted through slits in center of top crust goes into filling easily.
Baked custard *Pumpkin pie*	Thin knife inserted close to center has no filling clinging to it after it is pulled out.
Puddings *Pie fillings*	A slightly cooled spoonful is thick and has no taste of raw flour or cornstarch.
Cooked *custards*	Custard coats a metal spoon lifted from the mixture.
Cookies	Cookie feels firm (not crisp) to the touch and is turning golden brown.
Macaroons *Meringues*	One removed from a pan holds its shape as it cools.
Cooked *cereals*	Small spoonful is evenly thick and has no raw taste.
Pasta	Piece removed from pot is barely tender (al dente).
Rice, white	One grain pressed between forefinger and thumb flattens under the pressure or is tender and tastes cooked.
Rice, brown	One grain feels tender but is slightly chewier than white rice because of outer coating.
Vegetables, *small*	Small piece is tender (or al dente, tender crisp) and free of raw taste.
Vegetables, *large*	Cake tester or fork inserted in thickest part goes in easily, indicating it is tender.

Baked potatoes	Fork or thin knife blade penetrates easily or potato feels soft when squeezed by hand protected by oven mitt or pot holder.
Stewed fruit *Baked fruit*	Cake tester or fork goes into thickest piece easily.
Broiled, fried, stewed, or barbecued chicken	No pink is visible after making a small cut in the thickest part (right to the bone); fork penetrates meat and joint between drumstick and thigh easily.
Roast chicken *Roast turkey*	Meat feels soft to the touch; joint between thigh and drumstick moves easily; meat is no longer pink.
Broiled, panfried, or barbecued meat	Small cut in the thickest part (right to the bone) shows meat is the desired degree of doneness. (Pork should no longer be pink.)
Roast meat	Meat thermometer reads the appropriate temperature for the desired doneness; a small cut in the thickest part (right to the bone) is the color associated with the degree of doneness.
Fish	Thickest part separates into flakes as it is touched by a fork and is still moist (dry flakes indicates fish is overcooked); fish changes from looking translucent to looking opaque.

MEAL PLANNING

(What goes with what in a menu.)

◆

It's the contrasts in a meal that make it exciting. That's one of the things professor Edith C. Rowles Simpson emphasized in our food labs at the University of Saskatchewan in the early '50s. Over the years it's been an important factor in all my meal planning.

Picture this — a white plate with poached chicken breasts masked with white wine sauce surrounded by fluffy mashed potatoes and creamed cauliflower. Pretty dull and unappetizing! Why? Because the color of each item is pale and white, the flavor fairly blah and the texture pretty soft and smooth. It's good-for-you food but there's a sameness that's boring.

Without changing the main components but with a little attention given to contrasts the impression is quite the opposite. For instance, how about white wine and chunky tomato sauce on the chicken; a small baked potato with its jacket opened enough to hold a little cottage cheese topped with chopped green onion; steamed bright green broccoli (from the same family as cauliflower) and cooked to be just tender with a little firmness to its bite. Now the meal has more appeal. It's the striking differences that made the change.

The skillful use of contrast is the key to creating appetizing food combinations. When you are meal planning think of contrasts in the following components:

• **Texture**   It's tiresome having only crunchy, chewy and crisp foods in a meal. There's more appetite appeal when the crunchy things are complemented with something creamy and soft, such as crisp melba toast with smooth soup; chewy ham with tender eggs. Go back to the lifeless chicken plate. Serving tender crisp broccoli rather than creamy cauliflower made it a better meal.

• **Taste**   If everything tastes the same the meal is a bust so the repetition of a flavor in several dishes is a mistake. Instead contrast sweet with sour, spicy with plain.

- **Color** A colorless meal like the original chicken one kills appetites. If you ever end up with something like it use edible garnishes in contrasting colors to give it life — strips of red or green sweet pepper; sprinkles of paprika; flakes of grated cheese or lemon rind; sprigs of fresh parsley or dill.

- **Temperature** When everything in a meal is ice cold it feels like a big chill. If the opposite is true and every item is piping hot it has a smothering effect. Experiencing both hot and cold in one meal is far more enjoyable. Even when the weather hovers around 30 C (86 F) meals are more interesting if they have at least one hot item.

- **Concentration** Since our daily need for food is consistent it's wise to consume about the same amount at our various meals each day. Heavy rich foods with lots of fat, protein and sugar one day followed by only light, watery ones the next is not the best plan. Rather than that balance the two in each meal. For instance if the entrée is baked ham, don't serve mashed sweet potatoes with marshmallows, creamed lima beans and corn, jellied cream cheese and date salad and a steamed fig pudding. Wow, something has to be lighter! Try baked ham with mashed sweet potatoes and chunky apple sauce, green beans, crisp romaine salad and raspberry mousse for dessert. A cool summer plate of chilled melon balls, thin slices of cooked ham, marinated zucchini slices, sliced tomatoes and strawberry sorbet leaves you wanting more. It needs something more concentrated. The easy addition of grainy hot bread and a few chunks of cheese will add additional calories and help prevent an empty feeling from settling in too soon after the meal.

PUTTING IT ALL
TOGETHER

(How to have everything ready at the same time.)

♦

If you're a novice cook, like my son Bob, getting several dishes ready at once is a bit of a problem.

One day when I called him long distance he was eating his self-made meal. "I'm having pork chops," he said.

"Good! And what are you having with them?" I asked.

"Nothing, Mom. When I do pork chops that's all I can manage."

There he was having bare-naked chops — no veggies, no salad. So I imagined he was full of only protein and would soon have scurvy because he wasn't getting Vitamin C. But, he said he was covered because he always had a daily dose of orange juice.

Now back to meals that are more than meat alone. The secret to getting several things on the table at the same time is a little advanced planning with a strategic line of attack.

The first thing to have in mind in this game of cooking, even for the simplest meal, is the menu. If you're new to cooking, then keep it fairly simple. To gain confidence at the beginning try to master a few basic dishes. And always remember, with practice there's bound to be improvement.

You might start by concentrating on main entrées, the principal part of the meal. For appetizers and desserts choose really simple items, such as juice for a starter and ice cream and cookies — the drop kind are easy to make — or fruit and cheese for the finale.

It's also perfectly okay to round out your meal by complementing the entrée with something you can buy that's ready-to-eat. What's available is more costly and may not be equal to home-cooked, but it will be edible.

And, when you're in charge of a whole production it's sure nice to pass a bit of the work on to someone else. (Have you noticed how great chefs always have sous chefs?) It certainly makes meal preparation easier. There's also an added bonus, I've observed that family and/or friends who cook together also have fun together.

Jim pitches in when we're having a dinner party. What a relief for me when he takes charge of the potatoes and the salad. Besides, his scalloped potatoes and cole slaw are better than mine. And when the diners at our table praise his work I love watching the combination grin of surprise and satisfaction that crinkles up his face.

Taking a few minutes to organize the plan for making a meal work is an all-important step. I often try to close my eyes and walk through the whole process, right from the shopping to the serving. When you can do that, cooking is a breeze.

Here's the routine I use for any meal, simple or complicated:

1. *Plan the menu.* At first include only one dish that requires particular attention and/or some special skill. Don't have two oven dishes unless your oven is big enough to handle them and they both bake at the same temperature.

2. *Read the recipes from start to finish before writing the shopping list.* It helps if you group the items under the following headings: canned goods; baking supplies; dairy products; meat, poultry and seafood; fresh produce; sundries.

3. *Now shop.* If you can buy everything at one stop, great, if not, the categorized list makes it easy going at the green grocer's or butcher's.

4. *Do as much as you can ahead of time.* For instance:
   - Rinse and dry salad greens, wrap them in paper towels, put them in plastic bags and store them in the refrigerator. They'll keep and stay crisp for several days.
   - Trim vegetables (and treat like the salad greens).
   - Scrub and/or peel potatoes and cover with cold water.
   - Marinate meat or grate cheese, if required. Refrigerate.
   - Make dessert ahead, if possible.
   - Have the coffee ready to go except for adding fresh water.

5. *Set the table.* When you have a few minutes to spare.

6. *Read every recipe again.* Start with the dish which takes the longest to prepare and cook. Follow recipe instructions step-by-step, then count down to "soup's on".

7. *Assemble ingredients and utensils.* Get out bowls, measures, utensils and ingredients.

8. *Preheat oven.* If it's needed for baking or roasting, and just how long this takes depends on the type, make and year of the appliance. (You'll find you get to know the idiosyncrasies of your own equipment.)

9. *Tidy up.* Do this as you go along to prevent chaos in the kitchen.
10. *Serve.* When everything is ready, dish the food as English cooks say (serve it) — hot food on hot plates and cold food on cold ones. And, enjoy!

SETTING THE TABLE

(Where to put the fork and spoon.)

The fork sits to the left of the plate and the knife to the right with the spoon beside it. That's the way Mom taught us and that's the way I set a table today. Still, crossing over from right to left to pick up my fork always has seemed strange.

Mom's rule was that the place setting should include what was necessary for the meal. In addition, she put all pickles, condiments, milk, butter, et cetera, on the table in appropriate dishes or jugs and not in their containers or packages. My table is set the same way, whether it's at the cottage, in our dinette, kichen or dining room.

• Put the bottom of place mats, if using, right to the edge of the table.

• When using a tablecloth, it's nice to have an even overhang around the table. I like it to be about 12 inches (30 cm).

• Set the plates and cutlery about 1 inch (2.5 cm) from edge of tables.

• The procedure for cutlery is to place it in order of use with the last piece to be used closest to the plate. Place knives to the right of the plate with the cutting edge toward the plate. Spoons go to the right of the knife or knives. The fork or forks go to the left of the plate.

• The glass, for water or wine, is placed just above the tip of the knife. Any additional ones go to the right and slightly down from the first.

• There's no steadfast rule about napkins. They are usually put to the left of the fork, with or without a napkin ring. Or they're pretty tucked into the wine glasses or artfully folded and placed in the center of each place setting.

INDEX

◆